ETHNOPOLITICS

ETHNOPOLITICS
A Conceptual Framework

JOSEPH ROTHSCHILD

1981
COLUMBIA UNIVERSITY PRESS/NEW YORK

Joseph Rothschild is Class of 1919 Professor of Political Science,
Columbia University

Library of Congress Cataloging in Publication Data
Rothschild, Joseph.
Ethnopolitics, a conceptual framework.
Bibliography: p.
Includes index.
1. Ethnic groups—Political activity. 2. Ethnicity.
I. Title.
JF1061.R67 306'.2 80–28059
ISBN 0–231–05236-7

Columbia University Press
New York Guildford, Surrey

Printed in the United States of America

FOR RUTH, *'eshet ḥayil*

CONTENTS

ACKNOWLEDGMENTS

The reading and research for this study was begun in the summer of 1976 with a "start-up" grant from the Ford Research Fund of the Dean of Columbia University's School of International Affairs (Mr. Harvey Picker). The preparatory work of that summer enabled me to design and prepare a colloquium and later a lecture course on the politics of multiethnic states—pedagogic exercises through which I learned at least as much from my students as they from me. Then came another small but appreciated grant from the Columbia University Council for Research in the Social Sciences, followed by a major, generous Fellowship for Independent Study and Research from the National Endowment for the Humanities (NEH) during a sabbatical-leave year, 1978–79.

The Lehrman Institute of New York City (Dr. Nicholas X. Rizopoulos, Executive Director) arranged two round-table sessions in the autumn of 1979 at which earlier drafts of the first four chapters were constructively criticized by people from academic and business life and from public affairs. Chapters five and seven were similarly subjected to helpful discussion at two seminar sessions of the Fellows of the Research Institute on International Change of Columbia University in the spring of

1980. The entire manuscript was read and commented on by Professor Urs Altermatt (Contemporary History) of the University of Fribourg, Switzerland; Professor Philip Oldenburg (Political Science) of Columbia University; and Mr. Yosef Lapid, a doctoral candidate in the Department of Political Science at Columbia University. Both the group discussions and the individual readings generated many helpful suggestions and warnings, which were applied to my final revisions of the manuscript.

All these institutions and individuals are herewith cordially and sincerely thanked for their financial and intellectual generosity and their sterling example of academic collegiality.

For speedy and accurate typing and proofreading, I warmly thank the ever helpful Ms. Penny Yee, formerly the Administrative Assistant of the Research Institute on International Change at Columbia University, and her competent staff of secretaries and student assistants. I am also grateful to Messrs. Richard Coffman and Michael Klecheski for preparing the Index.

Joseph Rothschild

Columbia University
New York City
February 1981

ETHNOPOLITICS

INTRODUCTION

This book discusses the causes, options, and consequences of bringing ethnicity into the political arena. The psychological and cultural dimensions of ethnicity, though consequential, interesting, and hence, meriting study in their own right, are here interpolated only to the extent that they bear on the translation of ethnicity into political space. This research-strategy was dictated by the need to keep the study manageable in scope and length and is legitimated by the consideration that the world of academic productivity—like that of commodity production—is characterized by a division of labor. Other scholars are better qualified to analyze the cultural and psychological dimensions of ethnicity. And even in its limited political analysis, this book does not pretend to be definitive; rather, it is presented as a conceptual framework for further research and analysis. Like most such conceptual frameworks, it is rather heavily taxonomic and theoretical.

Ethnicity is a plastic, variegated, and originally ascriptive trait that, in certain historical and socioeconomic circumstances, is readily politicized. Such fertile circumstances abound in modern and transitional (modernizing) societies. Not only are such societies characterized by asymmetrical, nonrandom, self-reproducing correlations between ethnic categories on the one hand and socioeconomic classes and political-power distributions on the other hand, that is, by structured interethnic inequalities (which was true of many traditional societies as well), but they also generate political entrepreneurs with a conscious and realistic interest in mobilizing ethnicity from a psychological or cultural or social datum into political leverage for the purpose of altering or reinforcing such systems of structured inequality between and among ethnic categories.

These ethnic entrepreneurs are given this opportunity and this opening by the ambivalent effects of modernization and of the technology-based industrialization that modern and transitional societies sponsor—effects that, on the one hand, tend to foster functional macrointegration and to encourage expectations of mobility, and yet in fact often sustain and exacerbate the very inequalities whose traditional legitimacy and seeming inevitability they simultaneously undermine. As a result, in modern and transitional societies—unlike traditional ones—politicized ethnicity has become the crucial principle of political legitimation and delegitimation of systems, states, regimes, and governments and at the same time has also become an effective instrument for pressing mundane interests in society's competition for power, status, and wealth. This triadic nexus among ethnicity, political legitimacy, and social interest means that, hypothetically, there are always several possible ethnic or ethnonational cutting edges potentially available for mobilization in a modern society—for example, Breton or French, Cossack or Russian or Slav or Soviet, Welsh or British, Italo-American or White Ethnic or unmodified American, racial or religious or linguistic or regional or other marker-criteria. The interesting analytical and projective problem is to determine why and when which ones are selected for this politicization by which sets of political entrepreneurs.

A related problem is to assess the balance of opportunities

and of probable success between, on the one hand, these entrepreneurs of politicized ethnicity and, on the other hand, ideologically nonethnic and antiethnic political entrepreneurs seeking to dissolve the ethnic allegiances and transform the ethnic conflicts generated and sharpened by modernization into either class consciousness and class politics (Socialists) or into ideological individualism and voluntary-pluralistic group politics (Liberals). Though the latter sets of political entrepreneurs purport to be more rationally scientific in their analyses of, and prescriptions for, modern society, they have either been defeated or checked by, or else obliged to come to a *modus vivendi* with, politicized ethnicity. Somewhat ironically, indeed, the tilt of this (im)balance toward politicized ethnicity has increased with the increasing pace of modernization and increasing levels of modernity in different countries.[1]

The politicization of ethnicity entails yet a further, related, irony and paradox. It stresses, ideologizes, reifies, modifies, and sometimes virtually re-creates the putatively distinctive and unique cultural heritages of the ethnic groups that it mobilizes—precisely at the historical moment when these groups are being thoroughly penetrated by the universal culture of science and technology. Politicization of ethnicity is thus a dialectical process that preserves ethnic groups by emphasizing their singularity and yet also engineers and lubricates their modernization by transforming them into political conflict groups for the modern political arena, where they must deploy cosmopolitan modern skills and resources. These two aspects of the dialectical process facilitate and reinforce each other, controverting the conven-

[1] This proposition is controversial and is defended in subsequent substantive chapters. Many American sociologists contest it. For a recent example of such an attempted refutation, see Gans, "Symbolic Ethnicity," pp. 193–220. In general support of my proposition are Nelson, "Ethnicity and Socioeconomic Status," pp. 1024–38; Krejci, "Ethnic Problems in Europe," pp. 124–71; Anderson, "Renaissance of Territorial Minorities," pp. 128–43; Esman, "Management of Communal Conflict," pp. 49–78; Isaacs, *Power and Identity*, passim.

tional assumption that secular modernization and ethnic identification covary inversely.[2] The result is a hybrid global tendency toward the universalization of scientific norms and of economic interdependence and yet also toward ever more particularistic ethnopolitical loyalties. The two pulls—which are intricately related to each other—impose great strains on contemporary states, most of which are demographically multiethnic.

These strains can be descriptively summarized here very briefly. The globalization of science, technology, and organic economic interdependence is an uneven and disorderly process, conferring advantages on some regions and groups and facilitating their structural consolidation of those advantages and headstarts, while relegating other regions and groups to marginality and subordination. But these actual differentiating results of the process contradict its potential egalitarian promise. Thus two sets of contradictions come into play as the modernization process develops: (1) among regions and groups that are rendered structurally unequal and (2) between normative promise and implemented results. To the extent that this process operates among states, its dual contradictions fuel tensions between the so-called first and third worlds. To the extent that it operates within states, these contradictions provoke conflict between advantaged, dominant population segments and disadvantaged, subordinate ones. This conflict is often over control of the state apparatus and sometimes over the exasperated decision of one of the contending groups to secede from an extant state that it perceives as irredeemably alien and hostile. In other words, both dominant and subordinate groups come to view the state as the gatekeeper of the contradictions and the controller of the conflict. Hence either exclusive or participant power over and in a state apparatus becomes for

[2] Isajiw, "Olga in Wonderland," pp. 29–39; Newman, "Theoretical Perspectives," pp. 40–54; Forbes, "Two Approaches to the Psychology of Nationalism," pp. 172–81; Petersen, "On the Subnations of Western Europe," pp. 177–208.

them a crucial need and goal. Their most convenient, feasible, and productive ideology for this quest is politicized ethnicity, which can readily be mobilized along the faultlines of the contradictions and the conflicts.[3]

But its instrumental utility in the struggle for power over and within states does not exhaust the potency of politicized ethnicity. Or, more precisely, ethnicity can be honed to that trenchant political cutting edge because it also fulfills other, nonpolitical, prepolitical, or only incipiently political, human needs—emotional, cultural, moral needs. Among these, ironically, is a need for some psychological distance and social autonomy from the technocratic rationality that fuels the scientific modernization process, catalyzes its contradictions and conflicts, and thereby prompts the politicization of ethnicity. Science, technology, material productivity, and the technocratic style of decision-making that they entail are today suspect—not only for allegedly veiling economic and political interests under their screen of claimed objectivity and rationality, but also for supposedly leaving man unfulfilled on some inner spiritual frontier.

That inner frontier is often described as a need or a quest by individuals to find meaning and understanding in their lives—meaning and understanding that, ultimately, are more satisfactorily and more rewardingly supplied through a sense of belonging to, and identifying with, ethnic groups than by functionally specific groups and activities. Though the rhetoric with which this argument is posed is often hazy, its import is clear: our modern scientific–technological world is so highly structured and overorganized that it actually presents itself to many individuals as chaotic. To avert the resultant threat of personal anomie and fragmentation, they draw a reintegrating identity from identification with their ethnic group, which is the only social entity left that defines and accepts them for what

[3] Cf. Rawkins, "The Global Corporation," pp. 73–84.

they are, rather than by what they do.[4] In this sense, the ethnic group is somewhat analogous to Robert Frost's definition of home, ". . . the place where, when you have to go there, they have to take you in" (from his poem "The Death of the Hired Man"). Though it is not analytically clear why ethnicity should be uniquely capable of fulfilling this psychological need for meaning and belonging in a threatening world, the virtual ubiquity of the contemporary ethnic revival—in symbolic, cultural, organizational, and political dimensions—suggests that, in practice, modern man has failed to find an equally satisfactory alternative to it.

The politicization of ethnicity translates the personal quest for meaning and belonging into a group demand for respect and power. Simultaneously, it gives a public instrumental direction to ethnicity's affective psycho-cultural energies. To politicize ethnicity is (1) to render people cognitively aware of the relevance of politics to the health of their ethnic cultural values and vice versa, (2) to stimulate their concern about this nexus, (3) to mobilize them into self-conscious ethnic groups, and (4) to direct their behavior toward activity in the political arena on the basis of this awareness, concern, and group consciousness. Such politicization of ethnicity may ultimately enhance, retard, or nullify the political integration of states, may legitimate or delegitimate their political systems, and stabilize or undermine their regimes and governments. But since it always brings new actors into the political arena and often introduces new styles of participation, its initial impact tends to unsettle and wrench established institutions and processes.

Many observers, indeed, have been so fascinated and/or alarmed by this initially destabilizing impact of freshly politicized ethnicity that they have interpreted it as launching an absolutist, zero-sum type of politics over uncompromisable values and

[4] Parsons, "Some Theoretical Considerations," p. 56.

rights (for example, to self-determination, group status, territorial control) and, hence, as more dangerous to civic order than class and functional interest-group politics are. Now, it is indeed true that the rhetoric and the style of ethnic politics are often strident, raucous, and replete with images of irreconcilability. More seriously, it is also true that the energies of ethnic politics have sometimes produced catastrophic violence. But all that was also once true of class politics in the premodern and prepoliticized-ethnicity era of peasant jacqueries and in the early phases of the industrial revolution. Moreover, at the time, many contemporaneous analysts of that industrial revolution also perceived its allocative conflicts over wages, profits, and rents to be noncompromisable zero-sum conflicts—and were subsequently proven wrong. I consider it prudent, therefore, to begin this study with an agnostic stance toward the charge that the demands and goals of politicized ethnicity are inherently and generically absolutistic, indivisible, and nonadjustable—and to test that allegation in the chapters that follow.

At this point, two caveats are in order lest erroneous or exaggerated inferences be drawn from the immediately preceding paragraphs. First, at the level of the individual: in modern conditions, even a person for whom ethnicity is a deep reservoir of meaning, belonging, and self-esteem will not deliberately bring his/her ethnic identity to the fore in every social interaction or political engagement. As a modern person, he knows that ethnicity is irrelevant to some situations and for some roles and even a liability in other circumstances. Hence, in such contexts, it would be pointless or even counterproductive to activate his ethnic identity—and he prefers other actors to ignore it as well (though they may not oblige him). Second and similarly, at the collective level, even highly politicized ethnic groups do not necessarily introject themselves into every political issue that may agitate a society. For prudential reasons they may adopt a low profile or, indeed, on occasion even leave the overt political arena for an interval. This is not tantamount to depoliticizing or demobilizing the group—any more than an individual's decision not to engage his ethnic identity in every social encounter is tantamount to his assimilation or "passing" out of the group. Quite the contrary. A group decision to withdraw temporarily from the political arena as a corporate combatant may be a sophisticated political strategy in the interest of group survival and/or consolidation. It may also embed a long-run intention, *reculer pour mieux sauter*. In any event, it illustrates that ethnic groups (like ethnic individuals) have a variegated and flexible repertoire of political options—more flexible, ironically, than states have. After all, a state apparatus could hardly take a similar decision to withdraw temporarily from the political arena.

In sum, therefore, the contemporary rise of ethnic individual identification and the trend toward ethnic group politicization do not mean that all other orientations, affiliations, differentiations, segmentations, or conflicts have been neutralized or eliminated. They interact with ethnicity—within individuals, within states, and across states. But the ethnic dimension has become increasingly salient in an increasing number of political conflict situations in modern and transitional societies. It refuses to be dissolved into another dimension, such as class, and demands to be faced on its own political plane.

* * *

For the purposes of this political study, it is unnecessary—indeed, it would be counterproductive—to indulge in elaborate definitional distinctions among an ethnic group, a nation, a nationality, a people, a tribe, and the like. *Politicized ethnicity*, *ethnopolitics*, *ethnonationalism*, *ethnoregionalism*, *ethnosecessionism*, and so on, are all terms used here in analyzing what happens when such entities bring their social, cultural, and economic interests, grievances, claims, anxieties, and aspirations into the political arena—the intrastate and/or the interstate arena.[5] Nor would it be helpful, or even possible, to separate out the notion of ethnic consciousness, solidarity, and assertiveness from religious, linguistic, racial, and other so-called primordial foci of consciousness, solidarity, and assertiveness (as is attempted, for example, in the United Nations' International Covenant on Civil and Political Rights, Article 27). After all, if religious, linguistic, racial, and other primordial criteria and markers were to be peeled off, it is difficult to see what precisely would be left to, or meant by, the residual notion of ethnicity and ethnic groups. Because this argument is further explicated and elaborated later (chapter 3, section 4), suffice it to state here that the terms *ethnicity* and *ethnic*—in various compound nominal and adjectival grammatical constructions—are used generically in this study to refer to the political activities of complex collective groups whose membership is largely determined by real or putative ancestral inherited ties, and who perceive these ties as systematically affecting their place and fate in the political and socioeconomic structures of their state and society.

[5] Wallerstein, "The Two Modes of Ethnic Consciousness," p. 168; and Bram, "Change and Choice in Ethnic Identification," p. 248.

Chapter One

ETHNICITY AS A POLITICAL PHENOMENON IN SEARCH OF SCHOLARLY ANALYSIS

1 · If it is to be effective over the long run—indeed, if it is to survive—political authority must be sustained by legitimacy. That is, it must be perceived by its wielders and its subjects as appropriate and rightful within its specified limits. The source of this legitimacy was formerly often derived "from above" the subjects of the political authority, from such principles and titles as divine right, inheritance, anointment, biblical analogizing, marriage, conquest, "enlightened" administration, and so forth. But the validity of such claims to legitimacy was ended in the Western world by a double revolution in modern European political thought and ideology. First, in the wake of the civil war in seventeenth-century Britain, Hobbes and Locke, though differing profoundly on many other issues, agreed in affirming the proposition that political legitimacy is derived "from below," from the will and interest of the governed. Then, in nineteenth-century Europe, the Lockeian concept that political authority is legitimately accountable to popular sovereignty—a concept that was initially ethnically indifferent—was transformed into the Mazzinian doctrine of the self-determination of peoples qua ethnonational communities. The engine

of this transformation had been the French Revolution and the subsequent Napoleonic Wars, which had changed the notion of "the people" from an a-ethnic aggregation of autonomous individuals into a national community of ethnic brothers. *Fraternité*, which had originally been a cosmopolitan appeal, became an ethnocentric and nationalistic rallying cry.

In the course of the nineteenth century, European politics was thus transformed from a series of dynastic issues—the War of the Spanish Succession, the War of the Austrian Succession, and the like—into a series of ethnonational "questions"—the Polish Question, the Irish Question, and so on. World War I and the resultant Paris peace treaties supposedly resolved many (but scarcely all) of these so-called ethnonational questions within Europe, but the demonstration-effect of the creation of a number of new national (or supposedly national) states on that continent predictably whetted the appetites of the Asian and African subject-peoples of Europe's colonial empires for their own states. Their demands, in turn, were largely granted after World War II, a development that, ironically, today fuels a demonstration effect in reverse, from the Afro–Asian world back to the Western one as the Scots, the Corsicans, the Basques, the Ukrainians, and others ask why they should be denied the independent statehood that has been conceded to Ghana, Algeria, Guinea, and Bangladesh. Nor are these Western ethnonationalists impressed by the conventional retort that a state of their own would be too small or weak to be viable. If the Comoro and Fiji Islands and Gambia can be made into viable states, so can Quebec and Catalonia.

Indeed, the old interwar discussion of the viability of states (a discussion that then had a revisionist, anti-Versailles edge) has been neutralized by the upsurge of post-World War II ethnonationalism as the international community has lowered its threshold requirements and definitions of what constitutes viability. States that would formerly have been deemed nonviable by virtue of their small size, awkward and indefensible frontiers, or meager human and material resources are now normally and as a matter of course subsidized and sustained by the international community. In a sense, the role of the state has been rendered paradoxical. On the one hand, we witness an explosive worldwide growth of state activity, with a concomitant disappearance of stateless societies. On the other hand, this hyperactive contemporary state is no longer expected to be autonomously viable, let alone self-sufficient. Yet it emphatically insists on boundary-maintenance between itself and all other states. And this insistence is in large measure a predicate of politicized ethnonationalism.

Though ethnic political consciousness is today geographically universal, it has not been historically universal. In the ancient and medieval worlds, rather few peoples resented or rejected rule by ethnic strangers, and as recently as 1714 the British repudiated a native dynasty and replaced it with a foreign king—and this at a time when their sovereign was not yet a figurehead and still exercised extensive political and administrative powers. But by the mid-nineteenth century, these same British refused to confer on their queen's husband, Albert, the honorific title of king-consort (which she had wished)—in part because he was a foreigner. Roughly contemporaneous, albeit more potent, examples of this modern surge of politicized ethnicity were the unifications of Germany and Italy on the one hand and the incipient disintegration of the Ottoman and the Habsburg empires on the other—all in the name of ethnocultural solidarity and cleavage. More recently, these same solidarities and cleavages have also fragmented the proclaimed cosmopolitan unity of several ideological movements.

Neither in Europe nor elsewhere are most of the states that were created in the nineteenth and twentieth centuries in response to these ethnonationalistic pressures true nation-states in the sense of incorporating within their borders all members of—but no more than—a single ethnic community. The facts of human demography are simply too intricate and convoluted to allow for such a neat and clean map of state borders exactly congruent with ethnic boundaries. Most of the world's states are multiethnic, and yet the moral force of the norm of ethnonational self-determination remains extraordinarily potent. Out of this tension between the reality of multiethnic states and the potentiality of self-determination demands, there emerge today's politics of ethnonationalism, which agitate old European and new Afro–Asian states alike and which draw their moral impetus from the linked Lockeian–Mazzinian propositions that "a people" (self-defined by various possible cultural, physical, or political criteria) has the right to determine its political allegiance, including the right to claim autonomy or sovereign independence.[1]

Though several newer "isms" have arisen in the twentieth century, ethnic nationalism, or politicized ethnicity, remains the world's major ideological legitimator and delegitimator of states, regimes, and governments. A state's legitimacy depends heavily on the population's perception of the political system as reflecting its ethnic and cultural identity. Indeed, at the margin of choice, today most people would rather be governed poorly by their own ethnic brethren than well by aliens, occupiers, and colonizers (though they hope, of course, to avoid such a stark dilemma and be well governed by their own people). Indeed,

[1] Cf. Walker Connor, "Politics of Ethnonationalism," pp. 1–21; Cobban, *The Nation State*, pp. 33–41. There does not now exist a universally accepted definition of this entity, namely, "a people," that is ideologically and normatively declared to be entitled to self-determination. In other words, the "self" of "self-determination" remains problematic. Cf. Buchheit, *Secession*, ch. 1; and Harris O. Schoenberg, *The Concept of "People" in the Principle of Self-Determination* (doctoral dissertation, Columbia University: Faculty of Political Science, 1972), passim. The problem of the various criteria by which an ethnic group may identify itself is taken up in greater detail in chapter 3, section 4.

to be ruled by ethnic strangers is perceived as worse than oppressive, as degrading. Political elites, in turn, seek to mobilize this sentiment in order to achieve statehood for their nation or to forge a nation from the population of the state. (The French are said to have been welded into a nation by their centralizing late medieval state, whereas the Italian nation preceded and created the modern Italian state.) Often, of course, competing elites will race each other to realize the one or the other possible pattern. Thus, it is valid to ask but impossible to answer comprehensively whether the Québécois, Scots, Basques, Croatians, or Ukrainians will achieve independent statehood before organic Canadian, British, Spanish, Yugoslav, or Soviet political nations are molded—or whether the latter process will carry the day; or alternatively, whether the respective ethnic and state elites will manifest the political prudence, will, and skill to design and effectuate institutional arrangements that might comprehend and legitimate dual political loyalties (see chapter 5, sections 2 and 3). (I omit any listing of developing countries undergoing the same dialectical strains.) This analytical distinction between the state (a political–legal entity) and the ethnic nation (a politicized cultural–historical entity) is critical throughout this study.

No type of society or political system is today immune from the burgeoning pressure of politicized ethnic assertiveness, with its possible legitimating or delegitimating effects. Communist and non-Communist, old and new, advanced and developing, centralistic and federalistic states must all respond to the pressures of this ascendant ideology, which can propel relatively prosperous (for example, Basque, Croatian) and relatively poor (Québécois, Welsh) groups alike into a sense of political grievance. The conventional academic wisdom used to claim that modernization and development would defuse and dissolve this allegedly primordial sentiment of ethnicity or, at a minimum, would relegate it to a species of folkloristic trivia. But today we must recognize that it is rather this conventional academic wisdom which has been reduced to triviality by the power of this ubiquitous and growing phenomenon of ethnopolitical consciousness and assertiveness. Even urbanization, contrary to former expectations, intensifies it. Marxists have difficulty coming to intellectual terms with this movement, which cuts across and negates their preferred, and supposedly more rational, class solidarities, while Liberals, in turn, are rendered uncomfortable by ethnic insistence that ascriptive group-solidarity obligations have priority over individualistic choice-preferences. Precisely because other scholars are devoting so much energy and attention to the study of this ethnonational phenomenon in the new states of the so-called third world, I propose to emphasize the no less significant and, indeed, potentially no less incendiary ethnonational question in some of the older states of the developed world.

2 · I have so far made no explicit distinction among terms such as *authority, regime, political system*, and *state* in discussing the repositories and generators of political legitimacy. In his discussion of political support–inputs into systems, David Easton has distinguished three objects of such support: the community (for example, "France" as a state); the regime (that is, the prevailing ideological values, constitutional rules, and authoritative structures of the political game); and the authorities (the government of the day and other occupants of formal political authority roles).[2] This classification can also be productively applied to the analysis of legitimacy in its contemporary ethnopolitical manifestation. When, for example, nineteenth-century French republican–secularists, royalist–clericalists, and Bonapartist–imperialists were ceaselessly seeking to dele-

[2] David Easton, *A Systems Analysis of Political Life* (New York: Wiley, 1965), chs. 11, 12, 13.

gitimate each others' regimes and authorities, none of them ever questioned (indeed, all vividly affirmed) the legitimacy of a unitary French state. In other words, the legitimacy of the political community per se was not then at issue.

Applying this typology to contemporary Western Europe suggests that, in at least one very serious dimension, the challenge to the legitimacy of several of its states is today potentially more serious than it was and at least as serious (though in a different dimension) as in the East European countries. With the possible exceptions of East Germany, the Soviet Union, and Yugoslavia (and even here some hostile wishful thinking may be at play), the other Communist states do not appear to be targets of domestic ethnopolitical repudiations and delegitimations as state entities. Even the most vehemently antiregime and antigovernmental Poles, Hungarians, Romanians, Bulgarians, and others, affirm the desirability and legitimacy of the Polish, Hungarian, Romanian, Bulgarian, and other, states, even as they long for different political systems. By contrast, the Basque, Breton, Scottish, Québécois, and other ethnonationalist movements in the Western world appear to be intent on delegitimating the historic Spanish, French, British, Canadian, and other, states as political communities per se. Thus we appear to be witnessing an historically ironic reversal of the situation between the two World Wars when it was the states of Eastern Europe that were racked by delegitimating secessionist and militant ethnonationalist movements while those of the West appeared to be solidly legitimate nation-states. The change in Eastern Europe is largely a product of the considerable demographic simplification imposed during and after World War II: the flight, expulsion, and exchange of many nationalities; the redrawing of some frontiers; and the Nazi extermination of Jews and Gypsies. In the West, on the other hand, many long-dormant, or at least quiescent, ethnic and national groups have recently reawakened to self-consciousness and political activism. Yet, just as the current travails of regime-legitimation in Eastern Europe have an economic dimension, so, too, are the would-be delegitimations of some Western states based in substantial part on resentment and alienation over discriminatory modes in the structural incorporation of certain ethnic regions into the metropolitan and international economies. Furthermore, the current Western antistate ethnonationalisms, though indeed supported by such traditional elites as the local clergy and humanistic intelligentsia, increasingly draw the endorsement of the modern industrial elite and the technocratic intelligentsia and—perhaps most interestingly—are for the time being tilting toward the general political Left in a problematic but potentially potent association. They thus appear to be delegitimating the regimes and authorities, as well as the states, into which they are currently incorporated, and it would be deceptive to dismiss them as merely parochial and reactionary *frondes*.

Indeed, though they are analytically distinct, the political and historical interplay among the following contemporary challenges to the normative legitimacy of conventional states and political systems merits study: politicized ethnicity, multinational corporations, countercultural youth movements, ecologism, the urge to find self-fulfillment in supposedly fraternal subsocieties, the attitudinal decline in the developed world of personal ego-involvement with one's country, and the widespread sense that the contemporary state is somehow out of phase with the world's travails—seemingly too small and weak to solve such global issues as inflation, yet apparently too big and remote to evoke that cathartic trust and identification by its citizens that the state requires if its political system is to function normatively. A fretful skepticism about the direction of life, the quality of human relationships, and the spiritual and cultural costs of material prosperity pervades many advanced industrial states. Even those political systems that have succeeded in fostering economic growth are not deemed to have thereby earned legitimacy, because the price they have extracted from their publics in terms of the desolation of deeper values is allegedly excessive.[3] In such an environment, it is not really so incongruous that politicized ethnicity, which used to be viewed as conservative if not reactionary, should be marching in step with movements of the Left and of the counterculture that also emphasize participation, autonomy, local power, and whose political style is also often strident and suspicious of the contemporary state.

3 · Politicized ethnic assertiveness is thus a valid but not exhaustive explanation of the contemporary state's renewed crisis of legitimacy. While it is historically and organically linked with modernization and industrialization, politicized ethnicity postulates ascriptive, culturally specific solidarities in contradistinction to the universalistic achievement criteria that are supposedly the norms instilled and required by science-based modernization and industrialization. Yet, while recognizing this antithesis, care must be taken to avoid certain conventional errors in its analysis and interpretation, such as the following.

A. The would-be resolution of this antinomy through a simplistic intellectual and political dualism that requires "rational," that is, nonethnic, performance in those aspects of behavior that are "essential" for the functioning of the modern economy and the polity, while permitting ethnic cultural diversity in those, presumably less essential, aspects that do not directly impinge on functional economic or political rationality. Ethnicity is not to be allowed to press to its "logical limits" lest it disturb civic

[3] Berger, "Politics and Antipolitics," pp. 32–33.

and interstate order.[4] This attempt to square the circle begs the question of what, precisely, is here the content of "rational," "ethnic," "essential," and "logical limits."

B. The relegation of ethnic identity to the status of the "primordial" *tout court*. The evaluational thrust of this interpretation can be in various directions, as follows: (1) to romanticize ethnicity as supposedly authentic, intimate, organic, and populistic; or (2) to demonologize it as allegedly irredeemably subversive of modernization, development, science, and universalism; or (3) to depreciate it as merely aberrant, vestigial, obsolescing, and destined to be dissolved and transcended by the inevitably cosmopolitan, enlightened, scientific values of modernity.[5]

C. Ignoring the problem. While anthropologists and sociologists had long studied other aspects of ethnicity, its political problematics were not probed by social scientists until fairly recently, when their eyes were at last forced open by the vivid capacity of politicized ethnicity to provoke intrastate and interstate conflict. Approximately half the world's states have recently been plagued by ethnic strife, and it has tended to be more violent than class or doctrinal conflict. Some social scientists have retrospectively speculated about the reasons for their profession's prolonged myopia toward the problem, and among the more plausible explanations that they have suggested are the following.

1. The circumstances of the birth of the modern social sciences in nineteenth-century Britain, France, and Germany in

[4] For example, see Francis, *Interethnic Relations*, pp. 113, 125. See also Eugene Litwak and John Dono, "Forms of Ethnic Relations, Organizational Theory, and Social Policy in Modern Industrial Society," unpublished essay, 1976.

[5] These several interpretive tendencies may be discerned in the writings of, respectively: (a) Harold R. Isaacs and Michael Novak; (b) Orlando Patterson and John Porter; (c) Ferdinand Toennies and Gabriel Almond.

environments where ethnic divisions appeared to be minimal and class or estate stratifications and gaps alone seemed to be sufficiently salient to merit and require analytical, moral, and political attention. Britain, the first industrial society, has particularly been preoccupied by the question of class (a preoccupation that has probably contributed to the persistent failure of the English to understand the essence of their Irish problem).

2. The related assumption that the so-called nation-state, that is, the uniethnic state, is normative. Indeed, even the usually restrained John Stuart Mill allowed himself flatly and prescriptively to declare that, "Free institutions are next to impossible in a country made up of different nationalities . . . especially if they read and speak different languages . . . The boundaries of governments should coincide in the main with those of nationalities."[6] The illusion that the uniethnic state is the norm tends to be perpetuated into our own day by the persisting habit of social scientists (despite Max Weber's alert against it)[7] of using the words *state* and *nation* interchangeably. Note also the general use of *international* where *interstate* would be more accurate and the similar preference for the term *nation-building* where *state-building* is really intended.

3. The stubborn intellectual authority of the French legist–royalist–Jacobin tradition, which insists that the state not only structures but also virtually creates the society and, in the process, validly imposes cultural homogeneity. This fetishism of a unitary state that abhors pluralism is, for its devotees, tantamount to a dictate of reason.

4. The similar, albeit independent, propensity in American political science of the development-and-modernization theorists to exaggerate the capacity of elites to plan and mold public values, identities, and allegiances in an integrationist direction.

[6] Mill, *Considerations on Representative Government*, pp. 287, 289.

[7] *From Max Weber: Essays in Sociology*, eds. H. H. Gerth and C. Wright Mills (New York: Oxford University Press, 1958), p. 172.

5. In anthropology and sociology, the tendency of the structure/functionalist school to overstress equilibrium and underrate conflict and change.

6. Communication theory used to encourage the optimistic but misplaced expectation that greater contacts among a state's different ethnic groups lead to greater mutual understanding rather than to greater alienation. While it is, indeed, true that intensive communications tend to integrate the populations of different geographic regions that belong to the same ethnic culture, it does not follow that they have this same effect among different and contrasting ethnic cultures. Indeed, the opposite appears often to occur, as the rate of particularistic ethnic mobilization is stimulated to outpace the rate of supraethnic statewide integration.

7. Somewhat similar to this misreading of the impact of communication intensification is a false analogizing from the medieval integration of, say, Anglo-Saxons and Normans into Englishmen to predicting similar assimilations among the populations of today's multiethnic states. This overlooks the greater ethnic self-consciousness and tenacity that mass literacy and communications instill.

8. Indeed, the assumption that all the late medieval and early modern integrations are irreversible may itself be false and may have contributed to the underestimation of the persistence and resilience of ethnicity. Witness here the contemporary revival of Occitanian, Roussillon, and Breton ethnic assertiveness in the supposedly paradigmatically integrated nation-state of France, as well as the upsurge of Welsh, Scots, Basque, Catalan, and Galician politicized ethnicity, respectively, in Britain and Spain. Elsewhere, too, today's latent and hence ignored ethnic tensions may yet be politicized and may surface tomorrow.

9. The social sciences have tended to exaggerate the capacity

of material gratifications to erode ethnic bonds and have underestimated the emotional tenacity of these bonds, which often serve human needs better than instrumental groups and satisfactions do. Furthermore, the capacity of ethnic groups themselves to function as instrumental interest groups in the political arena was for long not appreciated by academics.

10. Related to the exaggeration of material gratifications was the end-of-ideology assumption. In the post-Cold War world, only pure pragmatism was supposed to inform political behavior. What was forgotten here is that pragmatic commitments are politically and emotionally rather weak precisely because they are merely pragmatic. Resurgent politicized ethnicity has, in a sense, turned the end-of-ideology argument upside-down: The power of formal socioeconomic ideologies may indeed have waned but only to be replaced by the ethnic ideology, not by pragmatism.

11. For the United States, the ideology and rhetoric of "the melting pot" for long blinkered recognition of the persistence of ethnicity. This error was then compounded when the historical experience of this immigrant country was fallaciously analogized to societies whose ethnic groups are autochthonous and hence repudiate any obligation to assimilate to a dominant core-culture other than their own indigenous one.

12. In Europe, ethnonationalism was muted in the immediate post-World War II years, in part because the Nazi experience had given "folkish" values a sinister reputation and in part because the enthusiasm for supranational European integration seemed to render ethnicity irrelevant. Scholars and students of public affairs misread this muffling as signaling the permanent demise of politicized ethnicity and as an implied confession that it was indeed reactionary and fascistic. Herein lies a double irony. The Europeanist movement can now be seen as having given unintentional and unanticipated encour-

agement to antistate and interstate ethnic (specifically ethnoregional) assertiveness (for example, the call for a Europe of ethnies), which, furthermore, today usually inclines toward the political Left.

13. In the so-called third world, much of the original scholarly fieldwork was undertaken in the years of the anticolonial struggle and the original euphoria of independence, when internal ethnic tensions were often muted. Now this honeymoon is over and in many (though not all) of the ex-colonial states interethnic relations have become more fractious than they were when that earlier research seemed to justify benign scholarly neglect toward their domestic ethnopolitics.

14. What might be called the Plato–Machiavelli mirror-of-princes syndrome flourishes among political scientists. The profession likes to imagine itself as the adviser to rulers and hence has a bias in wishing to see states and governments and elites succeed in achieving stability, modernity, and integration while recalcitrant obstacles, such as particularistic ethnicity, tend to be faulted as atavistic.

15. Finally, the two powerful ideological traditions of Liberalism and Marxism also contributed to the prolonged ignoring and dismissal of politicized ethnicity. The former has classically insisted that the basic problem of politics lies in the relationship of the autonomous individual to the state, and it rejects the notion that groups (other than purely voluntary associations) have corporate moral and legal rights. Indeed, since ethnic groups usually claim their members by ascriptive obligation rather than allow them a free choice, they are perceived by Liberals as quite menacing. Marxists, in turn, have long articulated a principled preference for analyzing society in terms of class interests and solidarities, and they continue to suspect ethnic allegiances as likely after all to turn reactionary, with their current leftward tilt in Europe proving ephemeral. Finally,

politicized ethnicity harbors a destabilizing threat to the multiethnic Soviet Union.[8]

4 · The approach that informs my study of politicized ethnic assertiveness, while much indebted to the earlier literature, seeks to avoid the three overall categories of error indicated above, specifically the following.

A. The suggestion that ethnicity can be compartmentalized and prevented from contaminating those "essential" areas of modern economic and political life that require "rational," universalistic behavior and values is deemed here to be intellectually facile and politically unsound. It was for long the traditional strategy of dominant elites in multiethnic states, such as Belgium, Canada, the Habsburg Empire, who sought to confine the use of the Flemish, French, and Slavic tongues to home, village, and menial exchanges while encouraging and requiring competence in French, English, German, and Magyar for entry into, and transactions in, the wider, supposedly more rational and universalistic, arenas of statewide economic, political, and professional life. But whereas this strategy was formerly in rare cases successful—note the near-extinction of Gaelic in the British Isles and of Euskara in Spain—today it no longer works (except toward immigrants). The Flemings,

[8] The listing above of some suggested explanations for the protracted delay in the social sciences' acknowledgment of the political potency of ethnicity in modern society draws on my own reflections and on essays by Burgess, "Resurgence of Ethnicity," pp. 265–85; Walker Connor, "Nation-Building or Nation-Destroying?" pp. 319–55; Walker Connor, "Ethnonationalism in the First World," pp. 19–45; Coulon, "French Political Science," pp. 80–99; Das Gupta, "Ethnicity," pp. 466–88; Halsey, "Ethnicity," pp. 124–28; Lijphart, "Political Theories," pp. 46–64; Van Dyke, "Individual, State, and Ethnic Communities," pp. 343–69.

Québécois, Ukrainians, and others now insist that, as the ancient inhabitants of their lands, they have a right to their native languages in all walks of life, including the most scientific, sophisticated, and universalistic of the professions. To be obliged to assimilate to an alien culture, as though they were recent immigrants, would be a humiliation and is no longer tolerable. What is at stake here is not simply the right or the pressure to use this or that language as a medium of communication but the whole issue of access to power and status for the respective contending ethnic groups—in other words, the politicization of ethnicity.

More generally, the compartmentalization scenario appears to misunderstand the meaning and the role of culture in social life. Culture cannot be so readily split and isolated from the daily decision, contacts, values, experiences, and patterns that people confront in their economic, professional, and political lives. The suggested compartmentalization of culture and of behavior into separate "ethnic" and putatively "rational-universalistic" sectors postulates an oversimplified and unrealistic world in which a supposedly autonomous ethnic culture is detached from the critical dilemmas, opportunities, promotions, demotions, satisfactions, and distresses of career, of market, and of public affairs. But in the fabric and texture of real life, these two sectors are always interwoven more or less densely.[9]

B. My difficulties with the "primordial" thesis require a somewhat lengthier explication. It is, of course, true that certain cultural or physical markers, such as language, religion, pigmentation, or tribal membership are primordial in the sense that people acquire them before they acquire more explicitly economic or political identities, self-perceptions, and allegiances. But initially these markers are simply the assumed givens of

[9] Cf. Deutsch, *Nationalism and Social Communication*, pp. 105–06.

life, not in themselves sufficient (though necessary) to mobilize those who share them into self-conscious groups that will be internally cohesive and externally competitive. Such mobilization occurs when these given cultural markers are infused with an intense, differentiating value, are elevated into an ethnic ideology. Thereafter the language or religion or customs or pigmentation are no longer simply "the way we do things" or "the way we are," but are appreciated as uniquely precious, binding those who share them into a special community pursuing collective goals. Some sharers of culture-markers never undergo this mobilization; some made it long ago; still others, in modern times. This last point means that not all contemporary ethnic groups, albeit mobilized along primordial markers, are necessarily ancient. The Yoruba of West Africa, for example, or the Slovaks and Belorussians of Central and Eastern Europe, or the Macedonians and Bosniaks of contemporary Yugoslavia are relatively new ethnic groups qua distinct self-conscious groups.

The emotional gratification and support that individuals draw from their membership in such a special community of shared, sacred ethnic values and customs can be quite profound. Self-esteem is sustained and enhanced by the resultant sense of belonging. And this deeply felt and deeply rooted personal ethnic identity can be an important political and psychological datum in an era of mass society, otherwise often characterized by shallow and intermittent attachments to transient people, volatile values, and insular functional-interest groups.

This ideologization of ethnicity through the sacralization of ethnic markers and the mobilization of the sharers of these markers is the achievement of ethnic leaders and elites. It occurs in times of social strain, competition, and confrontation, when the ethnic leaders persuade the bearers and sharers of the ethnic culture-markers to perceive their fate in ethnic, rather than in individual or class, terms and convince them that without ethnic communal solidarity their distinctive values, customs, and traits are endangered, their personal life-aspirations are jeopardized, and the very survival of their group is imperiled.[10]

Once so mobilized, ethnic groups may assert various types of political demands—or no corporate political demands. Traditionally dominant groups may mobilize politically in defense of their dominance. Subordinate groups may seek dominance within the existing state, or secession from it, or autonomy (political and/or cultural) within it. On occasion, a traditionally dominant group that sees its power slipping will also opt for a kind of secessionism, for example, the recent enclave-propensity of the Lebanese Maronites or the suburban flight of the middle class out of American inner cities. Relatively moderate is the frequent demand of ethnic groups that the social status, economic lot, educational opportunities, and civil rights and liberties of their members as individuals be improved within the broader multiethnic society. More radical is the demand for the redistribution of the society's assets among the ethnic groups as corporate entities. Here, in other words, the demand has been escalated from access for individuals to control for groups, from reward for performance within certain accepted structural perimeters to the power to set the perimeters.

This process, by which an ethnic group moves from (1) an aggregation of sharers of primordial markers, through (2) mobilization, and on to (3) politicization, is extremely difficult to reverse, at any rate in our modern, literate times. This means, for example, that, once politicized, an ethnic group is unlikely thereafter to be satisfied with economic concession alone; once corporate demands have been put on the political agenda, the upward mobility of individual members no longer suffices.[11]

[10] Trent, "Politics of Nationalist Movements," p. 164; Argyle, "Size and Scale," pp. 31–37.

[11] Brass, "Ethnicity and Nationality Formation," p. 237. An apparent exception to this empirical rule of the irreversibility of modern, militant, ethnic politicization may be the case of the South Tyrolean Germans in northern Italy. See Katzenstein, "Ethnic Political Conflict," pp. 287–323.

On the other hand, this point does not mean that every ethnic group necessarily takes this process through the highest possible level of political militancy. Much depends on its members' and leaders' perception of the state's social and political system as a whole—its nature, flexibility, and resilience; the benevolence and strength (or the reverse) of its authorities; and the possibilities and necessities of coalition politics. In short, the ethnic group's strategic decisions are in large part responses to the state's, the regime's, the government's capacity to earn and to project legitimacy.

Earlier in this section it was stated that primordial attributes and markers are necessary but not sufficient for the consolidation of ethnic groups. We are now in a position to state what else is needed: (1) elites with a capacity and an interest (religious, economic, social, or political) in mobilizing those who share the objective markers into such a self-conscious group and (2) competition over relatively scarce and valued resources and goals within the larger society, a competition that may precipitate into mobilization both dominant ethnic categories who feel themselves challenged and subordinates who perceive themselves as disadvantaged. Often, indeed, the mobilization is initiated by the traditional religious or aristocratic elite of a hitherto peripheral ethnic population whose values and position are threatened by the intrusion of competing modern values pressed by an alien, cosmopolitan regime. In time, this traditional elite may, or may not, be displaced by an alternative one—still indigenous but now modernizing and based on entrepreneurial or intellectual achievements.

An agglomeration, or category, of sharers of primordial markers that is without an elite, or whose incipient elite is consistently coopted away, will not be mobilized into an ethnic group unless and until this pattern changes. Examples here are the Belorussians of the former Polish–Lithuanian Commonwealth, the Slovaks of old Hungary, or the Amerindian populations of several Latin American countries, who for long used to lose their potential elites to Polish, Magyar, and Hispanic assimilation and hence remained, throughout that time, simply peasant sharers of their primordial languages and customs.

Thus, since the formation, consolidation, and politicization of ethnic groups is a mobilization process, always led by elites and usually crystallized in response to the challenge of modernity as represented by competing groups and alien values, it is not helpful to label ethnic groups as primordial *tout court*. Contemporary ethnicity is, rather, a highly conscious, political, and new mode of interest-articulation and conflict, which nevertheless also retains its quality of sacredness. Ethnic groups are simultaneously both primordial and modern, because in social life tradition and modernity are not necessarily mutually exclusive, nor is their interplay a zero-sum game. Indeed, technological modernization may even reinforce traditional, primordial bonds, as when radio and television broadcast sacred texts to communicant masses to deepen their sense of belonging to a special, precious, unique, organic collectivity and thereby to catalyze them into political assertiveness. Conversely, this politicization of the primordial bonds arms the ethnic group to survive under the exigencies of modern conditions.[12]

C. The third conventional error in the analysis of politicized ethnicity that I wish to avoid and correct is ignoring the issue. That intention is *ipso facto* expressed by the decision to undertake this study, but a word of explication is nevertheless in order. The long myopia of the social sciences toward politicized ethnicity, for which some explanations were suggested earlier, has been corrected. The bare fact of the existence of ethnic assertiveness by ethnic groups is now acknowledged. But it is still often ignored in the sense of being explained away as merely epiphenomenal or dependent and secondary. Occasionally it is

[12] Huntington, "The Change to Change," p. 295.

still trivialized as false consciousness; sometimes ethnic groups are simply redefined in terms of their (usually subordinate) class and occupational roles, and their ethnic allegiance is declared to be a symbolic expression of those roles; occasionally there are suggestions that ethnic solidarity is simply another mode of communications, and ethnic competition, another mode of conflict. Hence they supposedly need not be studied for their substantive content and issues but can be neatly subsumed under established, formalized communication theory and conflict theory. It is as if early in the industrial revolution the new social classes had been misperceived as simply another expression of *ancien régime* estates, and the new capitalist society, as simply a different but not intrinsically interesting mode of stratification.[13] But, while stratification may indeed be almost as old as human history, industrial capitalism was then incontrovertibly something new. So, too, today, while primordial ethnic markers may be traditional, politicized ethnicity is quite original and different from the immediately previous lines of allegiance and conflict. It has become the most keen and potent edge of intrastate and interstate conflict, displacing class and ideological conflict, and it asserts itself today, dialectically, as the leading legitimator or delegitimating challenger of political authority. Scholarly recognition of ethnicity's political potency, and scholarly acknowledgement that it is neither vestigial, nor obsolescing, nor definitionally reactionary, will also entail scholarly reexamination of conventional academic notions of political integration, development, and modernity.

[13] Glazer and Moynihan, "Why Ethnicity?" p. 33.

Chapter Two

THE EMERGENCE OF CONTEMPORARY ETHNOPOLITICS

1 · To argue that ethnicity is not simply primordial and that ethnic groups and ethnic conflict are not mere masks for socioeconomic classes and class conflict is not to claim that ethnicity is purely political or that the ethnic structuring of a society is utterly independent of its socioeconomic structures. Rather, it suggests that monocausal explanations of phenomena and exclusive claims for but one line of identification and cleavage are likely to prove distortive. Not only did the former exclusive preoccupation with class misunderstand the nature and tenacity of ethnic solidarities and cleavages, but also it even underestimated the significance of certain nonethnic socioeconomic identities and fissures alternative to class, such as those that divide professionals from businessmen, entrepreneurs from managers, skilled from unskilled workers.[1]

Practicing politicians have generally been alert to the pitfalls of any exclusivist categorization of people, even when many academics were writing as though they were not. Thus, even in the heyday of strict class analysis, regimes and parties of varying ideological hues were giving recognition—territorial, political,

[1] Dahl, "Pluralism Revisited," p. 193.

juridical, educational, cultural, fiscal—to ethnicity and ethnic communities. While the regimes and parties had ultimate intentions toward their ethnic publics and constituencies that varied and changed, they never ignored them through any fixation on class.

Today the danger of distortion through fixation seems to run in the opposite direction. The contemporary fad of "everybody is an ethnic; we are all ethnics," by implying a nonexistent equality, threatens to conceal the real nexus between ethnicity and the structural allocation of power, status, and wealth in society. Modern societies are generally characterized by several overlapping patterns of stratification and cleavage, and the proper task of social scientists is not to become preoccupied with the intricacies of only one such pattern but to explore and exhibit the interconnections among them. Thus, all societies are stratified economically, most societies are also stratified ethnically, and many are stratified racially. The purely, exclusively economic society, in which the only socially significant differentiation is that of class, that is, of economic wealth and economic power, with all citizens otherwise belonging to the same homogeneous ethnic (for example, linguistic, religious, racial) community, is extremely rare. Ironically from the perspective of dire class-conflict theory, where it does exist or come close to existing, for example, in Iceland, Luxembourg, Portugal, or Norway (consideration of her Lapps being put aside for the moment), it tends toward a relatively consensual rather than a starkly polarized political environment. (This is true even of Portugal, which in the 1970s navigated a difficult political decompression from half a century of dictatorship, followed by a painful decolonization trauma, with less violence and bitterness than most multiethnic polities with analogous problems inflict on themselves.) But even these few uniethnic, purely economic, societies are characterized by cultural differentiation (in the sociological, not the anthropological, sense of culture) corresponding to, and growing out of, their economic differentiation. Thus, to cite noncrucial dimensions, their working classes and their upper classes are likely to cultivate quite different culinary, esthetic, and recreational habits and preferences.

There are, indeed, historical examples suggesting that such cultural differences, originally sociological, may become so sharp and so patterned as to take on a near-anthropological distinctiveness; for example, the habit of the German and Russian nobilities in the eighteenth and nineteenth centuries, respectively, of conversing among themselves only in French. This custom, together with their genealogical claims to a special type of ancestry, suggests that these nobilities were then implictly bidding to separate themselves even ethnically from their national bourgeoisies and peasantries. The English and French nobilities, though not differentiating themselves linguistically from their countrymen, nevertheless also for long insisted on their descent from an ethnically distinct group of conquerors—respectively Normans and Franks. Lower class cultures may also hover between sociological and anthropological articulation. Witness here the old cloth-cap "uniform" and the distinctive argots of European urban proletariats.

For the student of ethnicity and its nexus with other lines of differentiation, this distinction between sociological and anthropological culture is of interest and utility—though somewhat more so for the study of developing rather than of developed countries.[2] Sociological culture is a function of the class and status position of its bearers. Thus, all other things being equal, the professional son of a beer-drinking, bowling worker is likely to change his leisure tastes to wine and tennis. Anthropological culture, on the other hand, consists of distinctive patterns of behavior and organization that are initially autonomous of class and status and are presumably primordial. Its bearers retain it

[2] Hoetink, "Resource Competition," pp. 9–25.

in a monoethnic society and supposedly seek to retain it in a multiethnic society, even through substantial changes in their social position—unless the social cost of such adherence is perceived as intolerable. For example, all other things being again equal, people are less inclined to change their religion or language than their beverage or sport as they become socioeconomically mobile. In modern Europe, for example, linguistic and religious frontiers have remained relatively stable (*toutes proportions gardées*) in comparison to sweeping socioeconomic revolutions. But all other things are, admittedly, not always equal, and the phenomenon of assimilating and "passing," of changing anthropological culture to adjust to changes in social position or to achieve a change in social position, is well known. It occurs because anthropological culture, though initially autonomous of social position, can become socially relevant in a multiethnic society. Not only occasional individuals, but sometimes also collective social categories, have engaged in this practice. As was mentioned in the preceding chapter, there was a time when the Belorussian and Slovak elites accepted Polonization and Magyarization more or less routinely, and any literate Latin American Indian was automatically Hispanicized. But in the current age of heightened ethnic consciousness and assertiveness, this strategy of "passing" has become rarer at both the individual and the group level. It is no longer perceived as necessary for avoiding status and aspirational discrepancy. Simultaneously, the politicization that accompanies and propels the new ethnic consciousness militates against the chances that the freshly revalued (anthropological) ethnocultural traits might remain simply private, albeit socially diversified, attributes and commitments.

A society may be uniform in its anthropological culture but differentiated in its sociological culture (Iceland, Luxembourg, Norway, Portugal, again), or it may be differentiated in both dimensions (Central and Andean America), or, hypothetically, it may claim a uniform sociological culture with discontinuous anthropological cultures (the Soviet prospectus of a culture "socialist in content but national in form"). A related problem of categorization arises from the consideration that, in the contemporary world of rapid and massive communications and close informational propinquity, the validity of pretenses to bearing authentic anthropological cultures becomes moot, indeed, precarious. For example, do Afro-American sartorial and tonsorial fashions, and soul food and music, suffice to place Black Americans in a distinct anthropological culture, when they share so many other behavioral and organizational patterns with Whites? The same question might be posed about the Hasidim of New York, who speak Yiddish and eat kosher, yet also learn to service computers and participate in pluralistic politics. Of course, the intensity of an ethnic group's solidarity and political militancy may be quite disengaged from the question of the primal authenticity and wholeness of its anthropological culture. Indeed, it is precisely when cultural traits are used politically for modern ethnic-group consolidation and competitive assertiveness that they are most likely to be modified, adapted, and reinterpreted.

Different anthropological cultures emerged out of a quondam condition of relative mutual isolation among human communities. With the end of that isolation, anthropological culture becomes problematic. The heirs of what were once internally integrated anthropological cultures now can, and usually must, choose whether or not to preserve them and, if the choice is positive, must decide which of their traits should be retained or restored or changed and how, in the teeth of external pressures and seductions. Thus, for example, most of the Jewish returnees to Palestine at the turn of the century decided that their national survival required the revival of the Hebrew language but became relatively indifferent to religious observances, whereas the Irish nationalists are allowing the Erse tongue to fade (they pay it symbolic lip service but do not use it) and yet identify emphatically with Roman Catholicism.[3]

2 · Though ethnicity bases its moral authority and its demand for member-loyalty on such primordial traits of anthropological culture as language, religion, and kinship patterns, at this point it is best to postpone a discussion of the substantive nature of these traits and of their psychological magnetism and to proceed first with a review of the political nexus between ethnic differentiation and other lines of stratification in a multiethnic society. Though the identifying and distinguishing criteria of ethnic, economic, social, and racial stratifications might seem, at the theoretical level, to be mutually exclusive or reciprocally irrelevant, in practice they coexist and interrelate in varying arrangements, shaped by the historical, political, economic, and technological experiences and capabilities of diverse societies.

Theoretically, even in a multiethnic society the allocation of economic possessions, social status, and political power might be ethnically (and racially) indifferent. And, indeed, in daily practice, there are many discrete economic transactions, social encounters, and political activities during which the actors do

[3] Streib, "Restoration of Irish Language," pp. 73–89. This article argues that the effort to restore Erse as a real language of use failed because it met neither social nor political needs. Hebrew was revived to supply a common tongue for Jews returning to Palestine/Israel from many different diasporas and speaking many different languages. In Ireland, this communication function was already supplied by English. Also, the political rationale for preserving Breton, Frisian, or Welsh as the languages of ethnic minorities in confrontation with dominant Establishments speaking a different language is absent for Erse, for the Establishment in the Republic of Ireland consists of English-speaking Irishmen, not of aliens. The upshot is that the Irish proclaim the revival of Erse to be their highly valued symbolic norm and yet evade it in practice.

not engage their ethnic identities and differences. But at the macrosocietal level this hypothetical image of an ethnically neutral distribution of resources does not correspond to reality, for the pattern of the distribution everywhere cross-corresponds with ethnic criteria. And it is precisely these asymmetrical correlations that transform ethnicity from a cultural or a phenotypical datum into a public issue and give a political bite to what might otherwise be bland socioeconomic statistics. Furthermore, the resultant pattern of ethnic stratification cross-cutting against socioeconomic stratification often dilutes the cohesiveness and political solidarity of economic classes. Hence the frequent case when the lower socioeconomic strata of relatively privileged ethnic groups are persuaded to distance themselves from the functionally similar strata of subordinate ethnic groups.

Today the engine of ethnic conflict is no longer this or that primordial cultural commitment per se (for example, which community worships God in the "true" way; which speaks a "nobler" or "richer" language); rather, it is the perceived ethnic inequalities and inequities in access to, and possession of, economic, educational, political, administrative, and social resources. And here a relatively favored ethnic group perceiving its domination to be threatened can become as militant as a deprived one struggling to end its subordination. The former will claim that its advantages are the product of its own virtues and must be defended against an assault by ethnic parasites. The latter will charge historic, ethnically biased, systematic neglect and exploitation. Furthermore, given today's intensification of communications and interactions, not only are the several contenders likely to be fairly well informed about their disparate resources and discrepant purposes, but also this very fact of widened information combines with the contemporary ambiance of competitive democratic emulation so as to render the situation of the advantaged groups the aspirational reference line for the disadvantaged.[4] No longer do the latter compare their current socioeconomic or political or educational station with that of their grandparents and appreciate the progress made; rather, they compare it with the levels being enjoyed by the dominants and resent the gaps that remain.

A basic question has, however, now been begged and an important caveat is in order. Since a cross-correspondence among economic, social, political, and ethnic criteria of distribution and stratification was stipulated above, is it valid to assume that the subordinates or dominants are fated to perceive themselves, the others, and the salient cleavages between them in specifically (because supposedly "natural")[5] ethnic terms? Must ethnocultural (anthropological) diversity become politically divisive? Was it inevitable, for example, that the Ulster and Lebanese civil wars had to be fought along ethnoreligious rifts rather than as class conflicts? Will a stratification between Magyar gentry and Slovak peasantry necessarily be experienced as an ethnic more than a socioeconomic one? Will aggrieved Welsh miners always funnel their sense of grievance against English owners or managers into an ethnonationalist rather than a social-ideological political party? And will other Welshmen always feel that an imperiled Welsh culture and Welsh landscape require to be protected and cleansed through widespread arson against English-owned rural cottages? Are Breton peasants bound to feel greater solidarity with Breton fishermen, shopkeepers, and workers than with the French peasants of the Ile de France? To ask the questions is immediately to answer them in the negative and to imply the caveat which must now be stated: In a cross-correspondential system of stratifications, alternative lines of cleavage and of solidarity are optionally available; which line emerges as politically most salient is deter-

[4] Young, *Politics of Cultural Pluralism*, p. 99.

[5] Cf. Rabushka and Shepsle, *Politics in Plural Societies*, pp. 64–65.

mined by historical, moral, political, structural-economic, and psychological contingencies (to be taken up seriatim in the rest of this chapter). This statement is, nevertheless, quite compatible with the argument made in the preceding chapter, namely, that since World War II there has been a general tendency (which, as always with general tendencies, has its exceptions)—including and especially in the developed world—for other lines of conflict to be displaced into ethnic ones. Though not a developed, but a still developing country, Nigeria is neatly illustrative here. In mid-1964, its trade unions virtually paralyzed the country with a transethnic general strike in support of wage demands. Two years later, interethnic civil war erupted. In Ulster, an analogous shift had occured even before both world wars. In 1907, the Protestant and Roman Catholic workers of Belfast had shown high class solidarity in a militant strike of dockside carters. But soon thereafter interethnic (Catholic versus Protestant) lines of conflict and violence became ascendant in Belfast, Ulster, and, indeed, throughout the whole island of Ireland. In Brittany, too, peasants have recently transferred their organizational-political energies from a long-standing emphasis on the interest-commonalities that were supposedly shared by all farmers in France to a staunch new ethnoregional perspective stressing transclass Breton solidarity to end and reverse "French" and "Parisian" exploitation and neglect of Brittany.[6] Why have this sequence and this tendency become frequent and general in our day?

3 · Historically, ethnicity was not a political problem in ancient and medieval empires. Even in the later, but still premodern, dynastic states of Europe, it was relevant only with respect

[6] Hechter, *Internal Colonialism*, p. 286; Berger, "Bretons, Basques, Scots," p. 172.

to administrative efficiency, not normative legitimacy. Thus, Joseph II's attempt to press German as the language of official transactions and communications on all his Habsburg subjects was really an exercise in rational statecraft, not a deliberate reach for ethnic domination. Yet, by posing the question of realm-wide education in an official language, this penchant for administrative rationality incipiently and unintentionally augured ethnic problems.

Ethnicity has become a potentially critical issue only since the French Revolution and the Napoleonic Wars, as modern states have sought to base their legitimacy on democratic claims and have simultaneously purported to be, or striven to become, nation-states expressing and enhancing specific national cultures. These pretensions and claims immediately posed the problems of ethnic assimilation, acculturation, discrimination, and rights; and ethnic response to the pretensions and claims led to many political upheavals, boundary changes, and interstate tensions. Nevertheless, in some of the older, early industrializing states of Europe and America, this potentially critical issue of ethnicity remained latent or secondary during the nineteenth and early twentieth centuries, being displaced by then more salient and more burning socioeconomic issues. In Britain at that time, for example, Scots and Welsh identifications did exist, but their political expression was channeled into, and masked by, ideological competition among the Conservative, Liberal, and Labour parties.[7]

[7] Seton-Watson, "Unsatisfied Nationalisms," p. 6. Note, however, that, even in that supposed heyday of class politics expressing economic issues and cleavages, the religious-confessional segments of several highly advanced and industrialized West European continental countries (for example, France, Belgium, the Netherlands, Switzerland) remained immune to such masking and reorganization along class lines. This was due to the strength of their politicized and affective religious bonds—Catholic, Calvinist, or Evangelical, as the case might be—and not to any supposed mildness of class tensions. Class tensions did divide the secular segments of these societies into opposing Liberal, Radical,

Since World War II, this supposedly "developed" pattern of the displacement of ethnic into socioeconomic identities and cleavages has been halted and substantially reversed—precisely in the developed countries. The prodigious postwar expansion in contacts and communications—both among and within the developed countries—has heightened their peoples' awareness of ethnic differences and imbalances. This informational effect is, in turn, compounded by the fact that the benefits and costs of the renewed postwar march of industrialization, urbanization, and modernization have been experienced differentially by various regions and ethnic groups. Governments that turn a blind eye to the resultant inequalities are accused of abetting discrimination; those that seek to correct them may be charged with practicing reverse discrimination. Either way, politicized ethnicity is energized. A Belgian or a Czechoslovak or a French or a Spanish government deciding whether to phase out or to subsidize an obsolescing mine or an unproductive factory or where to improve port and rail facilities or whether or not to protect a regional viniculture, will be perceived and judged as making a decision pregnant with ethnic consequences. Even if the operational decision is actually taken by an independent public-sector enterprise or a politically nonresponsible multinational corporation (in a non-Communist country), the political hazard of aggravating ethnic grievances will nevertheless be incurred by the particular country's government. Thus, when Bretons and Slovaks now ask why their ethnoregions are un-

---

and Socialist political camps but not the religious-confessional ones. However, since World War II, the new ethnic politics in Belgium has divided all the large older parties—Catholic, Liberal, and Socialist—along ethnolinguistic lines (Dutch/Flemish versus French/Walloon). Precisely to avert such fragmenting tendencies, the Swiss political parties—confessional as well as secular—have become increasingly attentive to the perceived need to achieve balanced linguistic and regional proportionality in their leaderships and their governmental delegations.

dercapitalized, or when Catalans and Croatians want to know why they should be overtaxed (as they see it) to subsidize other ethnoregions of their current multiethnic states, they are addressing ethnically charged political questions, requiring political explanations, to their governments. They will no longer be satisfied with "pure" economic or historicist or globalist accounts that might seek to evade the ethnopolitical issue behind rationalizations of supposed inevitability. To the extent that the parties of the classical Left Opposition are also often perceived as evading this issue in Western Europe, they too lose prospective militants to ethnoregional movements. The latter tilt ideologically leftward but are wary of the traditional parties of the Left.[8]

4 · Morally, the authority of the state has been thinned by a still more diffuse process, one that might be summarized under the old adage that familiarity breeds contempt. In former times, citizens and subjects came into contact with the state on

[8] Lijphart, "Political Theories"; Beer, "Social Class of Ethnic Activists"; and Berger, "Bretons and Jacobins," all three in Esman, ed., *Ethnic Conflict*, pp. 55–59, 156–57, 172–74.

The dynamics of this differential impact of change and its "ethnicization" is examined generically below, chapter 4, section 3. Here the following description of its political impact in Yugoslavia—whose constituent republics are really ethnoregions—is neatly illustrative of the point made in the text above: "Although the developed republics fought for the maximum retention of funds, the underdeveloped areas . . . demanded that the federal government assume a more active role in the distribution of development money. Intense competition among the republics for investment funds led to a growth of regional nationalism, and the rhetoric of politics and economics tended to merge. In 1971, the since-deposed Croat leadership demanded that foreign currency earned within each republic be controlled at the republic level . . . . In socialist states, economic issues are more legitimate topics for discussion than purely political matters, such as nationalism. Thus many arguments couched in the language of economics thinly concealed nationalistic particularism . . . . In November 1971, the economic and political issues merged into a demand for Croat autonomy." Klein, "Role of Ethnic Politics," pp. 349–50.

relatively rare, solemn, and respect-inducing if not awe-inspiring occasions. But today's developed welfare state, with its myriad demands, services, programs, and collections, impinges on its public's consciousness as a ubiquitous, prosaic, often arbitrary, and sometimes erratic bureaucratic presence.[9] As a result, an inverse relationship sets in between, on the one hand, the public's dependence on the state and the governmental apparatus and, on the other hand, its respect for them. Meanwhile, the prestige of other authority structures—academic, economic, religious, parental—is also often under assault. The beneficiary of this discrepancy, pressing itself forward to fill what might otherwise become a vacuum in moral authority and symbolic loyalty and providing an instrumental and a sentimental haven from all this overload and alienation, tends increasingly to be the citizen's ethnic group. While the overt behavioral obedience of citizens to states and to state authorities is not necessarily withdrawn (though it often is), the moral allegiance to the state that undergirds such obedience is changing and thinning—particularly in advanced societies, where, today, that allegiance is often either shared with, or transplanted to, the ethnic group. Poor ethnic groups level charges of having been traditionally neglected and exploited by an insensitive state apparatus; rich ones resent its recent intrusiveness; both types demand greater control over the allocation of their resources. In Western Europe, the loss of overseas colonies may have accelerated this transference of allegiance, not only for the conventionally cited economic reasons, but also in the psychological dimension, by dimming the aura of the former imperial state and eliminating the psychic reward that its ethnic groups used to draw from participating in its great imperial adventure.[10]

[9] Beals, "Rise and Decline," p. 164.

[10] Mazrui, *Post-Imperial Fragmentation*, pp. 9–14; Esman, "Perspectives on Ethnic Conflict," p. 375.

A dubious, albeit logical, corollary of this shift in "terminal"[11] political identification from the state to the ethnic group is the burgeoning demand that decision-making be localized, in order that specific ethnic problems, grievances, and aspirations might be addressed. This demand comes against the background of a massive postwar shift of decision-making power in many advanced Western states from relatively open and accessible legislatures toward arcane and unrepresentative technocratic bureaucracies whose normative operational ideology is the supposedly apolitical principle of cost-effective rationality in making allocative investment and infrastructural decisions. Ethnic groups often perceive this shift in decision-making power as disfranchising them, this technocratic bureaucracy as unaccountable to them, and this principle of rationality as insensitive to their particular needs, aspirations, and grievances. Hence, "local control" has become a virtual shibboleth of politicized ethnicity. However, though seemingly democratic, the net effect of such a process of dismantling "big and remote" bureaucratic government in favor of "community control and human scale" because "small is beautiful" might, ironically, prove to be particularly malign for the subordinate and disadvantaged ethnic groups that now often press for it in a risky association with disgruntled elements of the economic Establishment and with environmentalists. These ethnic groups' vulnerabilities and disabilities might well be aggravated by such a redistribution.

5 · Politically accelerating this moral erosion of the state's authority in favor of the ethnic group's is the pervasive sense in the developed world that, despite its fussy intrusiveness and its posing as a universal problem-solver, the state is really no longer competent to perform many of its traditional and

[11] This term is Rupert Emerson's, who uses it apropos the nation, not the ethnic group. See his *From Empire to Nation*, pp. 95–96.

necessary functions. The preceding chapter mentioned that the old question of the viability of small states has of late simply gone by the board, as states of all sizes are now arbitrarily rendered viable by the political stances of the international community. As with viability, so too with security, which is also no longer posed, in the developed world, as primarily a function of a state's own size, population, natural resources, and technological capacity, but more as a function of its alliance and alignment configurations. Hence—so runs the argument—if the external security of all small and medium states depends ultimately on the umbrellas of their superpower patrons and the credibility of their alliance arrangements, rather than on their own capabilities, then a relatively small but ethnically "pure" Brittany, Catalonia, Corsica, Croatia, Quebec, or Wales need to be no less secure from foreign aggression than a medium-sized multiethnic France, Spain, Yugoslavia, Canada, or Britain, since it could get the same level of protection. Indeed, it sometimes even appears as though small states have somewhat greater room for maneuver than medium ones, for the latter seem to be more closely monitored by their superpower patrons and more constrained by webs of obligations. Though there are flaws in this line of reasoning, and though it clearly does not apply to all extant or proposed states, it has acquired sufficient plausibility to be often mobilized for ethnosecessionist arguments against contemporary multiethnic states. In Western Europe and Canada its reception has been facilitated by the mood of detente, which tends to be misperceived as guaranteeing the security of any and every state on the two continents and thus as implicitly licensing ethnosecessionism from multiethnic states.

Furthermore, quite apart from such ultimate and drastic questions as security and viability, small states and their citizens do not seem to be seriously disadvantaged (relative to medium states) in today's world when it comes to more prosaic matters such as access to credit and trade markets, interstate labor, and professional mobility.[12] This observation also fuels ethnosecessionist speculation.

Ethnosecessionism having now been mentioned, four caveats about it must here be interpolated, as follows:

1. In general, this subject is most taboo among the new, ex-colonial, states that have achieved sovereign independence only since World War II and for whose governing elites even a hypothetical discussion, let alone an attempted implementation, of secessionist self-determination evokes fears of strategic truncation, "Balkanization," and, in many cases, infinite divisibility. Stated geographically, this means that ethnosecessionism is most vehemently proscribed in Africa and Asia, whereas in the older states of Europe and in Canada, while admittedly controversial, it is a much-discussed option, by no means taboo.

2. Though the states for which it presses would indeed be smaller than the multiethnic ones from which they would be carved (except in a few third world cases where secessionism is coupled with vast irredentism), they would not necessarily be drastically small. Everyone knows that Bangladesh, for example, is a huge state. But fewer people appreciate that Quebec is comparable to Sweden in population, natural resources, urbanization, and other important indicators. So, too, Scotland, Wales, Occitania, the Basque land, Croatia, the Ukraine, and some other ethnoregions that might yet bid for independence or autonomy can boast resource bases that compare favorably with those of many already existing states.

3. Secessionism need not inevitably become the level to which politicized ethnicity will escalate its demands. Yet, wherever secessionism is asserted, it always seeks to legitimate itself by appealing to the normative principle of ethnic self-deter-

[12] Cf. Abbott, "Size, Viability, Nationalism," pp. 56–68, and Leff, "Bengal, Biafra," pp. 129–39.

mination—such is the latter's moral power in today's world. "Mere" economic or administrative regional grievances without an acknowledged ethnic edge, such as those that wrack southern Italy and northern England, are not acknowledged as warranting secessionism, nor do they attract mass support if articulated simply as georegional grievances. At the margin, an aggrieved region may even have to invent an ethnic identity or revamp an old one, to justify its claims.

4. Even where it is asserted as a right, secessionism will not necessarily be adopted as a strategy or carry the day. If its prospective economic and institutional costs are prohibitive, then its potential constituents may nevertheless—their ethnic sentiment and the logic of the self-determination ideology notwithstanding—settle for a level of redress and satisfaction (cultural, psychological, administrative, political) somewhat short of independent statehood. Thus, for example, even the once categorically secessionist Parti Québécois leadership has recently sought to assuage the anxieties of its public about the possibly prohibitive costs and impacts of unqualified separation from the rest of Canada by devising the somewhat equivocal formula of "sovereignty with association." And such dilemmas of would-be secessionists, in turn, emphasize and bring into play the resources and options that metropolitan regimes still command. Nevertheless, since ethnic groups that are concentrated in ethnic regions form the only kind of social segments for whom political secession and separate statehood are feasible (unlike social classes, age cohorts, or sex genders, for whom it is not—*pace* the Lysistrata legend and the more recent "dropout" of the under-thirty generation), it follows that ethnosecessionism always remains a potential option, to be brandished as a serious goal or as a bargaining maneuver.

In Europe, indeed, ethnic groups that are concentrated in ethnic regions are learning to apply a subtle political calculus short of secessionism, while some of them reserve that option as a potential threat. Expectations that the existing European multiethnic states would be dismantled between the upper millstone of suprastate institutions (the European Community, the West European Union, NATO in the West, CEMA and the Warsaw Treaty Organization in the East) and the nether millstone of substate ethnoregionalism[13] have so far proven vastly exaggerated and erroneous. The suprastate bureaucracies have generally paid deference to the sensitivities of the existing states and regimes (whose creatures they are) and shunned collusion with political ethnoregionalism. After all, their respective styles and goals are not particularly compatible, as the suprastate commissions are self-consciously rationalistic, reformist, and technocratic, while the ethnic movements often cultivate emotional, radical, and sometimes antitechnological, populistic reflexes.[14]

Nevertheless, the European ethnic movements have been able to manipulate the network and the ambiance of suprastate actors and extrastate linkages to apply leverage—short of secession—to their several states. The Basques and Catalans, for example, helped to generate an environment obliging Spain to liberalize its political system as one prerequisite for full membership in the European Community. And any specifically regional concessions that Madrid makes to them will probably also be demanded by the Galicians and may well have an interstate impact by putting France under some pressure to grant concessions to her Basque (and other) ethnoregions or face ETA violence. (ETA are the initials of the clandestine separatist organization *Euskadi 'Ta Askatasuna*, whose name means Basque Homeland and Liberty.) The Tyrolean Germans intruded themselves into Austro-Italian interstate relations and,

[13] For example, Neal Ascherson on the Op-Ed page of *The New York Times*, July 12, 1978, p. A19. The term *ethnoregionalism* is to be read as referring to a political phenomenon, not as a mere geographical-administrative expression.

[14] Scheinman, "Interfaces of Regionalism," pp. 65–78.

by extension, into the fate of Austria's application for associate membership in the European Community. In Switzerland, the Jurassien movement drew support from the Francophone regions of Belgium and Canada in its successful internal-secessionist bid for a separate, new, French-speaking canton carved out of Bern. The Celts of Britain and France also cooperate across state frontiers to embarrass their metropolitan governments. Similar examples could be multiplied. Furthermore, the capacity of West European ethnic movements to exert such leverage may be enhanced by direct elections to the Euopean parliament (the first of which were held in June 1979), since such institutional innovations generally entail politico-structural consequences. One may yet see ethnic parties holding trans-state caucuses at Strasbourg, just as Socialist and Christian ones do already.[15]

Thus, while it is premature and unrealistic to speak today of a political "Europe of ethnies,"[16] nevertheless, when one considers that the institutional and political possibility of exercising such ethnoregional leverage is only a generation old in Western Europe, then the results are interesting and quite impressive. In effect, the ethnoregions have become a part of the West's intrastate and interstate political process. This may, in time, exercise a demonstration-effect on East Central and Eastern Europe, where it is watched attentively.

The political leverage of the ethnoregions is likely to prove particularly potent—for good or ill—where it is linked to functional problems, for example, industrial obsolescence in Wallonia or energy control in Scotland or capital deficits in Slovakia or ominous demographic trends in the Baltic and Central Asian republics of the Soviet Union; in other words

[15] Rudolph, "Ethnic Sub-States," pp. 537–57.

[16] Cf. Guy Héraud, *L'Europe des Ethnies* (Paris: Presses d'Europe, 1963), and the Vienna quarterly *Europa Ethnica* (1961–current).

(and in a reversion to the theme with which this chapter opened), where ethnicity interacts with other interests and cleavages, imparting to them its distinctive emotional edge and, in turn, being intensely politicized by them. Without this linkage of ethnic and functional problems, each of these two categories of problems could be analyzed, approached, and possibly solved with lower risks than is now the case.

6 · Structural theories that analyze this interaction between ethnicity and other cleavages and that seek to explain the widespread post-World War II tendency for other lines of cleavage to be displaced into ethnic ones are still controversial. Where the cross-correlations relegate an ethnic group to the lower rungs of the socioeconomic structure (for example, the Welsh, Bretons, Slovaks, Chicanos, and Québécois), the theory of "internal colonialism" is a suggestive analytical tool. Where a socioeconomically favored ethnic group comes to perceive itself as aggrieved or jeopardized (for example, the Basques, Catalans, and Croatians), theories of "relative deprivation," "mirror image interactions," or "possessive nationalism" are more helpful. As of now, no single structural theory supplies a truly comprehensive explanation of politicized ethnicity. Yet structural theories are a necessary complement to more ideational (yet also valid) theories such as those positing the inherent logic of self-determination, the universal demonstration effect, and others, if ethnopolitics is to be understood.

The theory of internal colonialism starts with the observation that the process of modernization and economic development is not a smooth, self-equilibrating flow but a discontinuous, disruptive pattern of waves that creates and leaves behind it discrepancies between advanced and retarded groups and regions.[17] Over time, these discrepancies are institutionalized into stratifications, as the advanced sector ("the core") provides itself with a diversified economy while relegating the backward one ("the periphery") to dependent, overspecialized economic functions (for example, monocrop agriculture or extraction industry or unskilled services). The periphery is left highly vulnerable to price fluctuations and to the basic investment decisions that the core reserves for itself. ("Core" and "periphery" may be, but need not be, understood in a geographical sense.)

Ethnicity enters the picture when certain cultural markers (of the anthropological type) that may distinguish the peripheral and the core populations from each other come to be perceived as identifying and categorizing the respective economic roles and functions of these two populations. It is in the interest of the core's elite to use this distinction and exploit these markers so as to maintain the peripheral population's instrumental dependency and restrict its access to the skills and resources that might enable it to challenge this stratification. Thus, the markers (pigmentation, religion, language, accent, and the like) are transformed from primordial givens into politicized discriminators, and the tagging of the peripheral population's traits as inferior becomes a self-fulfilling social prophecy. This development does not necessarily entail deliberate discrimination against individuals. Rather, the periphery as a region or as an ethnocultural population being structurally disadvantaged, individuals in it and from it are to that extent also competitively, cumulatively (and quite impersonally) disadvantaged in many market situations, including access to good incomes, jobs,

[17] See Hechter, *Internal Colonialism*, especially chs. 1, 2, 11, 12; Holland, *The Regional Problem*; Carol A. Smith, ed., *Regional Analysis*, chs. 8, 11, 12, authored, respectively, by Katherine Verdery, Gordon Appleby, and Carol A. Smith; Williamson, "Regional Inequality," pp. 3–84; Galtung, "A Structural Theory of Imperialism," pp. 81–118.

schools, housing, credit, and capital. Ethnic stratification, in other words, while very palpable, is anything but "purely" ethnic. Eventually the process comes full circle as the alleged cultural inferiority of the peripheral population ("lazy," "feckless," "shifty," "unruly," "wild," "clannish," "parochial," "backward") becomes the elite's alibi for restricting investment among it.

Investment includes, of course, quality education. Even a would-be benevolent core establishes its own culture as defining the standards and norms for success and socioeconomic mobility. Peripheral cultures come to be stereotyped, not only as second class, but also as second rate. Indeed, some ethnic groups who value themselves and their traditional culture highly try to evade this being judged according to the dominants' cultural norms by avoiding, or at least postponing, their entry into the modernization process, which the dominants press and control and which would devalue the peripheral culture. Whether such a categorical avoidance strategy can remain feasible over the long run is problematic. Transitional examples of it are the Mennonites of North America, the Masai of Kenya and Tanzania, and, less drastically, the Québécois of Canada before World War II.

The circle is broken when the peripheral group reappropriates the cultural markers that have been manipulated to keep it subordinate or marginal and uses them as foci and levers to end and possibly reverse this relationship. Thus, structural challenges by a peripheral-subordinate ethnic group against the core-dominants are preceded by a cultural-psychological mobilization within that group, a mobilization in which it revalues and ideologizes its ethnic culture from a datum or perhaps an embarrassment into a beacon and a weapon. It would now no longer accept assimilation even if the dominants were belatedly to offer it. Rather it turns its newly honed weapon of ethnicity outward to delegitimate prevailing arrangements—arrangements that are no longer accepted as "natural" or "inevitable" but are now perceived as flowing from the deliberate policy decisions of the dominants—and to demand such political and structural changes as would enhance its integrity and autonomy as a distinctive culture-bearing ethnic group. If it is also geographically concentrated in a particular region, it may press secessionist claims, either as a strategic goal or as a bargaining stance. This process characterized the third world's challenge to the overseas colonial system a generation or two ago, and it today propels many cases of ethnic confrontation in the developed world.

However, not all core/periphery, dominant/subordinate socioeconomic stratifications are characterized by this use of ethnic-cultural markers of the anthropological type for purposes of "internal colonial" gatekeeping, discrimination, and control—and eventual challenge. Mention was made earlier of ethnically homogeneous societies (for example, Iceland, Luxembourg, Norway, Portugal) and even in multiethnic societies the lower socioeconomic strata may and do include substantial numbers who are not ethnoculturally distinct from the dominants. In Britain, for example, many industrial workers are English-speaking members of the Church of England. Others, however, are Welsh Nonconformists, Scots Presbyterians, Irish Catholics, and Black or Brown immigrants. The following cautious generalization may be hazarded to subsume either pattern: (1) modern socioeconomically subordinate strata who are not ethnically different from dominants experience their condition in class terms and organize accordingly; (2) populations whose socioeconomic subordination also correlates with ethnic stratification may respond either in class or in ethnic terms (or may not respond organizationally at all, either remaining passive or seeking assimilation), depending on which ideology, as presented by which counterelite, is accepted by them as more relevant under prevailing historical and political circumstances;

(3) for the historical, moral, and political reasons sketched above, and psychological reasons to be outlined below, ethnic elites articulating ethnic ideology and proposing ethnic symbols have greater resonance with populations of the second variety in the present era in the developed world.[18]

One obvious, though not necessarily fatal, flaw in the structural theory of internal colonialism is that the notion of a unitary core is oversimplified, for it implies that the economic (industrializing) and the political (state-building) cores are identical. Whereas this was historically the case in Britain, France, and Belgium, where England, the Ile de France, and the Francophones, respectively, played both roles, it is not true, for example, of Spain, Yugoslavia, or Nigeria, where the politically dominant cores (Castile, Serbia, the Hausa-Fulani north, respectively) were and still are economically secondary to more industrialized and more modern regions (Catalonia and the Basque-land, Croatia and Slovenia, the Yoruba southwest and the Ibo southeast). The second type of "crossed" situation often results in greater politico-ethnic tensions than the first, where the political, economic, and cultural core/periphery slopes all converge. It is more vexing for an ethnic group to be politically dominated by those whom it considers to be its economic and cultural inferiors (which is the Basque or Catalan perspective on the Castilians and the Croatian perspective on the Serbs)

[18] The contingent quality of this generalization may be illustrated by the different strategies of Irish and Welsh immigrants into the United States in the nineteenth century. Both populations arrived with distinctive 'old country' linguistic traits and church (chapel) affiliations. But the cultural markers of the Welsh were never used for stereotypical discrimination against them and hence soon eroded away, and the Welsh in the United States (unlike the Welsh in the United Kingdom) early ceased to function as a self-conscious ethnic group. The Irish in America, on the other hand, politicized and rallied to their markers in response to their quite different reception and treatment. Thus it was not the primordial authenticity but the utility and relevance of the markers in a particular historical setting that decided their fate. The example is drawn from Patterson, *Ethnic Chauvinism*, p. 112.

than for an ethnic group that knows it is disadvantaged in these several dimensions to accept its subordination (as with the Slovaks relative to the Czechs). The "crossed" situation was, in a modifed way, the background to the Bangladeshi secession and revolt against West Pakistan, for the Bengalis regarded themselves as culturally superior and as the earners of the foreign currency (jute and tea exports), which was then "parasitically" invested by the politically dominant West Pakistanis in their half of the old state. The "convergent" situation, if stable, entails less cognitive dissonance and less relative deprivation and thus is psychologically less humiliating to the subordinated group and is also politically less amenable to successful challenge by it since, definitionally, this group has fewer levers available in all dimensions.

This generalization holds true, however, only if, and as long as, a core area remains vigorous and dynamic. If and when a core loses its dominant grip—because of a flagging of its own energies or resources, or because of secular changes in worldwide flows of investment and trade, or because of damaging decisions by multinational corporations and other actors over whom a particular core lacks control, or because of some combination of such factors—then even an ethnic periphery that has historically been "convergently" subordinate in all dimensions is likely to become more militant in politicizing and pressing its grievances and aspirations against a core whose legitimacy and attraction ebb in tandem with its power and productivity. This becomes particularly plausible in today's conditions of universal suffrage and *de jure* democracy. It would appear to be the dynamic background to Flemish militancy against traditional Francophone domination in post-World War II Belgium and to the heightened Slovak assertiveness against the palsied Novotny regime in the Czechoslovakia of the 1960s. And even a long-established, supposedly solidly integrated modern "nation-state" may find itself wracked by ethnopolitical and ethnoregional fissures under such conditions—witness today's Scots and Welsh reassertiveness against the once-vigorous but of late faltering English core of Great Britain.

A traditionally dominant core that finds itself under reactive attack by a formerly acquiescent subordinate ethnic group or periphery responds in one of the following three ways:

1. It may deny that the markers and values and discriminators it had used to establish and sustain its domination were ethnic in any exclusionist sense and insist that they were always intrinsically and potentially universal. In other words, it admits that these markers were culture-bound—but only in the sense of expressing the culture of modernity, or earlier the culture of industrialization, and not any particular ethnic culture. This protest by a dominant group is usually subjectively sincere and objectively has substantial merit—but does not resolve the political confrontation. It has been, for example, the response of Israel's Ashkenazic elite to the remonstrations of her Sephardic Black Panthers, of the American middle class to Black and White ethnic charges of structural discrimination, of the English in Great Britain to their Celtic neighbors' protestations, and of the Russian "elder brothers" to the complaints of non-Russian Soviet nations that many Soviet institutions, procedures, and programs are but a screen for Russification and Russian dominion. What appears to happen in such cases is that the dominants' habituation to power seduces them into diffusing or extending their sense of their own ethnic particularity into a generalized ideology of legitimation.

2. The dominants may, by their behavior if not in words, concede the validity of the subordinates' allegations and thus the illegitimacy of the established system of markers and controls. America's Affirmative Action innovations of the 1970s symbolize this response. A more vivid expression of it was the dismantling of the overseas West European colonial empires after World War II—a process that was preceded, accompanied,

and facilitated by an erosion among the European metropolitan publics of confidence in the legitimacy of traditional colonialism and imperialism. A hitherto dominant ethnic group may seek to orchestrate this response so as to retain its economic hegemony even as it yields (or shares) political power to (or with) its erstwhile subordinates.

3. The dominants may respond in mirror-image terms to the subordinates' new ethnic militancy and politicization by possessively insisting on the legitimacy and maintenance of their own ethnic sway and rejecting the desirability of greater equality, let alone of a reversal, in the power imbalance. They may claim, and indeed believe, that what is being demanded of them is not really this or that discrete concession or issue-compromise, but rather the surrender of their entire ethnic value-universe, group identity, and future existence. Once the confrontation is so presented, that is, as being over ultimates, then it becomes a zero-sum struggle that is virtually incapable of resolution through pragmatic give-and-take. Even supposedly neutral procedural rules that ordinarily are accepted as a fair method for resolving disputes, such as the democratic canons of "equality" and of "one person, one vote," are here tagged as substantively tainted since they foreordain certain outcomes that the prospective losers will not accept as tolerable. Ethnic groups, after all, regard themselves as collective entities, not as aggregations of individuals, and cannot accept an otherwise impeccable procedure or negotiating formula that jeopardizes their very future or even their positional advantage. It is such perspectives and anxieties that render the Ulster, Lebanese, and Israeli-Palestinian ethnopolitical conflicts so intractable.

But ethnic dominants may adopt militant, possessive stances and perceive their future as imperiled even without explicit political challenge by subordinate ethnic groups. This may happen when their socioeconomic resources and levers attenuate or when their own norms and standards, which they had prescribed for the whole society as supposedly objective and neutral but had also honed as stratifying devices to secure their own domination, come to be used by others to erode that domination. This is the case, for example, when ethnic subordinates excel dominants in the educational, professional, and other high-cultural tests and hurdles that the dominants had originally designed. In such situations, the dominants may (but do not necessarily) respond with the politics of aggressive *ressentiment*, fueled by the experience and the emotion of relative deprivation—a condition in which capacities (political, economic, social, or cultural) fail to match expectations. Subordinates, of course, also often find themselves in this condition.

While this theory of relative deprivation makes a helpful statement about the potential for ethnic militancy and ethnic conflict, it cannot predict the occurrence or the initiation of actual conflict. Hence, it supplements, but does not replace, historical, moral-ideological, political, and structural theories and analyses of ethnicity. Nevertheless, in connection with the immediately preceding discussion of reciprocal ethnic militancies' locking themselves into ultimate-value confrontations, it does here put on our agenda the fifth explanatory dimension, signaled at the end of section 2 of this chapter, for interpreting today's rising ethnic assertiveness in the developed world—that is, the psychological dimension.

7 · Psychologically, ethnicity has one advantage over other modes of personal identity and of social linkage, namely, its capacity to arouse and to engage the most intense, deep, and private emotional sentiments (for example, "would you want your daughter to marry out?").[19] This is not to say that ethnic identification will always be experienced by everyone at such a

[19] Foltz, "Ethnicity, Status, and Conflict," p. 105.

high emotional level, for that, too, depends on context, and experience has shown that the intensity of ethnicity varies over time and among ethnic groups and varies situationally for individuals. But it does mean that, even when latent, ethnicity is potentially intense and that the ethnic chord is relatively easily plucked thanks to its resonance with deeply felt personal relationships and needs. And it also means that, when once activated, ethnic identity, ethnic interest, and especially ethnic anxiety tend to neutralize and to subsume emotionally more abstract commitments to functional social groups. In other words, class interests, while indeed concrete in social and political systemic terms, are psychologically less palpable in the emotional life of people than ethnicity is. Thus an individual might "identify" himself as a taxpayer in the dictionary sense of "associating his interests with those of others" in that category, but he will "identify" himself ethnically in the alternative dictionary definition of "linked in an inseparable fashion; conceived as united in spirit, principle, outlook" with his ethnic brethren. In today's political world, relatively fewer people than was formerly the case are immune to the psychological charm of their ethnic identity, are truly nonethnic cosmopolitans à la Voltaire or Trotsky.

But to stress the emotional potency of the ethnic bond is not to disengage it from hard interest-leverage. In fact, the political genius of ethnicity in the contemporary developed world lies precisely in its ability to combine emotional sustenance with calculated strategy. A circular process has set in: as governments become increasingly sensitive to ethnopolitical demands, ethnic groups are thereby given an incentive to organize themselves into cohesive interest groups for the extraction of desired policies and outputs, and as this ethnic consolidation proceeds, governments render themselves yet more responsive to it. Thus ethnicity becomes both instrumental and affective, while class solidarity, which had formerly also combined these two qualities, has become flattened into prosaic, one-dimensional interest-instrumentality—and even there is weakening. Yet its fortunes could rebound in an environment of prolonged economic malaise.[20]

In sum, the relationship between the emotional component and the interest component of politicized ethnicity is dialectical. Neither is a mere epiphenomenon of the other, and neither functions alone. Shared cultural values and shared material interests together energize the moral solidarity and felt fraternity of ethnopolitical groups. Once such groups have been consolidated from among the sharers of primordial cultural markers (see chapter 1, section 4), then the achieved solidarity and fraternity become the bases for intragroup obligations, for intergroup demarcations, and, finally, for pressing group interests in the teeth of competition and resistance.

The psychological power of ethnicity to galvanize an individual's salient identity, and the accompanying political potency of ethnic-group organization and assertiveness, do not covary directly with the vitality of the so-called primordial cultural roots of ethnicity.[21] Thus Basque ethnopolitical militancy waxes, but linguistic competence in the Euskara tongue nevertheless wanes. Jewish ethnopolitical assertiveness is similarly far stronger today than Jewish religious observance is, despite the thorough cultural integration of most diaspora Jews into the cultures of their host societies. Even intermarriage does not necessarily attenuate political ethnicity, for the children of mixed marriages

[20] Bell, "Ethnicity and Social Change," pp. 167–71; Ballard, "Ethnicity: Theory and Experience," p. 199.

[21] "[D]rastic reduction of cultural differences between ethnic groups does not correlate in any simple way with a reduction in the organizational relevance of ethnic identities, or a breakdown in boundary-maintaining processes." Barth, "Introduction" to *Ethnic Groups and Boundaries*, pp. 32–33; "[T]here appear to be continuing psychological needs to identify ethnically even when ancestry is mixed and the cultural and social supports of such identification have withered." Pettigrew, "Three Issues in Ethnicity," p. 31.

often adopt intense ethnic commitments, and many ethnic leaders are the products of such marriages.

Indeed, the potential psychological intensity of ethnopolitical commitments, anxieties, and aspirations contains a possible and, alas, easily aroused nemesis—namely, overethnicizing all or most public issues, policies, decisions, and goods in highly charged contexts. And this, in turn, entails the likely danger of stereotyping one's own and the competing ethnic group(s) into starkly polarized images of virtue and menace, images that telescope past conflicts and misproject their oversimplified recollection into the present context such as to exacerbate it. This exacerbation flows in part from the tendency of the several stereotyping actors to behave toward their stereotyped "targets" in a manner that elicits from these latter actors reactive behavior corroborating the initial stereotypes. Stereotyping thus interacts in a vicious cycle with the above-mentioned frequent anxiety of ethnic groups that their differences with competing groups are not really over the discrete questions that are seemingly on the agenda but actually over hidden ultimates, indeed over their very survival. The resulting complex of emotional intensity, inappropriate stereotyping, and eschatological anxiety can lend a malign quality to ethnic conflict, rendering it peculiarly recalcitrant to political therapy.

But since stereotyping is, alas, a universal weakness and propensity, why assume that in a given conflict-context the salient stereotypes will be ethnic ones rather than social-role stereotypes? Stereotypes are overgeneralized half-truths, half-falsehoods, that evoke an aura of plausibility, become psychologically useful, and hence highly resistant to correction. But economic classes and status strata and political camps—and not only ethnic groups—also develop them about each other. Why should the ethnic stereotypes eclipse the other possible candidate-images?

As before (sections 2 and 6, above), the answer is a contingent one: in a cross-correspondential system of multiple stratifications, alternative sets of stereotypes, like alternative lines of cleavage, are indeed potentially available, and which will emerge as politically protrusive depends on context. Nevertheless, that said, it must also be said that the current context in the modern developed and developing worlds gives a premium to the ethnic alternative. First of all, ethnic groups today generally have better networks of communal organization, information, and leadership than most other types of groups do. This facilitates ethnic mobilization and the activation of ethnic stereotypes in social-conflict situations—all the more so in the current environment of often weak political consensus.[22] Secondly, recent empirical research indicates the following "Greshamite" flow-pattern of stereotype displacement: (1) Social groups tend to develop stereotypes of each other, for example, peasants perceive urbanites as ambitious, conniving, greedy, and slippery, whereas urbanites perceive peasants as phlegmatic, slow-witted, good-hearted, and stolid; (2) where the social groups belong to the same ethnic category, these stereotypes remain social-role stereotypes; but (3) if the different social groups also overlap with distinct ethnic groups, then these stereotypical attributions are retagged from social-role into ethnic ones— and once this happens, then little evidence is needed to sustain them as ethnic labels.[23]

Thus, to attempt to move the definition of a social conflict from ethnic to social-role is to undertake the difficult task of pushing up a psychological-stereotypical gradient, whereas to define the conflict as ethnic is to slide with the gradient. Hence ethnic elites using ethnic symbols and ideology to mobilize publics have an inherent psychological advantage over their

[22] Pinard, "Communal Segmentation and Communal Conflict," p. 362.

[23] LeVine and Campbell, *Ethnocentrism*, pp. 159, 174; and Pettigrew, "Three Issues in Ethnicity," pp. 37–49.

would-be competitors. An interesting but abortive modern effort to push against the gradient was that of the prewar Jewish Socialist Bund in Eastern Europe to persuade Jewish workers to see Polish and Russian workers as their appropriate allies against their alleged enemies, exploiters, and misleaders, namely, the Jewish bourgeoisie, the rabbinate, and the Zionists. Lenin's success as a revolutionary derived in part from his ability to neutralize the gradient temporarily by synthesizing class and national-ethnic grievances, aspirations, and mobilizations.

Thus, not only do the historical, moral, political, and structural-economic factors summarized earlier give an advantage to the ethnic cleavage in a contemporary conflict situation where alternatives are available, but so does the psychological factor. Returning to the set of questions posed above at the end of section 2 of this chapter, this is one of the reasons why the Ulster and Lebanese civil wars are fought as ethnoreligious and not as poor-versus-rich conflicts, why Slovak and Breton peasants eventually came to experience their resentment of Magyar landlords and French technocrats in ethnic instead of class emotive images, etc.[24] And this is also one of the reasons why political and economic tensions between the advanced industrial

[24] Some sociologists have detected a variant of this tendency among blue-collar workers in the northeastern United States, who allegedly describe others, especially antagonists and intruders, in ethnic stereotypical terms while still identifying themselves as "working men." But this is a fluid pattern, subject to change. "These [stereotyped] beliefs about other ethnic groups are important for [blue-collar] men's social and political outlook. By contrast . . . , a concern with one's *own* ethnic origin is of secondary importance in [blue-collar] men's understanding of contemporary America. Ethnicity has an impact on [blue-collar] men's social behavior, on their friendships and leisure pursuits. And it may incline them to favor one political candidate over another. But ethnicity is not a major way in which [blue-collar] workers interpret the operation of contemporary America." David Halle, *America's "Working Man": Work, Home, and Politics Among Blue-Collar Property Owners* (doctoral dissertation, Columbia University: Faculty of Political Science, Department of Sociology, 1979), pp. 442–43.

states and the third world so often arouse ethnic and racial passions.

* * *

Having here brushed in broad strokes some middle-level components of a theory of emergent ethnopolitical assertiveness in multiethnic societies characterized by complex stratifications, it now becomes appropriate to proceed to itemize in somewhat greater detail the possible modes for organizing the ethnic structure itself of such societies.

Chapter Three

THE POLITICAL ORGANIZATION OF ETHNICITY: CATEGORIES, PATTERNS, MODELS, AND CRITERIA

1 · The actual organization of ethnic stratification and of ethnic structures was for long a particularly neglected aspect of the generally neglected study of politicized ethnicity. It was as though scholars, honorably offended by bigotry and committed to egalitarianism, were too embarrassed to explore the precise and often successful manner in which ethnic criteria and cleavages that they abominated as irrational, immoral, and undemocratic are used to organize and structure societies. Hence they would often seek to dilute and sanitize this distasteful problem by subsuming it into the study of generalized stratification. Or they might treat it as an epiphenomenal aspect of class structure, class conflict, and false consciousness. Or they would psychologize and moralize it under the themes of prejudice and discrimination. This last-mentioned approach was particularly gratifying and hence lingering because it implied a comforting would-be remedy to the supposed pathology being described, to wit: Change the prejudiced hearts and minds of people and you will end ethnic discrimination.

But none of these tangential approaches proved quite satisfactory. Ethnic stratification manifests certain *sui generis* operational and theoretical issues that are slighted, blurred, or distorted by attempts to fold it into analyses of other types of stratification. Similarly, the monocausal class approach errs in denying intrinsic significance to ethnicity and ethnic differences in the structure of social relationships. Finally, the psychologistic-moralistic fallacy not only greatly exaggerates the general capacity of psychology to explain (or explain away) political and other power structures, but in this case it was also often morally naive in a politically consequential, though surely unintended, sense. For its recommended therapeutic emphasis on correcting prejudiced minds and hearts through exposing the unscientific nature of the guiding prejudices conveyed the implication that systems and institutions need not be changed. In other words, by its stress on attitudes, it neglected the examination of the nexus between structures and the real economic, political, and social interests that they embed, generate, protect, and sustain.[1] Even at the psychological level itself, this approach was often preoccupied with the attitudes of the prejudiced discriminators and neglected those of their victims.[2]

Since the mid-1960s, new and revised approaches have corrected many of these distortions. Political turmoil has drawn scholarly attention to the attitudes and beliefs of subordinated ethnic groups. Indeed, it is today often claimed that in the final analysis it is the changing consciousness of the subordinates, more than the attitudes of the dominants, that will define the field of ethnic confrontation and determine the eventual cast of ethnic stratification. And this stratification is no longer relegated to various tertiary and epiphenomenal positions in

[1] Cf. Schermerhorn, *Comparative Ethnic Relations*, pp. 6–7; Lieberson, "Stratification and Ethnic Groups," p. 208; Katznelson, "Comparative Studies," pp. 135–37; Kuper, "Theories of Race Relations,"pp. 19–28; Kuper, ed., *Race, Science, and Society*, p. 26.

[2] Exempt from this stricture is the work of Dr. Kenneth B. Clark on what he terms the pathologies of Black ghetto dwellers.

academic and political analysis but is now assigned central and autonomous significance. Finally, a new emphasis on the organization and structure of ethnicity, rectifying the former moralistic preoccupation with its ideology and psychology, has rendered political science one of the central disciplines in the investigation of this subject and has stimulated the truly comparative study of its institutional arrangements.

This is not to claim that political, organizational analysis has any exclusive capacity to explore and explain the problematics of ethnicity—only to endorse its rightful place in this collaborative endeavor. For example, the skepticism expressed above over the old fixation with correcting the prejudiced attitudes and discriminatory behavior of individuals is also valid on the reverse tack. Thus, if, hypothetically, the structure of society were to be changed so as to eliminate hierarchical ethnic stratification, it does not necessarily follow that this would *ipso facto* entail the disappearance of ethnic prejudice, even though the hypothesized change would seem to render such prejudice irrelevant as a defense of hierarchical institutional interests. Despite evidence that attitudes are heavily shaped by structures of power, such an inference (of prejudice inevitably eliminated through a change in social structure) would be overly optimistic, given the present state of psychological knowledge about this relationship. This and other open problems of ethnicity require further study. Such study now necessarily comprehends an organizational dimension.

2 · Formal, legal variations in the organization of ethnicity can be sketched in broad strokes. First of all, as mentioned earlier (chapter 2, section 1), a few small states are uniethnic and thus of no interest to this chapter. Iceland, Luxembourg, Norway, and Portugal were the examples cited. Some other states are multiethnic, with the ethnic factor operative at the

cultural and social, but not at the formal public-institutional and legal levels. Here citizenship is held directly and individually and the law is blind to ethnicity. In a third category of states, citizenship is still held directly and individually, but public law takes cognizance of ethnicity. The United States might here serve as an illustration of a society partially and tentatively translating itself from the second to the third category through its Affirmative Action commitments to protected ethnic groups. The Soviet Union and India are older members of this third category. A fourth category consists of states in which the citizen's access to the public realm is no longer even formally direct and individual but is mandatorily mediated through his corporate ethnic segment. Yet the proclaimed intent—authentic or spurious as the case might be—of the public authorities is to regulate the several ethnic segments in such a manner as to achieve or maintain collective equality among them. Malaysia, Lebanon, and episodically the now defunct Habsburg realm are instances of this class. Finally, a fifth category of states modifies the preceding one in the direction of openly structuring the ethnic segments into inegalitarian—dominant and subordinate—statuses. Here the dominant ethnic group may be the demographic majority (for example, the Greeks of Cyprus), or a minority (the Whites of South Africa), or a plurality (the Magyars of old millenial Hungary).[3]

Of course, hierarchical, inegalitarian, ethnic structuring may, and usually does, exist without such formal, legal sanction. Indeed, the felt need thus to mandate and charter it may betoken a sense of defensiveness and possibly of weakness on the part of the dominant segment. In other words, categories two, three, and four—not only five—in the just-listed formal typology of multiethnic states also manifest patterns of politically

[3] The typology above is an elaboration on that outlined by Edelstein, "Pluralist and Marxist Perspectives," pp. 45–46.

significant ethnic statification. A checklist of such patterns might read as follows[4]:

1. A politically dominant majority versus a subordinate minority or several such minorities—as on Cyprus (Greeks > Turks), Sri Lanka (Sinhalese > Tamils), historically in Canada (Anglophones > Francophones, speakers of other European languages, Métis, Amerindians, and Inuits [Eskimos]), contemporary Czechoslovakia (Czechs > Slovaks), Israel (Jews > Arabs, Druze), and Pakistan (Punjabis > Sindhis, Pashtuns, Baluchis). This pattern is at times more intricate than it initially seems, for such a particular state's locally subordinate minority may draw assertiveness from perceiving itself as part of a larger regional or universal ethnic reserve, for example, Cypriot Turks anticipating support from their brethren of nearby Turkey, Canadian Québécois drawing cultural and psychological sustenance from France and from an even larger Francophone world, Pakistani Pashtuns counting on fraternal Afghan aid. Alternatively, a locally dominant majority may apprehensively feel itself to be a vulnerable regional minority, for example, Sri Lankan Sinhalese contemplating the Tamil multitudes across the Palk Strait in southern India, Israeli Jews pondering the capabilities and intentions of the Arab world.

Because it is a province of the United Kingdom rather than a sovereign state, Ulster was not specified among the examples listed above. But there, too, a subordinate Catholic minority hopes, and a dominant Protestant majority fears, that the Catholic Republic of Ireland, which shares the island with them, will engage itself in Ulster's ethnic conflict.

2. A politically dominant minority versus a subordinate majority—as in most colonial situations (Europeans:autochtho-

[4] The following taxonomy extends and amends an original sketch by Clifford Geertz in the volume edited by him under the title *Old Societies and New States*, pp. 117–18.

nous peoples), in Jordan (Beduins:Palestinians), Liberia before 1980 (Americo-Liberian descendants of repatriates from the United States:indigenous tribes), on Taiwan (mainland immigrants from 1949–50:natives). This pattern of ethnic stratification becomes increasingly rare in developed states as the subordinate majority builds the consciousness and the resources to challenge it.

3. A dominant central core or plurality (not a majority) versus an aggregation (not a coalition) of peripheral ethnic segments. Here the core group views itself as the historic, institutional, and symbolic creator, and hence appropriate hegemon, of the state. Examples include the Soviet Union (Great Russians vis-à-vis other nationalities), Yugoslavia (Serbs vis-à-vis Croatians, Slovenes, Macedonians, Bosniaks, and several non-Slavic minorities), interwar Czechoslovakia (Czechs vis-à-vis Slovaks, Ruthenians, Germans, Magyars, and Poles), Ethiopia (Amhara vis-à-vis several different Hamitic-Cushite peoples), Iran (the Persians of the central plateau vis-à-vis the peripheral Arabs, Kurds, Azers, Turkmen, Baluchis, Lurs, Bakhtiaris, Qashqais, and tribal nomads), Iraq (the Sunni Arabs vis-à-vis the Shiite Arabs and the Kurds), and Indonesia (central Javanese vis-à-vis west Javanese, outer islanders, and local Chinese). Perhaps the United States, with its so-called WASP political and cultural core-Establishment and its hyphenated ethnic peripheries, might also be located in this pattern.

4. A bipolar balance, with one ethnic group politically and the other one economically dominant. Examples are Malaysia's Malay/Chinese, Guyana's Black/East Indian, and white South Africa's Afrikaner/Anglophone dispositions. The bipolar pattern is characterized by a special set of tensions and inhibitions. On the one hand, the political dominants, who are either the autochthonous or the earlier arriving ethnic group, are inclined to deny that the economic dominants, as immigrants and latecomers, have any legitimate claims to real political power or

governmental authority. Moderates in the politically dominant ethnic group who might be prepared to relent somewhat on this position risk being outflanked by their own camp's ethnic militants. On the other hand, the other ethnic group has the potential capacity to use its economic muscle to inflict unacceptable damage on the state and hence on its politically dominant ethnic segment. Finally, residential and ecological distributions tend to be such as to preclude territorial separation or autonomy, even if this were not already banned by the ideology of the political dominants.

In theory, this deterrent situation might be expected to lead either to pragmatic and acknowledged cooperation or to paralysis. In practice, two other solutions have been developed and often applied, either sequentially or simultaneously: (a) The menace of an external third party (for example, Sukarno's Indonesia, the Black majority of South Africa) is exploited by the political dominants (the Malays, the Afrikaners) to freeze the prevailing domestic political asymmetry and thus apply an interim muzzle on the appetites of both their own militants and the economic dominants cum political subordinates. (b) The political dominants use their political power and governmental leverage to contain, challenge, and intrude upon the other segment's economic primacy—as the Malays have done to the Chinese in Malaysia, the Blacks to the East Indians in Guyana, and the Afrikaner Boers to the Anglophones in South Africa. This development is sometimes interpreted as supposedly turning Marxism upside down, by demonstrating the superiority of political over economic power. Because it is implemented incrementally and formally legally, this pressure on the economic dominants is translated into severe strains between accommodationists and would-be resisters within their ranks.

Belgium is a rather special subcase of bilateral ethnic balance without bipolarity. Temporarily putting history aside, here neither political nor economic domination can any longer be attributed to either Francophone Walloons or Dutch-speaking Flemings. Nor does either community have an exclusive claim on the moral authority that derives from indigeneity, and hostile neighbors can no longer be evoked to smother domestic commotion. Another difference from the more general bipolar pattern is that the two ethnic communities are geographically separated (except in the Brussels/Bruxelles environs). Nevertheless, many other traits of the bipolar pattern are present: political acrimony runs high, policy consensus is brittle, and the danger of ethnic radicals outtrumping moderates is ever present. The experience of two German occupations in two World Wars assuaged class conflict but aggravated ethnoregional and ethnolinguistic strife. An extremely latitudinarian political elite, systematically coopting would-be outbidders and "splitting the difference" of conflicting ethnic demands, has so far preserved a precarious domestic balance—but at the price of much public cynicism and of fraying the regime's legitimacy.[5]

5. An economically strong but politically vulnerable "pariah" ethnic minority, performing commercial and entrepreneurial functions that are conspicuous, remunerative, important, but socially disparaged, versus a politically dominant yet economically unskilled agricultural majority, usually consisting of warrior nobles who disdain, and of peasants who lack the resources for, entrepreneurial activities. The "pariah" ethnic minority was often invited into the society from outside by the native rulers or nobility, or by colonial administrators, on condition that it not assimilate—for such an alien, unassimilated, "bourgeoisie" was less likely than a native one to challenge the political power of this "feudal" ruling elite. At the same time, the prohibition on assimilation fitted well with the initial desires of the "pariah" ethnic group itself. Furthermore, the fact that such an ethnic

[5] Zolberg, "Splitting the Difference," pp. 104–6; Lorwin, "Segmented Pluralism," p. 149.

group was usually part of a wider, trans-sovereign diaspora network was perceived by its hosts and by itself as an economic and cultural asset.

This, in short, is a synopsis of the historic "outsider" roles of Jews in eastern Europe, Greeks and Armenians in the cities of the Ottoman Empire, overseas Chinese in Southeast Asia and the Caribbean islands, Lebanese in West Africa, Indians in East Africa, and Yankees in the antebellum American South. It is a synopsis of a story that has probably run its course, for it depended on a number of now rapidly vanishing cultural and political ingredients: the "pariah" ethnic group's monopoly of mobility, secular literacy, and entrepreneurial skills; the host community's disdain for those traits and values, and for the liquid wealth that they generate, as allegedly polluting and corrosive (a disdain that in Western philosophy goes back to Plato and Aristotle and whose analysis merits a separate study);[6] the "pariahs'" readiness to remain at best tolerated but always vulnerable alien enclaves, and the like. These several conditions are now evanescing; hence this classic pattern of ethnic stratification becomes increasingly fragile and the situation of the ethnic "pariahs" ever more precarious—in both socialist and capitalist societies.

Nevertheless, one particular case of its survival, albeit in a much modified form, merits mention here because it teaches a general political lesson. The Chinese minority in Thailand is wealthy, resented, and the target of restrictive legislation passed

[6] Widespread and deeply ingrained is the cluster of prejudices claiming that tilling the soil is morally cleansing, that fighting in its protection is dignified, but that buying and selling is corrupting—especially in an urban ambience. Thus, farmers are stereotyped as honest and solid, warriors as brave and selfless, but merchants as slick and grasping. Even in the highly capitalistic, urbanized, industrialized, and commercialized United States, this Jeffersonian ideology remains potent and, together with certain structural-constitutional arrangements, helps to give the farm lobby (4 percent of the population) its disproportionate political leverage.

at the behest of Thai nationalistic youth pressures on the political system. Yet this legislation is not enforced, thanks to instrumental arrangements whereby the Chinese merchants make upper-level Thai politicians and administrators their silent partners and lower-level bureaucrats and policemen the recipients of their quiet largesse. Thus economic power in need of political protection and political power in search of wealth meet to form an informal but effective, concentrated system, held together by exploiting the very conflict that originally generated the restrictive legislation, continues to simmer, and remains potentially incendiary. Either the expulsion or the assimilation of the Chinese "pariah" community would eliminate the *raison d'être* of this mutually useful arrangement. The general political lesson here is that the political integration of antagonistic ethnic groups can be pragmatically effective without being ideologically harmonious and that not all ethnic conflict is necessarily system-disruptive.[7]

6. Multilayered gradations by power and size, as in Kenya today and formerly in the cisleithanian (Austrian) half of the Habsburg Empire.

7. A multiplicity of ethnic groups of varying size, power, and levels of politicization, compounded by a multiplicity of loci of contact and conflict among them, and by a multiplicity of the very criteria of ethnic differentiation (for example, language, religion, race, caste, and custom), such that no valid generali-

[7] "Thus a sort of 'antagonistic symbiosis' is established between the political elite and the pariah entrepreneurs in a typical transitional setting. The [Chinese] pariah entrepreneur cannot be liquidated because his activities finance the new [Thai] elite's growing leisure and luxury. Neither can he be assimilated, for such a step not only means the destruction of a useful scapegoat in a transitional process but also considerable financial loss for the elite as well. Militant economic nationalism has resulted, not in the defeat of the enemy, but in a precarious cooperation between the antagonists." Joseph P. J. Jiang, "The Chinese in Thailand," *Journal of Southern Asian History*, 7, no. 1 (1966): 64–65. See also Schermerhorn, *Comparative Ethnic Relations*, pp. 55–56.

zation about ethnic stratification for the state as a whole is feasible. India might here serve as an example. This situation is not to be confused with sheer fragmentation, as in Zaire.

A point made parenthetically in the preceding paragraph merits some elaboration. In the organization of ethnic politics, the locus of interaction of the several organized ethnic groups may be as important a dimension as the several planes and columns of their stratification. Thus, in the United States and in India, the locus of ethnic political interaction is at the level of subfederal political-administrative units, while the central government does not depend on a fixed pattern of ethnic endorsement and/or rivalry. *Per contra*, in Malaysian and Guyanan politics, the organized ethnic political competition is precisely for control of the central government, which thus necessarily depends on fixed, predictable, but segmental ethnic support. Whereas in the former situation ethnopolitics tend to be fluctuating, with the central government functioning as an *ad hoc* arbiter, in the latter they are likely to be tense, with the central government an inevitable partisan.[8]

This point may also help to clarify some of the supposed mystery behind Switzerland's success in achieving peaceful ethnopolitics, a success that is too often misattributed exclusively to cultural, rather than to structural and cultural, factors. Most Swiss collective political goods are at the disposition of the several cantons—most of which are uniethnic (unilingual). The central government has avoided becoming a locus of ethnopolitical competition by deliberately eschewing jurisdiction in ethnically sensitive and potentially contentious linguistic, religious, educational, cultural, and welfare issues. This parallels the Swiss policy of international neutrality, which is also in large part predicated on a desire to avoid dilemmas that would be ethnically divisive domestically. Such organized ethnopolitical com-

[8] Donald L. Horowitz, "Three Dimensions of Ethnic Politics," pp. 237–39.

petition as occurs in Switzerland takes place within the very small number of multilingual cantons (4 out of 26). It is, however, quite plausible that this convenient situation will change. More mobility, accruing from more modernization, may render more cantons multilingual and require more federal regulative and allocative involvement in ethnically sensitive issues. Simultaneously, more modernization and development will continue to attract large numbers of foreign laborers, most of whom come from Latin countries and against whom hostility is greatest among the Germanophone Swiss.

Finally, this point about the importance of the locus of organized ethnopolitical competition entails one more corollary. In certain phases of their historical development, certain ethnic groups that are socioeconomically disadvantaged may deliberately prefer to focus their political aspirations on the local governmental arena, slighting the central one, because local municipal government allocates and draws the kinds of goods and services that are most relevant for the needs and skills of such ethnic groups in the given historical phases. Central governmental office does not become a palpable political magnet until such an ethnic group has socioeconomically advanced to a point where there is a better reciprocal fit of resources and requirements. This was the sequence of political address by most immigrant ethnic groups into the United States and by the postindependence Sephardic immigrants into Israel.

Returning for a bird's-eye survey to the typology of patterns of ethnic political stratification, one notes that several of those patterns frequently engender corresponding sets of stereotypical images. Thus, in the configuration of dominant majority versus subordinate minority, the dominants often depict the subordinates as immature and backward, whereas a dominant minority perceives the subordinate majority as smoldering and primitive. "Pariah" minorities, in turn, are now portrayed as secretly strong, fiendishly clever, and hence a menace to the simple and unsuspecting native hosts. In the bipolar pattern, each ethnic camp rhetorically concedes some aspects of cultural-behavioral superiority to the second one, while reserving other aspects of superiority for itself, for example, "they are more enterprising, but we are more honest"; alternatively, "they work with greater stamina, but we are cleverer"; or "they are more freely in tune with nature, but we are more rationally disciplined"; and so forth. But note that, beneath their rhetorical symmetry, these comparisons are affectively and evaluatively quite unbalanced.

3 · While the preceding typology of patterns of ethnic stratification has substantial classificatory value, its analytical power is somewhat impaired by two significant, but correctable, shortcomings: it may be too narrowly political and it is relatively static. The first of these flaws was already anticipatorily repaired in the previous chapter's exploration of certain "crossed" relationships wherein ethnic groups that value themselves as the culturally and economically superior ones of their respective states nevertheless find themselves in the vexing and, indeed, humiliating position of political subordination (see chapter 2, section 6). Sometimes the situation is even more convoluted. For example, in wide western districts of the Tsarist Empire on the eve of World War I, Russians can be said to have been politically dominant, Poles culturally dominant, Jews commercially dominant, with Belorussians and Ukrainians constituting respective demographic majorities. Amplifying the political model of ethnic stratification into a multidimensional one will not only subsume such situations but may also rectify the blemish of staticism. Yet the model must not become so intricate or fluid as to be unmanageable for analytical purposes.

Societies may stratify their ethnic groups according to models of vertical hierarchy, of parallel segmentation, or of cross-patterned reticulation. Only in the first of these, in the vertical-hierarchical model, is there a categorical correspondence among all dimensions—political, social, economic, and cultural—of ethnic superordination and subordination. In other words, here all members of a particular ethnic group will be consigned and confined to the poorer, menial, disparaged, and powerless rungs and roles of the society, while another ethnic group monopolizes all positions of high wealth, status, prestige, and power—with structural and, if necessary, coercive sanctions enforcing these rigidly hierarchical arrangements. Indeed, in Weberian ideal-typical terms, all potential funnels of ethnic mobility—again, political, social, economic, and cultural—are here restricted by ascriptive criteria; the society is suffused with imposed deference, tends toward caste-type relations, and is highly repressive. It is today generally considered to be morally and politically illegitimate. Its very rigidity may convey a deceptive impression of stability (as in the antebellum American South or, more recently, in South Africa until the mid-1970s), but when it begins to crack, the disintegration is difficult to halt short of collapse and revolutionary upheaval, since neither normative procedures of gradual, peaceful change nor trans-ethnic institutional solidarities were allowed to develop. Indeed, the past compounding of political, social, economic, and cultural ethnic cleavage-lines will now also compound the intensity of the convulsion.[9]

In the model of parallel ethnic segmentation, each ethnic community is internally stratified by socioeconomic criteria and each has a political elite to represent its interests vis-à-vis the corresponding elites of the other ethnic segments. Solidarity within, and cleavage-lines between, the several segments are both strong. To lift a well-known phrase out of its original context, one might say that "separate but [almost] equal" is the

[9] Ibid, pp. 232–34.

organizational ideology of this model. Less rigid, and today adjudged to be more legitimate, than the vertical-hierarchical one, its segments relate to each other in a manner comparable to an interstate system—that is, by constant diplomatic adjustment, punctuated by occasional confrontations. The fact that this ideal-typical projection (like the previous one) is a logical construct with which no empirical situation coincides exactly does not preclude its analytic and heuristic utility. *Toutes proportions gardées*, it was formerly approximated in the *millet* system of the Ottoman Empire and today there are certain trends toward it in federal Yugoslavia.

Neither the vertical-hierarchical nor the parallel-segmental model exists in pure form in real life. In actual systems approximating the first model, some members of the subordinate ethnic groups manage to defy ascription, acquire skills, and permeate upward, and thereby precipitate occasional status panics and redoubled prejudice among unskilled and unprivileged members of the dominant ethnic stratum. In actual systems of the second model, the theoretical equality of the segments is compromised by real power differentials among them, though it remains true that within each segment there will be elites and plebians. One might say that the horizontal and vertical cleavage-lines postulated respectively by these two ideal-type schemas tend to shift toward the diagonal and thus approach the third itemized model of stratification, the cross-patterned reticulate one.

In this reticulate model, ethnic groups and social classes cross-populate each other—but the distribution is not random or symmetrical or egalitarian (see chapter 2, section 2). Each ethnic group pursues a wide range of economic functions and occupations, and each economic class and sector organically incorporates members of several ethnic categories. But a certain amount of overrepresentation and underrepresentation of ethnic groups within economic classes and political-power clusters is possible—indeed, likely. Furthermore, though it facilitates functional transactions across ethnic boundaries, this pattern does not assume (though it allows) ethnic assimilation or even a high level of mutual ethnocultural sympathy. Indeed, precisely because here the members of ethnic groups compete intensely for certain rewards that they all value highly and do not regard as ethnically particularistic or exclusive—such as scarce educational, professional, and monetary places and successes—the subjective components of ethnic conflict, such as pejorative stereotyping and panic-mongering, may become quite heated, albeit surreptitious. Furthermore, ethnic groups that find themselves disproportionately allocated to the lower socioeconomic strata are liable to infer that, despite its rhetorical commitment to fluidity, this system is in fact structured to their detriment. In the vertical-hierarchical and parallel-segmental patterns, interethnic relations are less competitive (though not politically easier) because fewer values are shared and hence contested. On the whole, ethnopolitics in Switzerland, the United Kingdom, and the United States correspond more readily to this cross-patterned reticulate model than to either of the other two.

The point here is that value-sharing resulting from crosscutting, reticulated cleavages is not necessarily conducive to harmony, nor is mutual isolation necessarily prone to conflict.[10] Indeed, where the social distance between ethnic groups is so wide and their cross-patterned integration so low that they share no, or few, value cultures, prestige assignments, status ambitions, or social goals, they may go their separate ways with relatively little conflict. In medieval Europe, for example, urban Jews and Christian peasants interrelated so little, shared so little, emulated and compared themselves so little, that they also clashed relatively little (the "Armleder" depredations of 1336–39 in Fran-

[10] For the opposite judgment, see Seymour Martin Lipset, *Political Man* (New York: Doubleday, 1959), pp. 85–90.

conia and Alsace being a deplorable exception). On the other hand, relations between medieval Jews and Christian burghers, who shared certain incipient bourgeois values and hence competed for certain resources, were chronically frictional and frequently explosive. Another comparison that might be made to illustrate this point is between contemporary Malaysia and Ulster. While Malay-Chinese relations in the former country are scarcely frictionless, nevertheless their peaceful regulation is somewhat facilitated by the fact that they do not share in assigning a high ethnic value to religion. The Malays do, but the Chinese don't. Thus, the government can subsidize the Malays' Islamic institutions without thereby offending the symbol-sensitivities of the Chinese (though these may regret the financial cost). In Ulster, on the other hand, where the two competing ethnic communities define themselves and each other in religious terms and as religious threats, the government does not have this luxury of being able to mollify the one without offending the other. Indeed, it can't even "split the difference" by supporting both the Catholic and Protestant churches without giving ethnic offense, since each camp would simply pocket its own subsidy as its rightful due but denounce the other's as a profanation.[11] Finally, to close this point on a lighter note, the difficult task of governing New York City is somewhat eased by the convenient fact that its strong ethnic groups do not share, and hence do not compete in, their symbolic demands on the municipal government. The Irish Catholics expect a green stripe to be painted down Fifth Avenue on St. Patrick's Day; the Jews, to have parking prohibitions suspended on Passover, and so forth. Each group's demand is relatively irrelevant and inoffensive to the other. Imagine the contrast if another ethnic group were sufficiently strong and

[11] Enloe, *Ethnic Conflict*, p. 20; Wright, "Protestant Ideology and Politics," pp. 213–80.

assertive to demand an orange stripe down Fifth Avenue on March 17!

In sum, the reticulate model, when used correctly and without the unduly optimistic expectation that it automatically guarantees the gradual and peaceful resolution of ethnic conflicts, is a more realistic, and hence superior, tool for the analysis of developed (not of all) multiethnic societies. It is neither static not exclusively political. It allows for, and indeed expects, diagonal, asymmetrical, and—most important—changing cross-correlations between ethnicity on the one hand, and class, status, and power distributions on the other, this being a more plausible expectation for developed societies than the rigid vertical and parallel compartmentalizations of the other two models. Indeed, the reticulate model could also accommodate a possible (though currently unlikely) depoliticization of ethnicity and its privatization as simply a datum of cultural diversity. It can also resolve some problems that are intractable anomalies[12] to one or both of the other models, such as (1) the phenomenon of the ethnic "pariah" groups, who are economically privileged and rich, yet politically vulnerable and exposed; or (2) the mobility of individuals from peripheral ethnic regions and subordinate ethnic groups into the state's central elite without "passing" in the sense of abandoning or repudiating their original ethnic cultures; or (3) the broader issue of the emergence of different types of subelites to lead and represent subordinate ethnic groups; and (4) their selection of different types of ethnopolitical strategies. Finally, the reticulate model indicates that the politics of ethnicity, be they conflictual, competitive, or cooperative, are a function of proportional resources (organizational, economic, ecological, technological, locational-strategic, cultural, demo-

[12] On models, anomalies, and paradigms, see Thomas S. Kuhn, *The Structure of Scientific Revolutions* (2nd ed.; Chicago: University of Chicago Press, 1970), passim.

graphic) and of proportional qualities (congruent or divergent goals, normative ideologies, political talents, levels of mobilization). These resources and qualities are possessed both by ethnic groups and by central elites who may or may not be ethnically representative or identified. But the model itself, validly, does not specify what their proportions are, and it leaves open various possible outcomes of their composite engagement—stable, evolutionary, or revolutionary outcomes.

A final reason for the high analytical utility and explanatory power of this model of cross-patterned reticulation is that it recognizes that modern societies that approximate this model will tend to "partialize" an individual's ethnic identity—without, however, nullifying its political potency. This is because such modern reticulate systems require and make many role assignments that are functionally deethnicized—professional roles, market roles, technical-competence roles, and the like. Hence, the unitary and total ethnic identity that had characterized men's social position and self-image in systems approximating the vertical-hierarchical and parallel-segmental models now becomes fractionalized—not only at the level of inner individual identity, but also in the dimension of overt cultural, social, economic, organizational, professional, and political participation. Individuals here recognize that their ethnicity is normatively not relevant to all situations and hence they no longer project it into every role and interaction (see the Introduction, above). But if and when these individuals discover or suspect that a cross-patterned reticulate system violates its professed norms, that is, that they are the targets of "totalistic" ascriptive and stereotypical judgments rather than of judgments and assignments based on their functional, partial role performances; or that their ethnic group as a collectivity is disproportionately and systematically relegated and confined to the lower and weaker rungs of the socioeconomic and political structures; or, alternatively, if their ethnic group is generally dominant, that its high and strong structural position is in jeopardy, then their ethnicity is likely to become intensely politicized and assertive—reticulate differentiation notwithstanding.[13]

4 · Before proceeding with the analysis of the dynamics of interethnic relations, engagements, and confrontations suggested by the several models, patterns, and categories of the preceding sections, I turn to a question that has so far been begged—intentionally so. This is the question of the focus, or criterion, of ethnic identification. The reader will have noticed that among the examples of ethnic groups that have been parenthetically cited so far are some that define themselves by linguistic, others by religious, and still others by racial and additional criteria or clusters of criteria. This has been deliberate. Ethnic identification and allegiance may attach themselves to any of several such criteria, and ethnicity does not exist as an entity totally separate from them—nor can they be declared to be necessarily separate from it. Thus, it is as pointless to search for the supposed essence of ethnicity apart from these several criteria as it is myopic to declare any of them exempt from ethnopolitical signification—for example, that such and such an issue or conflict is "purely religious" or "essentially linguistic." In other words, the possible ethnic significance of these marker-criteria is given, or withheld, or withdrawn, not by their content, but by their social and political context, that is, by their bearers and the neighboring bearers of different markers in sustained, and usually competitive, contact with each other. The several criteria or foci of ethnic identification and signification will now be listed—in no particular order of importance, frequency, or chronology, and without judgment of their "scientific" validity. No single one of them is either indispensable or necessarily

[13] Breton, "Structure of Relationships," pp. 60–61.

sufficient for ethnic-group solidarity and politicization. They are as follows:

1. Race—that is, shared phenotypical features such as pigmentation, stature, and facial or hair type. Though today race has a potent capacity to evoke political and psychological bonds of proclaimed brotherhood, it is, ironically, the least primordial of all the possible criteria of ethnic identity and solidarity, for it had no inherent cultural meaning, let alone political significance, predating its use as a device for imposing and enforcing stratification and segmentation—and eventually for challenging such racially elaborated systems of superordination and subordination. But once used for these purposes, it became over time a tenacious focus of both identification and of alienation, domestically and globally. Examples of race used today as a politicized ethnic criterion are furnished by urban politics in Britain and the United States, by the statewide political systems of Malaysia and Guyana, and by the continental Senghorian concept of *négritude*, as well as by the global political passions that linger from the era of colonialism.

2. Kinship—that is, assumed blood ties and alleged common ancestry, such as is generally claimed by clans, tribes, and occasionally by whole nations. Although the articulated myth here asserts that the sentiments of solidarity are a consequence of the common descent, the reverse may well be the real historico-political sequence: established solidarities were legitimated and reinforced by the invention of kinship and ancestral symbols. If the stipulated kinship group is coterminous with a state's population, the political system's legitimacy is buttressed; in the more frequent cases where kinship groups are either subunits of a state or stretch across frontiers, they may have a disruptive effect. Examples of both these situations are provided by the phenomenon of so-called tribalism in Africa.

3. Religion—assessed here as a leaven of social allegiances, not as a formal belief-system about ultimate essences. There

was a time, early in the modern era, when religion was the principal focus of solidarity and cleavage and of incipient ethnic consolidation, even in the countries that now compose the developed world. Since then, in this developed world, which is also a heavily secularized world, religion has yielded center stage to language—in the United States to nostalgia for the fractionally transmitted linguistic-cultural heritage of immigrant ancestors—as the leading catalyst of ethnicity. For example, from the seventeenth through the nineteenth centuries, the Dutch-speaking Catholic Flemings felt greater solidarity with the Francophone but also Catholic Walloons to their south than with their fellow Dutch-speaking but Protestant neighbors to the north. Accordingly, they were then amenable to membership in the political unit that eventually became Belgium, instead of throwing in their lot with the Netherlands. In the twentieth century, however, the language breach has moved to the fore as Belgium's most divisive problem. Canada is another country currently undergoing severe ethnolinguistic strain. Earlier in this century, language-anchored ethnonationalism fragmented both the Austrian and the Hungarian halves of the Habsburg Empire—the common Catholic religion of most of its peoples and several other potential bonds not sufficing to hold it together against the centrifugal pull of linguistic particularism.

There are, of course, exceptions to this trend from religion to language as the cutting edge of politicized ethnicity in the developed world. Ulster is a vivid one, but Lebanon is not an authentic exception, for it is not a developed country. Cyprus is problematic, for here the linguistic and religious criteria separating Greek from Turk are now so overlapping that neither the actors nor an observer can today disaggregate them. This, incidentally, was not always the case in Greek-Turkish relations elsewhere. When the states of Greece and Turkey decided to exchange their respective ethnic minorities in the 1920s, they opted for religion as the identifying criterion, and, as a result, among the almost 2 million people compulsorily exchanged, there were sizable fractions of Turkish-speaking Orthodox defined as Greeks and of Grecophone Muslims defined as Turks.[14] Modern Jewish self-definition has oscillated between the religious and linguistic criteria. On the one hand, the magnet of the ancestral religion pulled Yiddish-speaking and local-language-speaking Jews out of Europe, and Jews speaking Arabic and Central Asian languages out of the Muslim world, into Palestine and then into Israel. On the other hand, within Israel this division between "European" and "Oriental" Jews remains quite recalcitrant—no longer as an overt linguistic separation, since all now speak Hebrew, but as a socioeconomic cleft that is, however, politically neutralized at times of external threat. Furthermore, while Hebrew has been embraced as the Jewish state's national language, persisting disagreement over the proper public political role of religion has so far prevented the adoption of a formal constitution by Israel. For diaspora Jews, specifying the criterion of ethnicity remains a problem (only the religious among them having resolved it)—yet there is no doubt that they, too, participate in the contemporary wave of politicized ethnicity.

4. Language. Two functions of language ought here to be distinguished: as a vehicle of communication and as a potential symbol of ethnic or cultural identity. These two functions are connected in the sense that a pair of languages used within the same cultural ambience will tend to approach one another as instruments of communication unless they become indicators of ethnic distinction and competition, in which case their differences will stabilize or even increase.[15] Only the second of the two functions of language is of interest to this study, and even here there are ambiguities, for language and the ethnic

[14] Psomiades, *The Eastern Question*, pp. 66–68; Ladas, *Exchange of Minorities*, pp. 377–84, 438–42.

[15] Petersen, "Comparison of Racial and Language Subnation," p. 166.

group that it potentially represents and delineates are not necessarily identical. Scots and Basque ethnic affirmation, for example, does not appear to depend on the vitality of the Gaelic and Euskara languages. On the other hand, the overseas expansion of Europe transformed some of its tongues into world languages that not only are widespread secondary linguae francae but also are the mother tongues of many peoples other than their original ethnic communities. Thus, Trinidadians speak English, Haitians speak French, and Chileans speak Spanish as their native languages but are not thereby rendered into Englishmen, Frenchmen, or Spaniards.

Two more caveats are in order here: (a) Not all language conflicts are interethnic; some are intraethnic. Thus, over the past century, there have been serious disputes within the Greek, Jewish, and Norwegian ethnic communities about the proper ethnonational language (Demotiki versus Katharevusa; Yiddish versus Hebrew; Bokmål versus Nynorsk). But the antagonists did not deny each others' membership in the same ethnonational community, even though the linguistic-philological differences at issue were wider and deeper than those that distinguish, for example, Croatian from Serbian speech. Yet this last-mentioned distinction has been reified into the political symbolization of a profound interethnic rift. We shall return presently to this matter of the politicization of potential criteria of ethnicity. (b) Not all language differences within a particular state necessarily lead to language disputes or to ethnic conflict. In Belgium and Canada they do, but in Tanzania and the Philippines they have so far not.

That said, it must nevertheless be acknowledged that the multilingual condition of many modern states is an uneasy one. Governments and dominant elites tend to suspect that it serves as a standing temptation to centrifugal ethnic counterelites. And counterelites do, indeed, often look and seize upon it as a political opportunity and lever. When a central government of a modern, or would-be modern, state seems to be at ease with the multilingual condition of its subjects, it has either decided that the linguistically "aberrant" groups are irrelevant or marginal to its overall policies (a decision subject to revision), or it has spun the problem off onto subfederal units for regulation (as in Switzerland), or it is presiding over a system of strict parallel segmentation as modeled in the preceding section (in which case the level of integration is problematic), or it is putting a brave face on its own weakness (which it presumably hopes is only transitory). A government committed to modernization under centralized direction is inclined to press for unilingualism (as in nineteenth-century France) or, at a minimum, for universal competence in a leading language (as in the twentieth-century USSR).

History may, however, already have turned a corner aborting such ambitions unless they were already realized before the advent of widespread literacy and political consciousness. Thus, as late as the French Revolutionary era, it was still feasible for the Jacobin and Napoleonic regimes to resolve to impose the French language on that full half of the population of France that then still spoke regional vernaculars or mature alien languages—and for republican governments to implement that resolution throughout the nineteenth century. So, too, it had once been possible for relentless English pressure to well-nigh extirpate Erse from Ireland. Today, however, it is already too late to impose Russian or Hindi on the politically self-conscious peoples of Soviet Central Asia or Andhra Pradesh in southern India—let alone on the even more modernized Ukrainians or Tamils. A neat illustration of this time variable is provided by old Hungary, where the government adopted a policy of vigorous linguistic Magyarization in the last quarter of the nineteenth century. It might have succeeded with the not-yet fully awakened Slovaks and Ruthenians if World War I had not intervened to save them from this assimilationist pressure, but it was already too late with respect to Hungary's politically more self-conscious Croatian, Serbian, and Romanian language groups. An era passed is an opportunity missed.

5. Customary mode of livelihood. This can become a criterion of ethnicity in relatively primitive economic environments (for example, Baggara migratory pastoralists vis-à-vis Fur sedentary agriculturalists in the western Sudan,[16] or the nomadism and characteristic crafts that historically have identified Gypsies, or the specialized trading and artisanal functions that identify the Dioula in West Africa, or hill peoples versus plainsmen). As such, this criterion can also be politicized if one group considers its customs and modes of livelihood to be more civilized than another's. Thus, the Bible states that the Pharaonic Egyptian agriculturalists regarded the shepherding mode of life of Jacob and his sons as "an abomination" and therefore confined them to the region of Goshen.[17] Contemporary examples of the possible politicization of such criteria are Arab-Berber tensions in the North African Maghreb, and the Javanese and Bengali propensity to preen themselves as the bearers of customs and cultures superior to those of their neighbors, respectively in Indonesia and on the Indian subcontinent.

6. Regionalism. This possible criterion of ethnic identification and signification sometimes flows out of the preceding one, as in the case of hill/plains tensions, or Javanese vis-à-vis Sumatran and other outer-island Indonesians, and often it flows into the next one—differential political experience. It is elusive. To what extent was the American Confederacy's bid for secession in the 1860s energized by a sense of ethnic distinctiveness

[16] Haaland, "Economic Determinants," pp. 58–73. This suggestion that modes of economic livelihood may, at times, function as marker-criteria of ethnicity is not to be confused with the observation that ethnic groups already identified by other criteria are often heavily concentrated in certain occupations, trades, and professions.

[17] Genesis, 46: 33–34.

flowing out of regionalism compounded by the South's customary modes of livelihood? What would have been the ethnic consequences if that bid had succeeded? To what extent was the earlier separation of the 13 American colonies from Britain predicated on a sense of separate ethnicity and, if so, what were its criteria? Or did their war of independence itself crystallize such a sense of ethnopolitical Americanism? And what about today's geographical-political separations of peoples who are much alike by several other criteria? Might East and West Germans, or North and South Koreans eventually grow to be ethnically distinct?[18] Would North and South Vietnamese have become so had their civil war ended in a draw?

Though speculative, such questions are not pointless. A distinct geographic region plus political institutions make a potent combination for the formation of ethnic groups. This combination has recently created an ethnopolitically self-conscious Macedonian nation, separate from the Bulgarians, in federal Yugoslavia. In earlier history, it had created three of the four Swiss ethnic groups (and the Swiss state itself) by distinguishing and separating them from their non-Swiss German, French, and Italian fellow linguals. In the interwar era, the governmental elites of restored Poland and enlarged Romania had been quite concerned lest the pre-1918 geopolitical separations of their "state nations" might have instilled lasting, protoethnic distinctions and alienations among the Poles who had been subjects of the three partitioning empires and between the Romanians of prewar Hungary and of old Romania proper.[19]

7. The preceding paragraph has introduced the last crite-

[18] Indeed, East German spokesmen occasionally claim to detect increasing linguistic differentiation between the two German populations, the East Germans supposedly developing a socialist German tongue, whereas in the Federal Republic the language is allegedly being corrupted by Americanisms.

[19] Rothschild, *East Central Europe*, pp. 29–31, 286–88; Rothschild, *Pilsudski's Coup d'Etat*, pp. 168–69, 179–80.

rion that may define and focus ethnic identification: a population's political experience within political institutions, eventually creating a politically derived sense of enthnonationalism, initially unbuttressed, or only minimally buttressed, by racial, kinship, religious, linguistic, or other prepolitical, primordial marker-distinctions. In other words, whereas it is conventional to say that ethnonations create or strive to create states of their own,[20] it is also the case that states may create ethnonations out of the demographic raw material, so to speak, of their populations (see chapter 1, section 1). If "the American people," or "the Swiss people," or "the French people" can be said to exist as real entities, they are the historical products of the political institutions, the states, that have shaped them into such peoples. If Guatemalans, Hondurans, Salvadorans, and Nicaraguans in Central America or Peruvians and Ecuadorians in Andean America distinguish themselves from each other as nations (occasionally even to the point of warfare), it is not because they differ from each other in terms of race, racial mix, religion, language or other prepolitical, primordial criteria but because they belong to different states. In other words, the old, and rather futile, debate whether nations can be said to exist before they are infused with national consciousness (for example, was there a Slovak or Belorussian nation in the eighteenth century?) is here turned upside down, and the suggestion is posed that ethnonational consciousness can be the product of shared historico-political experience, even in the absence of other shared focal criteria of ethnonationhood differentiating a given population from others.

Admittedly, the effort to consolidate ethnonationalism around the focus of shared political experiences and institutions is likely to require a sustained uphill press against the often diffusive

[20] *From Max Weber: Essays in Sociology*, ed. by H. H. Gerth and C. Wright Mills (New York: Oxford University Press, 1958), pp. 176, 179.

tendencies of the other itemized criteria and foci of ethnicity. Although this effort fails frequently, it is not necessarily doomed to failure. And its occasional successes confirm the proposition that political institutions and processes are not only the creatures but can also be the creators, over time, of ethnonational groups and distinctions, that they are not merely the epiphenomena of the other marker-criteria but have autonomous potency as foci of ethnicity.

Indeed, the reverse impact of political institutions and political decisions on the other "raw" marker-criteria of ethnicity themselves (as well as on derivative ethnopolitical consciousness) has been historically consequential. The reader will recall from earlier allusions in this chapter that today the ethnopolitical chasm between Greek and Turk on Cyprus is profound. But it is of recent vintage and is the product—in its religious and linguistic, as well as its political dimensions—of explicit political decisions and institutions. Before the British occupation of the island in 1878, both communities spoke a unified Cypriot dialect and used each other's places of worship with ecumenical latitude. The British, entering the picture with different concepts, undermined this symbiosis by handing control of education and culture on the island over to the ministries of the Greek and Ottoman mainland states. These then "antagonistically colluded" to segmentalize the two Cypriot communities and alienate them from each other. Small and manageable ethnic-communal and marker-criterial differences were sharpened and politicized into major ethnic cleavages by the political decisions of political entrepreneurs.[21] Similarly, there was a former time when Hindi and Urdu were regarded as two styles of one language. Then, at the turn of the century and as a consequence of political decisions and political divisions, the Hindus pressed the Sanskritizing of their version, and the Muslims the Persian-

[21] Pollis, "Intergroup Conflict," pp. 585–92.

izing of their version, of the language. Eventually two languages were created out of one for political reasons, and then each of them absorbed peripheral dialects—again as a product of political pressure.[22] The revival of Hebrew as the spoken mother tongue of Jews in Palestine and Israel was also the cultural consequence of political decisions and political motivations.

5 · The preceding discussion has shown that ethnic consciousness and assertiveness do not flow automatically out of primordial cultural or naturalistic data and differences but that they are the products of political entrepreneurship. How does this political, or politicizing, edge cut into and across the several criteria of possible ethnic identification and, in turn, how do the dynamics of that engagement relate to the several structural models, patterns, and categories of sections 2 and 3 of this chapter? The strategies and tactics selected by the political entrepreneurs of ethnicity for these engagements and confrontations are discussed in later chapters. But a brief comment on their opportunities is appropriate here. The most plausible inference to draw from this chapter's analysis and the examples cited therein is that politicized ethnicity surfaces and hardens along the most accessible and yielding fault-line of potential cleavage available, given the historical circumstances and the prevailing stratification. Thus, in Belgium, the common religion yields salience to the linguistic split, as it did in the division of Pakistan and in the earlier fragmentation of the Habsburg Empire. In Ulster and Lebanon, on the other hand, the common English and Arabic tongues fail to reconcile ethnic groups that are politically mobilized along religious-sectarian criteria. In Guyana the common English language fails in the face of the

[22] Das Gupta, "Ethnicity," pp. 476–77.

racial articulation of cleavage, whereas in Nigeria and Zaire commonality of race does not guarantee the state against the centrifugal danger of regionally and tribally organized ethnopolitics. In the United States, race and supposed kinship (in the form of ancestral or immigrant origins) supply the most accessible fault-lines. Often fault-lines overlap and compound into clusters. Thus, religion plus language overlap on Cyprus, Sri Lanka, and partially in Canada; race plus language in Malaysia; language, historic and socioeconomic regionalism, plus differential political experiences and styles in Spain and Czechoslovakia; to this last-itemized cluster, religion should be added as another overlapping fault-line for Yugoslavia, and race, as well as religion, for the Soviet Union.

There is no point in multiplying these examples of divisive ethnic fault-lines and their clustering. There is, however, a point in emphasizing that the criteria marking the fault-lines are historically variable in their significance, strength, salience, and hence availability for politicization. They are variable not only relative to each other (for example, religion compared to language in different eras and areas) but also cumulatively, as a whole. Hence the political militancy and solidarity of ethnic groups, like the militancy and solidarity of economic classes, is historically and situationally contingent. Ethnic groups who perceive secular historic trends and/or governmental policies to be jeopardizing their very survival or who fear being swamped on their own ancestral territory by other, alien ethnic groups can be politicized to a highly militant edge indeed. But when the issue is the interethnic division of shares in "normal" politics, then such high levels of group militancy are more difficult to achieve—and are perhaps not even desired by the mobilizing political entrepreneurs. In the latter contingency, moreover, these entrepreneurs of politicized ethnicity may be bidding not only for bigger immediate shares for their group and power for themselves but also for an opportunity for their group to make a qualitative new contribution to the multiethnic macro-society, enhancing its variety and resiliency.

One additional caveat is in order lest the preceding point about the contextual variability of ethnic marker-criteria and their correspondence with accessible fault-lines be misunderstood. In one sense, indeed, it may be argued that, whether the marker-criterion selected by political entrepreneurs for contrastive ethnic mobilization in any given case be religion or language or race is intrinsically irrelevant, since any and every one of them can be sacralized into a symbolic focus of ethnic mobilization and politicization, and this process is more or less the same whichever marker-criterion is selected. In other words, Belgians can be mobilized to as intense a level of political militancy along their fault-line of language as Ulstermen along theirs of religion or Malaysians theirs of race, and so forth. Nevertheless an important political-contextual qualification is here very much in order. If a particular state apparatus or regime—for example, India's—has ideologically, formally, and constitutionally committed itself to secularistic goals and values under which some ethnic marker-criteria are aprioristically relegated to political illegitimacy while others are tolerated as licit, then the selection of one or another marker-criterion by a challenging and oppositional counterelite becomes very crucial indeed. In the example here cited, the selection of religion as the criterion for group mobilization and politicization by any Indian counterelite—be the fault-line of religion ever so accessible and convenient—would be a provocative attempted delegitimation of that state's political system and regime; the selection of language, on the other hand, would be an exercise, albeit militant, in "normal" ethnopolitics. *Mutatis mutandis, toutes proportions gardées*, and with all other appropriate qualifications and caveats, a similar statement could be made about alternative marker-criteria in the Soviet Union. Other states, in other historical and ideological contexts, have occasionally defined other potential marker-criteria as politically taboo—noncore languages and regionalism, for example, in France during the Third and Fourth Republics and in Spain during the Franco era. This point once again illustrates the potency of political institutions and political decisions in affecting the configuration of ethnic groups, the cutting edge of ethnic conflict, and the very content of ethnicity per se.

Chapter Four

THE DYNAMICS OF INTERETHNIC RELATIONS, ENGAGEMENTS, AND CONFRONTATIONS

1 · This chapter is intended to infuse dynamic political-behavioral content into its predecessor's structural analysis of various types and patterns of multiethnic systems.

Whichever model of ethnic stratification a particular multiethnic state approximates (see chapter 3, section 3), the relations, engagements, and confrontations of its constituent ethnic groups are the product and expression of sustained and regular contacts among them. Contacts that are no more than intermittent or occasional do not yield systems of stratification. Moreover, in addition to continuous, or at least regular, contact, stratification requires and implies the following: (1) that the ethnic groups be ethnocentric—otherwise they would merge, or one would dissolve itself into another, as, for example, the original early medieval Bulgars and Varangians, who allowed themselves to be absorbed into the sea of the Slavic peoples among whom they had settled in the Balkans and in Russia; and (2) that the ethnic groups compete as ethnic groups for scarce goods and goals that they share in valuing highly—otherwise there would be no rationale for the ethnic stratification. Furthermore, in practice if not necessarily in theory, (3) some element of power differential usually pertains between and among ethnic groups in such sustained contact with each other. Equality is extremely rare and appears to exist only in conditions of low population density and economic complementarity—as sometimes between nomads and agriculturalists, Beduins and market-oasis dwellers.

The competition of ethnic groups for scarce goods may be direct or at one step removed from the objects and goals themselves. For example, the Spanish conquerors of the Aztec and Incan empires are famous, or notorious, for the extraordinarily high value they placed on gold and silver. The Amerindians, on the other hand, while appreciating the ornamental potentialities of these metals, did not assign to them a high intrinsic or exchange value. Hence, at this level the latter groups were more or less indifferent to the former's values. Their conflict and subsequent stratification ensued from the decision of the Spaniards to exploit their greater power to appropriate the labor of the Amerindians—which these also valued—for the extraction of more precious ore out of the mines. In other words, once a second group is perceived as instrumental by the first for the achievement of the first group's valued goals, then the competitive condition for stratification is met, even in the initial absence of primary competition over directly shared, jointly valued, goals.[1]

In modern multiethnic states these three conditions of ethnocentrism, competition, and differential power may be hypothesized as present. Also ordinarily present are certain regulative values that condition and inform the system of stratification, defining the perimeters of legitimate political behavior on the part of its dominant and its subordinate ethnic groups. Though these regulative values vary among systems, and though they

[1] While the historical examples are mine, the theoretical components of the two preceding paragraphs are condensed from Noel, "Origin of Ethnic Stratification," pp. 157–64. Note that they are compatible with the structural theory of internal colonialism (chapter 2, section 6).

occasionally break down, nevertheless a generalized consensus appears to exist about their outer limits—at any rate within the universe of developed states. Thus, the infliction of genocide and mass expulsion by dominants and the perpetration of indiscriminate terror by subordinates are now generally regarded as beyond the margins of legitimate ethnic political behavior. As for more precisely targeted, "surgical," violence in the prosecution of ethnic conflict, the burden of cultivated liberal sympathies and judgments today often weighs more heavily against dominants than subordinates, greater tolerance being shown for the assassination of gendarmes or other forms of forceful protest by aggrieved ethnic militants than for overtly repressive governmental and dominant-group measures against them.

Though violence and overt force were often instrumental in establishing many contemporary systems of ethnic stratification, and though they remain today latently available even while normally and normatively screened, they are neither the only nor the conventional regulators and enforcers of interethnic relations, engagements, confrontations, and stratifications. If we persist for an interval with the heuristically convenient, albeit somewhat oversimplified, image of ethnic domination and subordination and ask what it means for an ethnic group to be dominant over one or more other group(s), our probe brings us back to values, norms, goods, and goals, as well as force and violence. The dominant group is the one able to define its own standards and cultural markers as normative for the society as a whole. The subordinates are thus confronted with the dilemma of either striving to meet those standards, that is, of competing with the dominants on the latter's home ground, as it were, or of challenging them, which requires a heavy investment in group solidarity. If, as sometimes happens, subordinates outperform dominants at meeting the latter's own values and standards (for example, in educational, professional, and cultural achievement), then the dominants are confronted with the dilemma of abiding by or subverting their own regulative and procedural values and rules. How the dominants resolve this dilemma may be substantially guided by whether or not the subordinates achieve a stance of group solidarity.

Only in the hypothetical, but rarely realized, model of pure parallel segmentation are these dilemmas absent, for here there is no general acknowledgment of the validity and desirability of any one set of values and standards; each ethnic segment here retains and cultivates its own. As for the cross-patterned reticulate systems, these might, admittedly, be accurately (but awkwardly) described in terms of relatively more and less favored or privileged ethnic groups. Nevertheless, since such systems are, after all, also provided with a set of generally valid standards, values, and norms (with the resultant dilemmas that were just sketched for all groups), the simple and clear rhetoric of "dominant/subordinate stratification" is here retained to distinguish between those who have the power to set these norms and those who must either comply with or challenge them.

Perceptions of the legitimacy of such systems of dominant/subordinate ethnic stratification may run the gamut from both parties judging the system and their relationship within it to be fully legitimate (in ideal-typical terms, the image of every group knowing its place and perceiving it as appropriate) to both parties viewing the arrangement as categorically illegitimate (in which case it is no longer viable). In between these two evaluative poles are several possible intermediate positions, combinations, and permutations, in which the parties may repose identical or discrepant degrees of legitimacy in the system. While ours may be an age characterized by a tropism toward ever lower levels of legitimacy-acknowledgement on the part of ethnic subordinates, it must be recalled that historically there have been important instances when dominants, or at any rate significant sectors of the dominant group, preceded subordinates in withdrawing legitimacy from the very arrangement that ratified their domination. In the case of the dismantling of the British overseas empire, for example, the Liberal and Labour camps in the metropolis had come to regard the colonial system of ethnic stratification as illegitimate and unjust at a time when its subordinate peoples still acknowledged it as at least partly legitimate and normative.

Indeed, some general theories of revolutionary change argue that in any system of power stratification—be it political, economic, ethnic, or mixed—the subordinates do not become militantly restive until after they have detected signals of declining self-confidence, lowered legitimacy, and internal division in the ranks of the dominants.[2] This is the supposedly universal eve-of-upheaval scenario, from France in 1789, through Russia in 1917, East Central Europe in 1956 and 1968, American ghettos and campuses in the 1960s, Iran in 1978 and beyond. Of course, the dominants' antecedent loss of confidence in the legitimacy of their domination may reflect calculations of long-run interest as well as normative or ideological *crises de conscience*. Their sophisticated sectors may become impressed by the costs and contradictions of a system in which the subordinates are poorly motivated, poorly trained, and potentially alienated. Such considerations may be as operative in systems of ethnic as of socioeconomic stratification, though in the ethnic system the lower socioeconomic strata of the dominant ethnic group, whose relative status is at stake, are unlikely to appreciate these arguments for elevating the ethnic subordinates to greater equality in order to render them less of a burden and liability on the system as a whole.

[2] Paul Kecskemeti, *The Unexpected Revolution* (Stanford, Calif.: Stanford University Press, 1961), passim; Serge Moscovici, *Psychologie des minorités actives* (Paris: Presses Universitaires, 1979), passim, and his full-page interview in *Le Monde Dimanche*, October 7, 1979, p. 16.

What, then, are the dynamics of interethnic relations, engagements, and confrontations in situations where the dominants' levels of legitimacy, self-confidence, and unity are either firm or are eroding? The answers depend on a number of additional interrogative and factual ingredients and are quite variform. (Here only the intrastate factors and actors are assessed, consideration of the international situation and pressures being postponed to a later chapter.)

1. Have the ethnic subordinates achieved political group solidarity, or do they scramble for individual or fractional advancement? In the former eventuality, the likelihood of confrontation is heightened.

2. How wide is the power differential between dominants and subordinates? The narrower the power gap, the greater the incentive for the subordinates to challenge the dominants, because the higher the chances of success. *Per contra,* the wider the power gap, the greater the likelihood that fear of dominant reprisal will prompt the subordinates to mute their hostility or to displace it onto still other subordinate groups. Such cool calculations may, however, be neutralized if either (a) the subordinates are driven by moral-eschatological imperatives, in which case they may discount even a wide objective power gap and challenge the dominants despite it, or (b) if the subordinates find themselves in the "cornered rat" situation, facing destruction, and hence with little to lose by counterattacking across a wide power gap. Furthermore, eroding dominant confidence in their own legitimacy automatically narrows the power gap, since an organic ingredient of power is the will to use it; effete will means compromised power.

3. How deep is the disparity in values? On the one hand, as argued earlier (chapter 3, section 3), shared norms and goals may in fact stimulate competition and conflict while mutual cultural isolation may be conducive to harmony. On the other hand, however, in a situation of outright political confrontation,

dominants may well be more amenable to letting themselves be challenged by, and eventually sharing power with, subordinates who partake of the same values and standards, since here not all will be lost.

4. How significant are the differences in ethnocultural traits and markers? In political reality, these differences are not objectively measured but are rather flexibly interpreted as profound or superficial by the actors in the light of their strategic perceptions and interests. Thus, in Israel, Zionist ideology requires that the political significance of the cultural differences between Ashkenazic and Sephardic Jews be minimized, whereas in South Africa the dominant Whites exaggerate the ethnocultural differences among themselves, the Blacks, the Coloureds, and the Asians into unbridgeable chasms—and this precisely at a time when they were in fact narrowing. Indeed, South Africa has on occasion redesigned its educational systems so as to reverse this narrowing. (Note here also the British fetishism for using pragmatically trivial speech accents for purposes of relatively rigid social stratification.) Ethnic subordinates may engage in similar behavior, emphasizing and celebrating certain ethnocultural traits and symbols in order to differentiate themselves from the dominants. In multiethnic systems, in short, the utility of reifying certain emblematic ethnic markers and criteria into devices of stratification, distance maintenance, domination, and challenge is shaped by political considerations and needs. Sometimes, indeed, such ethnocultural emblems have to be virtually invented or reinvented to suit political exigencies. One recalls here the Nazis' revival of the synthetic yellow star to identify even assimilated Jews who had become otherwise virtually indistinguishable from their gentile neighbors in Western Europe.

5. What impact will the respective evaluations by ethnic dominants and subordinates concerning the desirability of their systemic integration have on the political dynamics of their

interaction? The several answers to this question entail the infusion of operational content into the three previously itemized models of stratification (vertical hierarchy, parallel segmentation, cross-patterned reticulation), together with an analysis of the various meanings and dimensions of integration.

2 · In a multiethnic state the term *integration* may refer to at least three possible and different phenomena:

1. "Life-chances" integration, such that differences in average mortality rates, literacy rates, income rates, employment rates, housing quality, and the like, among the society's several ethnic groups tend to narrow. This is a meaningful hypothesis even though full equalization of such indicators is unlikely to be reached and even though not all indicators necessarily point in the same direction. Thus, an ethnic group's infant mortality disadvantage may decline but its unemployment liability rise, or the society's allocation of educational opportunities may become more egalitarian but its residential distribution more segregated.

2. Cultural integration, either in the sense of acculturation to a dominant, putatively "rational," norm in the socioeconomically and politically "essential" areas of life, while tolerating ethnocultural particularities in supposedly marginal, private, areas (see chapter 1, section 3), or in the sense of full assimilation, wherein ethnocultural particularities disappear or become even privately irrelevant, and intermarriage eventually ensues. As suggested earlier, this latter scenario is today highly unlikely, and even if it is approached, does not necessarily entail the disappearance or even the attenuation of the political expression of ethnic assertiveness (see chapter 2, section 7).

3. Political integration, which occurs when its several constituent ethnic groups grant and acknowledge the system's legitimacy. Either they may do this freely and voluntarily, or they may have been coordinated into such legitimation by the

more or less subtle and effective exercise of the dominants' authority. Either way, this is neither a unilinear nor an irreversible process. An ethnic group may withdraw its imputation of political legitimacy if its own expectations change, or if the system changes to the group's detriment, or if the dominants lose their effectiveness. And it may do this without simultaneously reversing its tendencies toward life-chances integration or cultural integration. Thus, Basque, Breton, and Scots ethnonationalists who seek to delegitimate and politically dis-integrate (literally) the contemporary Spanish, French, and British states do not necessarily revert to their ancestral, ethnically characteristic, occupations and languages. Indeed, of the three dimensions of integration, this political one is currently the most volatile. Political integration, like political legitimacy, is not a condition but a process that must be constantly rewon and reearned.[3]

Moreover, these three dimensions of integration can be linked in varying constellations with the three models of stratification. Thus, virtually by definition, statistical life-chances integration is extremely low in systems approximating the vertical-hierarchical model of ethnic stratification, whereas acculturation to the dominants' norms might, paradoxically, be quite substantial here, especially if these dominants have earlier destroyed the autonomous culture(s) of the subordinates and imposed their own as exclusive. In systems of parallel segmentation, on the other hand, the reverse situation may well pertain, the life-chances statistics of the several ethnic communities approaching each other, but their cultural integration (of either the acculturation or the assimilation variety) remaining low. In the cross-patterned reticulate model, finally, acculturation to dominant norms is likely to be high, but full cultural assimilation may not

[3] Hechter, "Theory of Ethnic Change," p. 22; Moshe Ater, "The Social Gap," *Jerusalem Post*, No. 619, September 12, 1972, p. 12; Schermerhorn, *Comparative Ethnic Relations*, p. 66.

follow at all, and statistical life-chances, while not starkly polarized, will also not reach utter equality. Indeed, even if "objective" indicator-equality is approached, social prestige differentials may still lag behind.

In none of the three models is the level of political integration merely a dependent function of the other dimensions of integration. In other words, the formerly conventional academic optimism that expected that, if statistical life-chances integration is achieved, then the other dimensions must also follow, is now conceded to have been misplaced.[4] However, the reverse of that old proposition is more plausible, to wit: an attempt to achieve political integration without also moving toward a tolerable level of life-chances integration is today likely to prove futile; progress toward life-chances integration seems to be a necessary, though it is not a sufficient, condition for political integration and system-legitimacy.

Even these analytical disaggregations of the components of the problem of ethnic integration do not do full justice to its complexity. For one thing, there are conventional differences between the approaches of immigrant and of autochthonous ethnic groups to integration. Immigrants and their descendants (other than "pariah" minorities) generally anticipate having to acculturate to a significant extent to the languages and some other cultural norms of their dominant hosts, whereas autochthonous groups today often insist that their indigeneity morally entitles them to refuse such acculturation, let alone assimilation. And since these autochthonous ethnic groups are also often geographically concentrated to the point of forming the local majorities in the regions of their immemorial settlement, their moral self-assurance in pressing their stances can be buttressed with considerable political leverage, sometimes

[4] See Gordon's comment on his own earlier work in his later essay "Racial and Ethnic Group Relations," pp. 84–110. Seemingly still subscribing to the old optimism is Francis, *Interethnic Relations*, p. 254.

including secessionist threats. Thus, in the historically and contemporaneously immigrant society of the United States, for example, while most ethnic groups now strive to preserve and to revive (and sometimes to invent) aspects of their ethnocultural heritages, none would seriously expect its members to receive a higher liberal-arts or free-professional education in a language other than English. In both Communist and non-Communist European multiethnic states, on the other hand, the native ethnic groups increasingly tend to demand precisely such a right to receive even the most advanced educations and enjoy the most elevated professional careers without having to submit to the alleged humiliation of having to retool to an alien language. In Canada, too, the Québécois consider themselves to be autochthonous for the purposes of this interethnic engagement with the Anglophones.

Two additional refinements should also be factored into the integration analysis. One is the consideration that the subelite of a subordinate ethnic group may be integrated with the dominants in one or more of the dimensions of integration without the subordinate masses' following suit and without that subelite's being thereby lost to its ethnic group. The other is the observation that the tactics of an ethnic group may at first glance appear to contradict its goals and yet on closer examination prove to be quite functional for the realization of those goals. Thus, ethnic groups may participate in elections—a politically integrationist tactic—to preserve or achieve ethnolinguistic and ethnocultural reserves or even autonomous politico-administrative jurisdictions (sometimes resorting to legislative obstructionism to get their way). Conversely, they may threaten to secede—a centrifugal tactic—to be bribed back with greater participatory integration. Alternatively, ethnic groups frequently accept a significant level of acculturation—in order to arm themselves with the resources to stave off full assimilation. The various options, tactics, strategies, and goals of ethnic elites and ethnic masses under diverse circumstances are examined later. Our immediate agenda remains the question of how the respective evaluations by ethnic dominants and subordinates concerning the desirability of their systemic integration impact on the political dynamics of their interaction.

Since dominants and subordinates may each endorse or reject the desirability of integration, four main judgmental combinations are possible (with secondary nuances within each):

1. Both dominants and subordinates may be negatively disposed toward cultural and social integration. Paradoxically, such dual rejection may in fact facilitate political integration, provided that the dominants are prepared to facilitate life-chances equilibration and provided that the subordinates are not already secessionist in their political aspirations. Switzerland has already been cited as an example of a state whose successful political integration is predicated on a mutual decision by its several language communities to shun ethnocultural integration. For those readers who might object that in Switzerland the level of life-chances integration is already so high that the French-, Italian-, and Romansch-speaking groups can no longer be adjudged as subordinate to a dominant German-speaking group, one could cite as an alternative example the United States, where the dominant WASP core no longer insists on implementing the melting-pot metaphor but has come to acknowledge and endorse the desire of several ethnic peripheries to preserve substantial expression of separate ethnocultures—for example, via ethnic day schools, afternoon schools, and Sunday schools. This partial ethnocultural and ethnosocial segmentation facilitates political integration. One might also list here Czechoslovakia, Yugoslavia, and India as states seeking to achieve political integration and system-legitimation via reciprocal dominant and subordinate respect for ethnocultural insularities, combined with efforts to achieve life-chances parity.

Some observers, however, allege that in Yugoslavia, at any rate, the secessionist alienation of some ethnic groups is already too far advanced for this strategy to succeed. In Israel, too, Arab disaffection appears to be so high as to render political integration problematic despite the mutual decision of the dominant Jews and the subordinate Arabs and Druze to go their separate cultural ways and despite the narrowing of the socioeconomic life-chances gaps among them. However, among Israel's Jewish cultural camps (Ashkenazic, Sephardic, secularized, religious), this formula of political integration via mutual cultural segmentation and life-chances approximation appears to be successful.

2. The dominants may sponsor, and the subordinates resist, integration. This is definitionally a more conflictual combination than the preceding one. It pertains when dominants presume that political integration will remain fragile without the underpinning of cultural integration or, to formulate the same point differently, that state-building will be rendered nugatory unless buttressed by nation-building. Allusion to one of its modalities was made in the previous chapter's discussion of the frequent unhappiness of modernizing governments over segmental multilingualism among their populations (chapter 3, section 4). If the dominants fail to press life-chances integration together with cultural and political integration, or if they fail to honor their own regulative values by, for example, inflicting residual discrimination on subordinates who enter the dominants' universe of cultural norms and values, their bona fides will become suspect and their chances of integrative success will be undermined. Alternatively, the burden of compromised good faith may rest with the subordinates if they withhold political loyalty from the state despite dominant tolerance of their collective cultural autonomy and their privileged life-chances station—as was the case with the Volksdeutsche ethnic groups in interwar East Central Europe. In any event, even without such nuanced

contingencies, in today's era of heightened ethnopolitical assertiveness, the likelihood of successful subordinate resistance to dominant integrationist pressure is high.

3. The subordinates may be the ones who press, and the dominants the ones who resist, integration—reversing the immediately preceding paradigm. This is often the situation on the morrow of the emancipation of a previously enslaved or otherwise legally disentitled subordinate group, which then expects other barriers to its full integration to be also removed—only to be repudiated and relegated "to its proper place" by the dominants. Such was the case with the Jews in several West European states in the nineteenth century and with Blacks in the United States after the Civil War. Initially they expected no more than an end to civil, political, and social discrimination against their members as individuals, that is, an end to unequal treatment violating the universalistic and regulative values that the dominants themselves purported to profess. Only after this expectation was disappointed did they recoil into collective strategies stressing group rights and group autonomies—sometimes to the point of reversing their original integrationist aspirations.

4. Both dominants and subordinates may endorse integration. But their congruent evaluations by no means ensure conflict-free interethnic relations and engagements. Once again the observation is in order that groups sharing values and goals are prone to compete and conflict for the appropriation of the scarce resources and goods that are defined as desirable by those values and goals and that are necessary for their realization. And modernization tends to intensify that competition. Thus, in the here-hypothesized combination of congruent affirmations of integration, the dominants, by definition, nevertheless have a headstart over the subordinates in the possession of strategic political, socioeconomic, educational, and other resources, places, and opportunities. They are likely to perceive

these advantages as theirs by right, that is, as the product of their own hard work and other virtues, and protect them accordingly. The subordinates, believing that the mutual agreement on the desirability of integration promises them a quick catchup, define the stations reached by the dominants as their own reference line of expectancy and resent the gaps that still must be closed, even if these gaps have already narrowed dramatically. Indeed, the remaining gaps are all the more frustrating and intolerable for being so tantalizingly narrow and hence seemingly bridgeable. Though economic expansion increases the available life-chances resources, places, and opportunities, it does not necessarily abate the competition, since some of the issues at stake are perceived in absolutistic-moralistic terms by at least some of the antagonists. Indeed, as is argued in the next subsection, economic expansion may even spur ethnic politicization and confrontation. Ironically, thus, an interethnic engagement that began with joint dominant and subordinate endorsement of integration may end with one or both camps behaving politically and socially in a manner that in effect negates this stated commitment and subverts the society's regulative values. Even in a system approximating the cross-patterned reticulate model of stratification, in which a modicum of integration in all three dimensions is necessarily and definitionally present, these dynamics stimulate ethnic-group mobilizations and the whetting of ethnic political strategies.[5]

Thus, none of the four itemized combinations of judgments

[5] The preceding four paragraphs, that is, the depiction of the four possible combinations of dominant/subordinate, negative/positive attitudes toward integration, are informed by the theoretical contributions of Schermerhorn, *Comparative Ethnic Relations*, pp. 82–83; Melson and Wolpe, "Modernization and Politics of Communalism," pp. 1112–30; Akzin, *State and Nation*, pp. 84–91; Brass, *Language, Religion, Politics*, p. 10; Hah and Martin, "Conflict and Integration Theories," pp. 373–78; Amersfoort, "'Minority' As Sociological Concept," pp. 220–22, 229–31.

about the desirability of integration is conflict-free. Least conflictual is the one in which both dominants and subordinates are reticent toward it. Most liable to mutual misinterpretations and reciprocal misunderstandings is the combination in which both purport to acclaim integration. In all four, the dynamics of the interaction are liable to have an impact on the dominants' and the subordinates' imputation of system-legitimacy and thus may prompt either or both to reverse their judgment on the desirability of integration. Hence, the four combinations should not be regarded as static; change is possible within each and from one to another.

3 · Economic expansion's capacity to aggravate ethnic tensions and conflict, while simultaneously increasing overall resources, places, and opportunities, is generated by the cultural and political dialectics of mobility. From the perspective of the dominants, economic expansion, by opening up potential new chances for upward mobility by the subordinates, embeds the risk of the dominants' being challenged and possibly leapfrogged for skilled, prestigious, and powerful positions. This risk is apprehended particularly keenly by the lower socioeconomic strata of the dominant ethnic group. Even if the dominants resist the resultant temptation to hone their society's mechanisms of ethnic stratification, discrimination, and possibly even of repression to a keener edge, nevertheless, at a minimum, the sociopolitical salience of ethnicity is heightened. Admittedly, even in nonexpansionary economic times some ethnic subordinates strive for upward mobility, particularly if a value-integrated educational system instills in them the requisite expectations and skills; but then the dominants can more easily use the objective paucity of suitable openings as their device and

alibi for evading this competitive challenge and consolidating their own advantage.[6]

From the perspective of the ethnic subordinates the dialectics of competition for mobility in a context of economic expansion develop as follows. As long as upward mobility was rare, slow, and precarious, those few individuals from the subordinate group(s) who achieved it tended to acculturate and even to assimilate to the dominants. Only exceptionally would they articulate political expectations on behalf of their (former?) subordinate brethren—and then only those of an ameliorative, rather than a power-demanding, tack. When, however, economic expansion and other general trends substantially increase the ethnic subordinates' opportunities for mobility, then their group perception of group goals, group solidarities, and group grievances tends to be whetted. Even the most successfully mobile individuals now find it politically opportune and/or emotionally rewarding to remain loyal to their ethnic roots. Indeed, it is precisely they, that is, the ethnic subelites, who most appreciate the utility of group solidarity for bolstering their own achieved successes and supporting their further aspirations. And these aspirations, in turn, now broaden from economic attainments to cultural recognition and political power.[7]

As always in the dialectics of social and political life, such developments entail their costs—often, initially unanticipated costs. The allusion here is not only to the previously discussed likely countermobilization of dominants and intensified frustration of subordinates accruing from the still remaining, albeit narrowing, gaps but also to more subtle tolls. Preoccupation

[6] Lieberson, "Stratification and Ethnic Groups," p. 205; Bonacich, "Theory of Ethnic Antagonism," pp. 547–59.

[7] Petersen, "Comparison of Racial and Language Subnation," pp. 145, 168.

with group solidarity and group advancement may sacrifice the opportunities of specially talented individuals in both dominant and subordinate groups. Furthermore, competitive mobility tempts consolidated ethnic groups to behave as publics or parapublics rather than as conventional interest groups. They hold their communal leaders and their officers of state accountable to themselves to a point where ethnic patronage tends to replace rationality and productivity in allocative public-investment and public-interest decisions.[8] In a period of sustained economic expansion, with its seductive surpluses, the insidious toll on the public ethos of such an ambience of collective ethnic "entitlements" to sectors of the public exchequer and the public realm may not be fathomed until too late. When state institutions are perceived as having lost their autonomy to ethnic annexation—be it by dominants or by subordinates—their legitimacy becomes compromised and their capacity to administer the society's regulative values is subverted.

The preceding cautionary lines are not directed at mere ethnic "ticket balancing" in partisan politics in multiethnic states, for there the consequence is ordinarily not the veritable appropriation by ethnic groups of sectors of the public realm. Nor are they intended to imply that the alluded-to dangers are present only in economic expansionary periods; rather they are intended to suggest that then these erosions may not be appreciated betimes. They are also meant to indicate that, when mobility opportunities give a premium to ethnic strategies, a momentum toward a self-fulfilling prophecy may be generated whereby (1) most social and political competition comes to be perceived and structured along ethnic lines, and (2) the state itself becomes a prize to be occupied and exploited by the contending ethnic groups, and (3) the momentum becomes cyclical as further emerging mobility opportunities—which are

[8] Cf. Jackson, *Plural Societies and New States*, pp. 11, 19–25.

particularly vivid during economic expansion and to which the educated younger generations are particularly sensitive—further reinforce ethnic mobilization both to seize these opportunities and to either retain or capture the state apparatus controlling access to them.

If one were to postulate the opposite situation, one in which no mobility opportunities are available to the ethnic subordinates owing to economic stasis and/or the dominants' unchallengeable power monopoly, then interethnic relations might be either paternalistic-deferential or openly conflictual, but they would not be competitive. Such a situation is approximated in systems of the vertical-hierarchical model of ethnic stratification. Here paternalistic-deferential interethnic relations rely on elaborated systems of etiquette to maintain social distance and status inequality between ethnic dominants and subordinates while allowing them intimate contacts and spatial proximity. Such systems, once cheap and functional from the point of view of the dominants, do not easily survive modernization and urban industrial economic development, which, as demonstrated above, stimulate competitive interethnic relations. Eventually the subordinates withdraw their imputation of legitimacy and the dominants respond by imposing spatial distance (segregation) to replace the evanescing social distance (etiquette) as a stratifying device.[9] But imposed segregation also eventually proves costly and dysfunctional as economic modernization proceeds

[9] Van Den Berghe, "Distance Mechanisms of Stratification," in the volume of his essays entitled *Race and Ethnicity*, pp. 42–53. He points out that in some of the older, preindustrial cities of the American South, little residential segregation was imposed on local Blacks, who could be relied on to keep their "proper" social distance from Whites. But in the newer, industrial cities of both South and North, characterized by competitive rather than paternalistic-deferential interethnic relations, residential segregation, that is, spatial distance, was imposed. It should here be parenthetically noted that concentrated and segregated groups tend to seem bigger and more menacing to each other than if they are dispersed and integrated.

to still higher levels. Moreover, it facilitates the political organization of the subordinates and the "ethnicization" of allocative public decisions. Sooner or later the dominants are confronted with the dilemma of either sponsoring (under subordinate pressure) movement toward cross-patterned reticulate interethnic stratification (as with current White/Black engagement in the United States) or of using their political monopoly of state power to repress the mobilizing and increasingly competitive subordinates, at the risk of civil upheaval, revolutionary confrontation, and system-disintegration (as in South Africa).

An exception to these conflictual pressures might pertain if the spatial segregation were to be authentically voluntary, that is, true self-segregation, and thus not an expression of imposed ethnic superordination and subordination or of politically enforced inequalities in life-chances and power. Such might be the situation in the previously itemized pattern of mutual reservations toward the desirability of cultural and social integration (section 2 of this chapter), as well as in the earlier discussed model of parallel ethnic segmentation (chapter 3, section 3).

In the secular type of economic expansion conventionally termed "modernization," the dialectics of mobility also tend to aggravate ethnic conflict and confrontation. The initial phases of modernization widen the inequalities between the dominants, who have a headstart in the possession of valued resources, and the subordinates, who lag. At the same time, however, the perceived potentialities of modernization erode the traditional, premodern legitimacy of those very same inequalities. At this stage it is the subordinates who experience the frustrations of relative deprivation, as their normative expectations outpace their experienced satisfactions. In later phases of modernization, the subordinates either narrow the gap by successfully competing within the dominants' own value-and-standard universe to exploit new mobility opportunities, or they challenge the dominants outright—politically, culturally, and structurally. Either way, it is now the dominants' turn to be afflicted by the sense of relative deprivation (see the earlier discussion of the later dynamics of internal colonialism, chapter 2, section 6, and the Introduction).

In an ethnically homogeneous society, these tensions and conflicts of modernization are experienced and expressed in class terms; in a multiethnic society, more probably in ethnic terms. If the multiethnic society is also one in which the several ethnic groups form concentrated regional majorities, the unity of the state itself may succumb to these ethnocentrifugal pulls provoked by modernization. But even if this threat of fragmentation is averted and the state succeeds in consolidating itself, it nevertheless must contend with conflicting, ethnically based, claims and grievances over the legitimate political meanings of the "equality" that modernization promises and the inequality that it generates. By the time the dominants concede legal equality and equality of opportunity based on merit, the subordinates may already be demanding equality of results and pressing ascriptive criteria to achieve it. Ethnic mobilization and countermobilization pursue each other; issues of equity and equality, rationality and entitlement, become snarled; dominants and subordinates each come to feel victimized; and regulative values and regime-legitimacy are frayed and strained.[10] In this imbroglio, ethnic identity and ethnic solidarity, having been stimulated by the dialectics of modernization, come to be perceived as politically more effective levers than class organizations for capitalizing on the opportunities and liabilities of that modernization process.

4 · What are the steps whereby ethnic groups may change or even reverse their judgmental positions on the legitimacy

[10] Cf. Burgess, "Resurgence of Ethnicity," p. 278.

of the state itself, or of its stratification system, or of its political regime, and on the desirability of one or another mode of integration with other groups? What are the linkages between such evaluational changes and their political-organizational consequences? These questions are here most acutely addressed toward changes in the perceptions and behavior of the ethnic subordinates.[11]

Legitimacy is an evaluative concept and acquiescence a behavioral stance. Though analytically distinguishable, they tend to be politically linked. A subordinate ethnic group may impute legitimacy to a political system and acquiesce in that system's ethnic stratification—in which case there is no tension between its evaluation and its comportment. Or a subordinate group may still impute legitimacy to the multiethnic state and political community in which it exists but challenge the prevailing stratification system and political regime. Alternatively, subordinates may regard the state, the system, and the regime as all illegitimate—and nevertheless acquiesce for prudential reasons, lest premature challenge at a time when the power gap between themselves and the dominants is still wide prove abortive, worsen their group's position, and possibly even jeopardize its very survival. Or they may continue to acquiesce out of sheer inertia despite their judgment of illegitimacy. Finally, the subordinates may deem a system illegitimate and proceed to challenge it—in which case there is again a correspondence between their evaluation and their behavior.

Acquiescence and challenge are both complex behavioral variables. Each may be rational or irrational. Acquiescence predicated on a clear-eyed calculation of forces leading to a decision to bide one's time until a more favorable constellation

[11] Apropos dominants, these questions have been tangentially addressed in the earlier discussion of structural theories of ethnopolitics, chapter 2, section 6.

might emerge is rational and instrumental. Acquiescence from sheer habitual dependency or apathy is irrational and immature (unless nonpolitical goods and values are deemed more important than political ones by the subordinates). So, too, with challenge. When predicated on an aware analysis of relative (and changing) strengths and vulnerabilities, of possible long-run gains and losses, or on a shrewd assessment that the squeaking wheel will get a quick oiling (that is, that rioting may yield some immediate benefits), challenge is rational. But when indulged in out of sheer uncalculated escapism, revanchism, rage, or macho-bravado, it is irrational and infantile.[12] (It is not intended here to equate this rational/irrational axis with moral/immoral. Irrational challenge can be moral, just, and heroic.)

In real-life political behavior, rational and irrational usually manifest themselves, not as alternative poles, but as mixed ingredients. Thus, the acquiescence of subordinates is usually predicated on both a rational calculation that disturbing the status quo would leave them, as the vulnerable party, even worse off than currently, as well as on an irrational, diffuse, sense of generalized inefficacy. "The mass of men lead lives of quiet desperation" was the way Henry David Thoreau depicted this latter stance.[13] Note that he did not state that most men are desperate—which would have implied a readiness to take action—but that they lead lives of quiet desperation—which suggests that they perceive their world as a given and hostile necessity, not as a contingent and negotiable construct on which they can make an impact or have an effect. So, too, serious political or revolutionary challenge by subordinates also combines a rational assessment of chances with a somewhat irrational, millenarian conviction that faith can and will move

[12] The argument of this paragraph extends a suggestion by De Vos and Romanucci-Ross, "Ethnicity: Vessel of Meaning and Emblem of Contrast," in their coedited volume *Ethnic Identity*, p. 384.

[13] Henry David Thoreau, *Walden* (1854), Chapter 1: "Economy."

mountains precisely because it is in part contemptuous of the realities—or seeming realities—of the status quo. As contemporary ethnopolitics manifest a generalized tropism away from acquiescence and toward challenge, the question is posed how this change in behavior is energized by changes in the mix of rational and irrational components in the changing moral, cultural, and political consciousness of dominants and subordinates alike.

Changes in moral and cultural consciousness precede changes in political behavior. And once such changes in consciousness have taken place, they do eventually entail different behavior. Thus, ethnic subordinates who come to perceive their society and especially its ethnic stratification as unjust and withdraw their acknowledgment of its legitimacy may still acquiesce in its arrangements for an interval—but now for purely calculated and no longer for normative reasons. Thus the moral quality of their acquiescence will have thinned. Not only does this change the entire tone of the political engagement between them and the dominants, but also this season of prudential acquiescence is inherently fluid. The subordinates' new moral-normative consciousness propels them to probe and test their own potential efficacy, especially if it is accompanied—as is likely—by a positive revaluation of their own, hitherto denigrated, culture.

Since persuasion is less costly and more effective than coercion, dominants have historically sought to persuade subordinates to devalue their own (subordinate) culture and competence as indeed inferior—for this, in turn, redoubles the subordinates' sense of political inefficacy. To the extent that this program is successful, the subordinates become the guards of their own prison. And, indeed, negative self-images instigated by dominants pervade the consciousness of many ethnic subordinates (and of other categories of subordinates, such as peasants and women, as well).[14] But in modern interethnic engagements this program meets with increasing resistance and only rarely enjoys lasting success, for the denigration of one's own ethnic culture now entails, at a minimum, psychological strain and guilt—particularly since there are always some upholders of the subordinate culture who eventually acquire prestige and authority for and from defending it.

A shift from disowning to affirming their own culture always precedes and then accompanies the ethnic subordinates' move from political acquiescence to challenge and is an essential step in their transition from irrational dependency toward a rational sense of efficacy.[15] As part of this cultural reaffirmation the

[14] In interwar Czechoslovakia, Yugoslavia, and Romania, for example, the Slovak, Croatian, and Transylvanian Romanian subelites, whose formative experiences had been in pre-World War I Hungary, where they had been treated by the dominant Magyars as inferior and incompetent, initially persisted during the 1920s with a political style suggesting that they had internalized the pejorative Magyar projection of them—aborting repeated opportunities to acquire or share power and preferring the sterile politics of boycott, abstention, and obstruction. See Rothschild, *East Central Europe*, chs. 3, 5, 6. For this phenomenon among such other disparaged ethnic groups as American Blacks and Japanese Burakumin, see, respectively, De Vos, "Ethnic Pluralism: Conflict and Accommodation," p. 38, and Donoghue, "Social Persistence of An Outcaste Group," p. 150, fns. 6 and 7. On the parallel phenomena of peasants' and women's "fear of success" due to having absorbed negative self-images instigated by dominants, see, respectively, Beqiraj, *Peasantry in Revolution*, pp. 11–12, and the works of Dr. Matina S. Horner. The mass media's role in this process of inculcating and absorbing negative group self-images is analyzed by St. Leger, "Mass Media and Minority Cultures," pp. 63–81.

[15] One of the many possible examples of this shift in cultural self-perception that could here be cited is the changing attitude of American Blacks toward the suggestion of the anthropologist Melville J. Herskovits that they are the bearers of a distinctive culture retaining African components. When initially published in the 1930s and 1940s, this theory was received warily and on the whole negatively by American Blacks, who then feared that it implicitly labeled them primitive and denied their integrationist aspirations. By the 1960s and 1970s, when American Blacks had come to revalue their African roots and reassess their place in American society, they also came to appreciate Herskovits' work.

subordinates also reappropriate their own history. Their reduction to subordinate status, or their conquest, or their discovery, by the dominants is downgraded from the starting point of their historical mindset into an episode—admittedly a painful, but in the long run a transitional, episode—in their older, longer, and ultimately vindicating history. And even in the rare case where that history is an unrelievedly oppressive, rather than a once-glorious, one—as with India's Scheduled Castes (Untouchables) and Japan's Burakumin—it, too, can nevertheless function as such a catalyst of cultural-psychological edification and political assertion.

Parallel and related to this revolution in their historiographic perspective, the subordinates also radically alter their definitions of themselves, the dominants, and their interrelationship. Often labeled a search for identity, this change in nomenclature is more than that; it is a change in consciousness, claiming the right to redefine the perimeters and the agenda of interethnic engagement. In other words, the power to name and to define is appropriated by the subordinates as a cultural precedent to their political assertiveness, as a necessary sloughing off of what is sometimes termed false consciousness, at other times cultural repression or colonization of the mind, preparatory to moving from political acquiescence to challenge.[16]

[16] American Blacks will again supply an example. Formerly they often referred to Whites as "The Man" and allowed themselves to be called "boy." No more. This change, and the accompanying refrain "Black is beautiful," were intended to convey a political, as well as a psychological, self-liberating thrust. Kuper, *Race, Class, and Power*, pp. 83–88; Tajfel, "Social Psychology of Minorities," pp. 11–17. The widespread ethnic trend to Africanize, Celticize, Hebraicize, and the like, personal names also expresses this sense that the power to name, being a power to define and redefine, incubates a political potential. The newly selected ethnic names usually symbolize strength, presubordination antiquity, and supposed ethnic authenticity.

The mythic thrust of a subordinate ethnic group's freshly assertive cultural-historical consciousness may be directly correlated to its particular political plight. Thus, a group threatened with fragmentation, either within one or between several states, has an incentive to emphasize the historic unity of its culture and to claim collective kinship descent from a putatively common ancestry. A group exposed to unwelcome assimilationist pressure may stress more its ethnocultural distinctiveness and is apt to try to revitalize its historic language from a dying rural or "kitchen" patois into a literary vehicle of modern communication despite the initial "objective" economic and professional disadvantages of such a program. Autochthonous groups that once enjoyed independent statehood or retain vivid memories of distinctive political institutions (for example, the Basque *fueros*, and Catalan *Generalitat*, the Scottish kirk and legal system) are more prone than immigrant and dispersed groups to entertain secessionist or parallel-segmental visions of political reconstruction. Challenged dominants respond by honing their own counter-myths, which are also directed to their particular predicaments and which may imply a more integrationist, or a more autonomist, or a more exclusionist-repressive policy toward the subordinates (see chapter 2, section 6). Once any ethnic group's new level of cultural consciousness, and of the political mobilization linked to that consciousness, pass beyond a certain threshold, these become highly resistant to being directed toward alternative perspectives and to being diverted with nonpolitical prospects—such as "mere" socioeconomic mobility for individual members.

An ethnic group may whet and link its developing cultural consciousness, its revised historiographic perspective, and its progression toward political challenge within an ambience of moral pacifism (as with the movements organized by Gandhi in India and Martin Luther King in the United States) or in a context of political violence (as in many anticolonial revolutions and secessionist conflicts). Also, the institutional setting that incubates the new subordinate militancy may be one of relative segregation and/or withdrawal (such as the Black chapels, churches, and mosques in the United States) or of direct interaction (as in urban labor and housing markets and in violent confrontations). Dominants often misunderstand the potentials of these institutional settings and misjudge the levels of politicized consciousness that subordinates can reach within them. (Such misreading is particularly likely in—but not confined to—systems approximating the vertical-hierarchical model of ethnic stratification.) Thus, dominants often fail to appreciate betimes that segregated institutions, which may originally even have been imposed on the subordinates as supposedly toothless and intended to inculcate apolitical attitudes and acquiescent comportment, can become authentic vessels of ethnopolitical consciousness and assertiveness—as with the above-mentioned Black chapels in the American South and conceivably some day with the Bantustans of South Africa. And when the dominants do, finally, recognize this potential and notice the changing consciousness and behavior of the subordinates, they often misproject again. From underestimating the subordinates' openness to change, they switch to exaggerating it. Whereas earlier their image of the subordinates had been one of contented subjects whom outside agitators are maliciously but vainly seeking to set astir, now it becomes one of rapacious fomenters of limitless violence. Note that neither image credits the subordinates with a capacity for rational political consciousness and behavior—goal-oriented, self-controlled, neither passive nor berserk.

Perhaps these misreadings are in part an outgrowth of the difficulty that ethnic antagonists experience in assessing the reciprocal influence of ideological and rhetorical violence, on the one hand, and of behavioral violence, on the other hand, in shaping each other's political conduct and consciousness. Indeed, not only ethnic but also other categories of political antagonists have difficulty in making this appraisal about their respective adversaries and hence in determining what is an appropriate counterstance for themselves to adopt. For example, in the 1920s and 1930s Hitler's crystal-clear rhetorical and ideological projections of violence were dismissed, as supposedly without programmatic content. From this fatal error of underestimation, the political world has recoiled into taking ideology and rhetoric very seriously indeed —sometimes perhaps too literally, for while it is, alas, true that violent words and images are often intentional preparations for violent actions (for example, "Jews are vermin to be exterminated," "the kulaks are a dying class," "offing the pigs"), it is also true that such violent images and rhetoric may, over time, become ritualistic substitutes for real violence (for example, the *modus vivendi* reached between European Catholics and Protestants during the seventeenth century even though each side retained the theological anathemas that it had pronounced against the other). Sometimes the flow is in the reverse direction, ideological images of violence being generated out of the experience of violence. Moreover, much political violence is uninformed and unguided by ideological content. Nevertheless, while it is possible for antagonists to move from confrontation to *modus vivendi* without ideological disarmament, in interethnic politics the converse is probably not feasible. In other words, it is unlikely that subordinate ethnic groups can move from acquiescence to challenge without a change in their consciousness, which means, in effect, without a change in their ideological comprehension of their situation. All in all, the openness and indeterminancy of these several possible correlations and noncorrelations help elucidate why ethnic dominants are often volatile and wrong in assessing the subordinates' actual and likely levels of political consciousness and assertiveness.

5 · So far, this chapter has taken ethnic groups as givens and has treated their respective positions in, and their perceptions and evaluations of, their interrelationships. And since these interrelationships are ongoing and in flux, the chapter has also discussed the corresponding and anticipatory changes in the several ethnic groups' levels and modes of cultural and political consciousness.

At this point it is in order to refine somewhat this assumed givenness of ethnic groups. Just as earlier it was pointed out that, though alternative lines of cleavage and solidarity are potentially available, there nevertheless exists today a propensity for them to be displaced into ethnic ones (chapter 2, sections 2, 6, 7), so, too, it is here appropriate and necessary to indicate that the givenness and boundaries of ethnic groups are contextual—not only historically contextual in a broad, secular sense, but also politically contextual in terms of the specific configurations of particular confrontations. For both the individual members of an ethnic group and for the group as a collectivity, the behavioral significance of ethnicity, and even the selection of the operative criterion of ethnicity, flow out of the contours of particular situations, as well as of overall, historically shaped, systems and heritages.

These contours of particular situations, by shaping which (if any) of several possible ethnic criteria and interethnic boundaries shall be salient, also help to determine how the confrontational antagonists identify themselves, recruit their allies, and select their leaders. And as the situations change, so do these identifications, allies, and leaders. Thus, for example, depending on the situational context, a certain group of Israelis might project themselves as the Moroccan community, or, more generally, as Sephardim (Orientals) vis-à-vis Ashkenazim (Westerners), or—in the context of the Arab-Israel conflict—as Jews. This parallels Lebanon, where situational context also determines whether the salient definitions and boundaries in a particular issue shall be regional-clannish (for example, Frangieh, Gemayel, Jumblat, Karami, *zu'ama*), sectarian (for example, Maronite, Greek Orthodox, Greek Catholic, Sunni, Shiite), or more broadly religious (Christian, Muslim, Druze), or generalized Arab, and so forth. One should also cite the Indian subcontinent for a particularly vivid illustration of this contextual argument. When it was being partitioned in the late 1940s, ethnoreligious criteria and boundaries were at a premium. But when Bangladesh was seceding from Pakistan in the early 1970s, language, custom, and regionalism were salient and Muslim Bengalis were appealing to the Hindu Bengalis of India for fraternal aid against the Muslim Punjabis of West Pakistan.

Though various possible perspectives and criteria are hypothetically available, once a specific confrontational situation has been perceived and defined in a particular manner by one of the parties—be it dominant or subordinate—this generates strong pressures for the other party to respond in mirror-image terms. A kind of antagonistic collusion may even set in between them to prevent alternative perspectives from emerging and to facilitate their respective mobilizations and enforcement of ethnopolitical solidarity. Witness Ulster and Lebanon. Or, for a past historical illustration of this mirror-image rigidification and how it can be broken, witness Europe's Thirty Years' War of the seventeenth century. There the antagonists persisted in defining the conflict as one between religious camps and escalated it relentlessly by summoning ever more allies in accord with that criterion—until a sufficiently powerful prospective participant, that is, the France of Cardinal Richelieu, rejected that perspective and changed the criterion, as well as the rules, of the confrontation.

A situational context may even generate hitherto unknown neoethnic amalgams whose durability and relevance beyond and outside the particular situation that generated them pose an interesting political and intellectual question. Thus, Muslims from various parts of India who fled into East Pakistan at the time of partition were definitionally amalgamated into Biharis by the host Bengalis. Maghrebi Berbers and Arabs working in France are collectively dubbed Arabs by the French. In Guyana, the refusal of British colonial administrators and plantation proprietors in the nineteenth century to recognize caste and linguistic distinctions fused that country's East Indians into one ethnic group. In the United States, too, the context of immigration amalgamated people whose original self-identification was parochial, provincial, religious, or social (peasant), into "Italo-," or "Polish-," or "Chinese-," or "German-Americans," and so forth. Then, in the 1960s, the different situational context of conflictual relations with Blacks and the WASP Establishment clustered several of these same groups together as the "White Ethnic" phalanx. Similar cases could easily be multiplied.

These several examples suggest that what is at work here is a kind of reductionism, initially imposed for purposes of convenience—mapping convenience, administrative convenience, as well as economic and political convenience—by outsiders, often by dominants. The examples also suggest that this phenomenon often takes place in an ambience of rapid, even drastic, social change, for example, migration, urbanization, or mobilization. What the examples do not answer with any consistency is the question whether the amalgamated identities, initially imposed by others, will over time become internalized as the authentic self-identities of those thus tagged and remain salient in other than the originating situation. Occasionally, this is indeed the case, as with the disappearance of caste and the emergence of a consolidated East Indian ethnic group in Guyana. Presumably the exigencies of its ongoing confrontation with the Guyanese Black community contributed to this outcome. More often, the amalgam remains volatile—operative in one context, only to lapse in another. A Berber worker returning from France, where he had been an Arab, to Algeria, may well resume his Berber identity. American "White Ethnics" in one political or social context return to their separate Italo-American, Polish-American, and the like, identities in another, and in a third context even revert to still more particularized, and older, Calabrian and Górale solidarities. In sum, various possible ethnic cohesions do not necessarily replace each other absolutely. Criteria and identities that are vestigial in one context may resume salience in another—as may nonethnic ones, such as social class.

Incidentally, it should not be supposed that amalgamation/fusion is the only process creating new ethnic groups. Its reverse, fragmentation/fission, can achieve the same result. Whereas in Guyana, as mentioned, the British obliterated communal distinctions among the Indian immigrants, in India itself they encouraged them and, by rigidifying certain criteria and boundaries that had once been fluid, midwifed the emergence of new, particularistic ethnic groups, such as the Sikhs. In each situation, political and socioeconomic convenience explains their policy.[17]

A word of caution is, however, in order. While it is valid to stress ethnicity's situational context rather than attribute to it a supposed immutable givenness, and while it is true that ethnic identities and group boundaries are potentially flexible and multiple, it would, however, be an exaggeration and an error to postulate them as infinitely elastic.[18] They are not changed like shifts of underwear.

Finally, it is here appropriate to discuss the effect of situational

[17] The preceding discussion of situational context and the generation of new ethnic groups through fusion and fission extrapolates from the theoretical contributions of Foltz, "Ethnicity, Status, and Conflict," pp. 104–05; Donald L. Horowitz, "Ethnic Identity," pp. 118–31; Fisher, "Creating Ethnic Identity," pp. 282–83; and Young, *Politics of Cultural Pluralism*, p. 42.

[18] This fallacy is illustrated in Patterson, "Context and Choice," pp. 305–49.

context in shaping the selection of leaders by ethnic groups. This effect operates in two reciprocal directions. On the one hand, the contours and the perceptions of an interethnic confrontation suggest how the ethnic groups should organize and position themselves and what qualities their leaders should be expected to manifest. This, again, is usually a mirror-image process. For example, during the first half of Britain's Palestine Mandate, Arabs and Jews perceived their competition as one in which it was crucial to have the ear of influential members of the British Establishment. Accordingly, they then selected high-status leaders of cosmopolitan polish, courtliness, and eloquence. By the second half of the Mandate era, they had come to perceive their confrontation as one to be slugged out on local ground, as it were, with competitive land-settlement activities, buttressed by military preparedness and occasionally accompanied by quasi-military violence. This revised contextual perception dictated the replacement of the Nashashibi and Weizmann type of leader by the more earthy Husayni and Ben-Gurion type.

On the other hand, the flow of the leadership-selection process is also in the reverse direction. Different possible candidates for ethnic-group leadership, boasting different talents, seek to persuade their ethnic constituencies to perceive the context of an interethnic engagement or confrontation in such a fashion as to give a premium to their respective types of talent. For example, in interwar Yugoslavia, Croatians were locked in confrontation with the Serbians. What was the essential nature of this confrontation? Stjepan Radić argued that it was basically a political contest to be determined at the ballot boxes and hence that his oratorical and charismatic gifts were the kind of leadership attributes needed by the Croatians. After him, Vladko Maček sought to persuade the Croatians that the conflict was essentially a constitutional-juridical one, requiring his legal and administrative talents. Finally, Ante Pavelić insisted that the correct perception of the conflict was paramilitary and hence that he, as the leadership-candidate commanding guerrilla-terrorist resources and Mussolini's endorsement, should be the Croatian people's appropriate choice.[19] Thus, not only do varying situational contexts tend to project to the fore different types of ethnic leaders, but also—reciprocally—different types of leadership-candidates seek to shape situational contexts and perceptions of same so as to enhance their own claims and aspirations.

* * *

The preceding point places on our agenda the need to analyze the elites and leaders of ethnic groups—their types, characteristics, motivations, strategies, options, goals, and dilemmas—a need to which the next chapter turns.

[19] Rothschild, *East Central Europe*, ch. 5.

Chapter Five

LEADERS AND LEADERSHIP IN THE PURSUIT OR THE CONTAINMENT OF ETHNOPOLITICAL CONFLICT: A TYPOLOGY

1 · Politicized ethnic assertiveness today appears to be keenest among those who have been least successful and those who have been most successful in meeting and achieving the norms, standards, and values of the dominants in their several multiethnic states. The former regress into ethnic militancy out of a sense of failure. The latter either recoil into it out of a sense of outrage that their demonstrated superiority as individuals in the cultural and socioeconomic "obstacle race" designed by the dominants has still not gained them full entry into the society's inner power sanctums, or they resolve to link personal external success to ethnic identification and service from a sense that their group has been denied its due place and its appropriate allocations in the overall political and socioeconomic structures. Either way, they perceive the dominants as having violated—indeed, betrayed—their own (dominant) regulative rules and conclude that this repudiation in effect changes the "race" from one in which individual talent and effort were rewarded to one in which ethnic group solidarity is henceforth at a premium. In effect, this reaction—which can be observed

in the Soviet Union as well as in the West[1]—is a special variant, at the level of the ethnic subelite, of a general point made in the preceding chapter's discussion of the dialectics of integration, to wit: that remaining gaps—power gaps as well as life-chances gaps—between ethnic dominants and subordinates are all the more frustrating and resented precisely when they have become tantalizingly narrow and hence seemingly bridgeable (chapter 4, section 2).

Particularly in developed states approximating the model of cross-patterned reticulation, society is today perceived by ethnic subelites as less "open" than the perception was a generation or two ago.[2] This changed viewpoint characterizes both immigrant and autochthonous multiethnic societies. And, somewhat ironically, the resultant sense of grievance over unfulfilled promises and unrealized expectations now propels these ethnic subelites into stances of politicized ethnicity precisely at a time when their own hold on "objective" ethnic markers and criteria such as kinship endogamy, religious observance, language competence, and traditional livelihoods has become tenuous. In short, without denying the authentic emotional energy that they invest in, and draw from, their rediscovered ethnicity, one may nevertheless suggest that these ethnic subelites return to their roots less for cultural sustenance than for organizational leverage. Indeed, their ethnic group remains of interest to them only if it is prepared to pursue a political strategy, articulating political and socioeconomic demands and grievances; it risks losing or alienating them again if it confines itself to an exclusively cultural agenda such as, for example, language revival only.[3]

[1] Rakowska-Harmstone, "Dialectics of Nationalism in the USSR," p. 10.

[2] Goering, "Emergence of Ethnic Interests," pp. 379–84. For data on this narrowing of personal mobility opportunities in East Central Europe, see Walter D. Connor, "Social Change and Stability," pp. 25–28 and *The New York Times*, November 1, 1979, p. A2; for perceptions of such a trend in the United States, see *The New York Times*, November 12, 1979, pp. A1, D8.

[3] Williams, "Cultural Nationalism in Wales," p. 24; Reece, "Internal Colonialism," p. 276.

A comment must here be interpolated about that other type, described above as recoiling into ethnic militancy out of a sense of failure. This does not include those genuinely traditional ethnic personalities who are morally rooted and psychologically secure in their respective ethnic (anthropological) cultures and unaffectedly indifferent to alternative values and norms—whether these alternatives purport to be universalistic or concede to being dominant-designed. Whereas such largely unacculturated and altogether unassimilated individuals may survive in any multiethnic society, they and their more or less autonomous cultures receive structural support only in the relatively rare systems approximating the model of parallel segmentation. While they are persistent, tenacious, and potentially even violent in the defense of their ethnic cultures and values, they are not "assertive" or "militant" in the sense of wishing to compete in, or redesign, any outsider's obstacle race.

No; the type referred to here as recoiling into ethnic militancy out of a sense of failure did seek, albeit unsuccessfully, to compete (or at one time vainly hoped to compete and succeed) and has subsequently bunkered itself into a depressive strategy of shunning further exposure to such competition. To ward off fears of failure, rejection, ridicule, and loneliness, this type develops a synthetic fantasy of stipulated ethnic warmth, brotherhood, and conformity. In contrast to the security and autonomy of the authentically traditional ethnic personality, its psychological stance is defensive and rigid. Tragically, the very choice of foreclosing further exposure and competition, although usually rationalized via an elaborated ideology of ethnic pride, tradition, and militancy, often only confirms an inner sense of inferiority, normlessness, and shame. To ward off further failure, which they apprehend as tantamount to annihilation, people of this type obsessively hypercathect their ethnic identity to the exclusion, or at any rate to the impoverishment, of other possible components of a full, multidimensional human identity. If they achieve power, they seek to impose the same flawed one-dimensionality on outsiders. Thus, the Nazi storm-troopers, having reduced and dehumanized themselves to one-dimensional executors of a *volkish*-racial destiny, also defined their Jewish victims as nothing but Jews *tout court*, denying them individual, rounded, multifaceted human identities.[4]

Even short of such catastrophic encounters, it is a generally useful *arcanum dominationis* in exploitative situations for a leader—including, in this case, an ethnic leader—to restrict the range of identities available to his followers, as well as his enemies, since this heightens the likelihood of his being able to extract compliance and lowers their opportunities for evading his exactions by maneuvering within a wide repertoire of possible roles and identities. Hence top ethnic leaders, whose own experience, range, and psychological profile may be quite different, have a place for the militants-out-of-a-sense-of-failure, with their closed and narrowed personalities, in the secondary and tertiary cadre-echelons of their movements and organizations.

The alternative type of person, who is propelled into ethnic assertiveness by rejection at the hands of the dominants despite his individual success in meeting their professed norms and standards or by an autonomous decision to link personal success to group-service, tends to be more rounded and less brittle and to integrate his ethnic identity more affirmatively and more organically with his other identities and roles. It becomes a means to expand rather than to contract or to limit his humanity. He is also a more plausible candidate for ethnic-group political leadership, despite the fact that he is not likely to be socially typical of his group (here a subordinate or a "pariah"-minority group) and despite the consideration that his command of its cultural patrimony may be rather weak. Indeed, he might once

[4] Devereux, "Ethnic Identity," pp. 66–67.

have been culturally well eligible to have "passed" into the ranks of the dominants but for their social rejection and his reactive political recoil or but for his free decision to forgo that route.

Before proceeding with an analysis of the strategies, options, and goals of different types of ethnic leaders, the just alluded-to phenomenon of "passing" out of one's native (generally subordinate) ethnic group into another (usually dominant) one merits some discussion. A broad historical reference to it was made earlier (chapter 2, section 1). Here the focus is on some of its sociopolitical and psychological aspects. "Passing," in effect, means that ethnic affiliation is perceived as a matter of calculation and manipulation for strategic advantage—mobility advantage and/or power advantage—rather than as an enduring dimension of identity. In some sense, therefore, it is the other side of the coin of the above-mentioned reactive ethnic militancy to secure organizational leverage. Since "passing" is an exercise in mobility, it is most practicable in multiethnic societies approximating the cross-patterned reticulate model—unless and until aborted by that traumatic rejection at the hands of dominants to which reference has been made. It is also feasible in societies of parallel segmentation that are ruled by relatively cosmopolitan and ethnically latitudinarian central elites, such as old, premodern Poland and Hungary. Would-be "passers" who are rejected in their quest often boomerang into ethnic militancy. Those who succeed are permanently lost to their native ethnic communities.

"Passing" appears to be rarer today than it was as late as a generation or two ago. In this era of heightened ethnic consciousness, it probably entails guilt feelings over deserting one's original ethnic community and anxiety lest those origins nevertheless be discovered. Furthermore, and more importantly, it is no longer perceived as a step necessary to attain upward socioeconomic mobility or as a plausible device to achieve political aspirations. Hence it has been replaced by acculturation and partial assimilation.

In contrast to the "passer," the acculturated or partially assimilated upwardly mobile ethnic does not deny his origins. Indeed, he often uses his cultural acceptability and access to the dominants to position himself as a broker between those dominants and his own ethnic group. His expected reward from his ethnic group for playing this broker role is its patronage for the economic, professional, and political skills he commands. Thus, ethnic lawyers, physicians, accountants, businessmen, politicians, and the like, combine self-interest with communal solidarity by training their fellow ethnics to come to them for the indicated services. Yet they must also protect their "universalist" flank lest this ethnic clientelism become an ethnic trap, compromising the entrée to the dominants that the broker role requires. The ethnic professional or politician who confines his practice or his appeal exclusively to fellow ethnics may be placing his general professional and political respect at risk. Brokering, in other words, necessitates balancing. Furthermore, as regards his more specific policy options, while the acculturated broker may be quite assertive in pressing his ethnic group's collective claims and grievances in the corridors of dominant power, as long as his broker role is viable he is precluded from behaving as a revolutionary or secessionist ethnic militant.

It is thus clear that, whereas in a uniethnic society whose stratification system is purely socioeconomic, an upwardly mobile individual is lost to his original class (for example, the illustrative professional son of a worker alluded to in chapter 2, section 1), in multiethnic societies characterized by cross-corresponding socioeconomic and ethnic stratifications, the upward mobiles are today likely to remain identified with their original ethnic groups—thanks to self-definition, external stigmatization, internal group-authority, or some combination thereof. (The phrase "likely to remain" is used because there is still some range of possibilities, depending on the character of the individual, of his group, and of his macrosystem. In states where the citizen is publicly and mandatorily assigned to a corporate ethnic segment, as described in chapter 3, section 2, he has no choice but to remain.) That said, it must, however, also be noted that ethnic groups vary profoundly in their several judgments upon their upwardly mobile members. For example, while some traditional Jews are, admittedly, indifferent or even skeptical toward high achievement in the external world, nevertheless modern Jewry as a whole and in general applauds those of its acculturated members who triumph in that world, with its dominant-designed obstacle races. Their success is adjudged to bring credit and benefit to the Jewish community as a whole, which thereupon tends to select its political leaders and brokers from among them. The Japanese in America manifest similar attitudes. Quite different, on the other hand, are the judgments of American Chicanos and Indians. They appear to fear that the material and emotional rewards of the outside world are likely to seduce their potentially upward mobile members into deserting and thus betraying the ethnic community. Hence they tend to discourage and to disparage—more or less subtly—high performance in, and high ambitions toward, that external world's system of norms, standards, and values. Until a generation ago Canada's Francophone community was similarly reluctant to have its ambitious young members compete and succeed in career patterns outside that community's traditional ones of agriculture, forestry, theology, humanities, and politics—lest they be lost to the ethnic group.[5]

Thus, our valid generalization that, in today's world of heightened and politicized ethnic consciousness, upwardly mobile individuals are likely to remain identified with their ethnic

[5] De Vos, "Ethnic Pluralism," pp. 17, 25, 33, and, by the same author, "Selective Permeability," pp. 7–24; Grabb, "Subordinate Group Status," pp. 268–80; McRoberts, "Internal Colonialism," p. 304.

groups, does not necessarily assuage the anxiety of most such groups. Their concerns are complex and somewhat ambivalent. On the one hand, they resent external discrimination against their members as, in effect, demeaning their group as a whole. On the other hand, they also fear assimilation of these members by the outside world as a threat to the groups's very survival. Even those ethnic groups that do endorse entry and success by their members in external competitions and value-systems and that do vividly protest the outside world's residual discriminations against those acculturated members nevertheless also develop more or less visible internal sanctions to retain these same members.

The psychological potency of such sanctions is a function of their capacity to link the individual's sense of identity with the group's continuity. He is made to feel that his own moral survival is jeopardized if he facilitates the extinction of the group by deserting it, by "passing" out—an act depicted and perhaps experienced as tantamount to patricide. And even short of such dire invocations against such drastic behavior, the ethnic group's sanctions are also intended to warn that even those who merely allow themselves to become excessively acculturated and who sever too many ethnic threads in the pursuit of upward mobility also risk alienation and anomie.

When such internal sanctions and warnings are reinforced and confirmed by unexpected, normatively illicit, external barriers in the lives and careers of talented and prospectively successful ethnics and when they perceive the dominant camp to be subverting its own purported regulative rules and values to keep their ethnic group subordinate, they may well veer from their anticipated broker and even "passer" roles into militant, possibly secessionist or revolutionary, ethnic leadership. In other words, such a highly politicized mode of ethnic reidentification and repossession can serve as their response and reaction to the double threat of deracination and exclusion. In effect, they resolve their incipient dilemma (thwarted personal ambition versus alienation from the group) by championing structural change to elevate the political and social position of their group and through this very process achieving a kind of public personal mobility and effectiveness for themselves without sacrificing their group bonds or group reference.

If and when they make this fateful shift, these largely secularized ethnic leaders generally (but not always) complement their own skills by also drawing on the resources of more traditional leaders who have all along preserved the group's specifically ethnic culture and historical mystique. The latter set of leaders must then be persuaded to modernize this culture and this historiology, synchronize them with the ideological thrust of the former's new ethnopolitical assertiveness, and thereby widen and deepen the solidarity resources of the ethnic movement.[6] In short, the two sets of leaders and their two types of skills jointly crystallize the ethnic group's cohesion by appealing to its members' sense of interest, of duty, and—above all—of group.[7]

[6] ". . . although the basis for historical mystique may exist in rich measure in the reservoir of folk tradition and myths of origin, the move from the oral repository of the traditional elders to the written page multiplies the potential mobilization of identity. This cultural educated class has many tasks to absorb its energies: the language must be standardized and a literature of verse and prose accumulated; history must be recorded and a vision of the future defined. . . . The history of the group must be unravelled and rewoven as epic poetry. The founding fathers, the great kings, the trimphant generals, the high priests must be rescued from obscurity and accorded their place of veneration in the cultural hagiography." Young, *Politics of Cultural Pluralism*, pp. 45–46. See also Anthony D. Smith, "Theory of Ethnic Separatism," pp. 26–31; and Hannerz, "Ethnicity and Opportunity," pp. 38–39.

[7] "Ethnic and nationalist movements are the expression of group interest. Political elites define the interest in terms of access to power and wealth. Cultural elites define the group in terms of where frontiers begin and end. The two leaders rarely merge in one individual; more often, each plays a different but complementary role. Political innovators easily capture our attention. Their cultural counterparts receive a passing glance because no one really believes

At this point, if they are to succeed, these ethnic leaders must either delegitimate and defeat, or harness and subsume, other would-be leaders offering competing, nonethnic or antiethnic, ideological and political perspectives. Such competitors, proposing rival symbols and programs—class programs, voluntary-pluralistic group programs, universalist programs, and the like—include not only the dominants but also alternative subordinate hopefuls. To foil or yoke them, the ethnic leaders depict all social grievances and deprivations as basically ethnic-group grievances and deprivations and their class and individual aspects as secondary or illusory. They seek to persuade their group that its subordinate condition is cumulative and irreformable without ethnic group consciousness, solidarity, dignity, and assertiveness. They may even insist that otherwise its security and very survival are jeopardized. (Dominant leaders also may wave this red flag of "sacred community in danger of extinction.") Some ethnic groups have better resources and/or more skillful leaders than others in this quest to mobilize, modernize, and give political focus, as well as ideological direction, to the

---

that the pen is mightier than the sword. Within this neglected category of actors are the great writers, translators, poets, and dictionary makers whose choice of tongue for their literary works can raise that language up the flagpole of identity. The virtuosity of the pen creates a symbol for new community frontiers and new interests—which are defined and defended by the thrust of the sword. The person who thus innovates linguistically in order to promote interests should be called a language strategist. . . . Political elites take the language fashioned by their cultural allies and make it a banner of challenge. Without the assistance of these manipulators of culture they would be unable to define their followers as ethnic or national groups. . . . Thus, the partnership stimulates the kind of movements that have created the world's nations and ethnic identities. The language strategists, whom we habitually praise exclusively for their contribution to literature and learning, are also political innovators standing unobtrusively behind the curtain during the most momentous acts in the human drama." Weinstein, "Language Strategists," pp. 345, 364.

culture and historical consciousness of the group and to the anxieties and guilts of its individual members.[8]

2 · The discussion has now been brought to the point where it is suitable to examine the linkages (if any) among (1) the assets and liabilities of ethnic leaders, (2) the resources and vulnerabilities of their ethnic groups, (3) the goals and strategies that the leaders recommend (or compete to recommend) to their groups, and (4) the responses and options of the ethnic dominants and/or of the central governmental elites.

Both publicistic and analytical literature often claim that it is a political asset and a democratic desideratum for an ethnic leader, or a candidate for ethnic leadership, to be socially typical ("descriptively representative") of his ethnic group[9]—in the way, for example, that Cesar Chavez is said to be a typical Chicano; or Gwynfor Evans, a typical Welshman; or William Wolfe, a typical Scot; or Carlos Garaicoetxea, a typical Basque; or Uktam Alimov, a typical Uzbek. Putting aside as somewhat casuistical the possible objection that leadership, by definition, negates typicality, one is nevertheless inclined to demur against the literature's overemphasis on social typicality. First of all, only those ethnic groups that are conditioned to suspect their upwardly mobile members of incipient desertion (see section 1 of this chapter) are prone to place such a high value on the real or pretended egalitarian typicality of their would-be leaders, whereas those ethnic groups that endorse external achievement

[8] Trent, "Politics of Nationalist Movements," p. 164, and Young, *Politics of Cultural Pluralism*, p. 140.

[9] Katznelson, *Black Men, White Cities*, pp. 26–28; Thomas Sowell, "Led, and Misled," Op-Ed page of *The New York Times*, April 13, 1979, p. A27. That this stipulated desideratum is most unlikely to be realized in fact is indicated by the statistical data and leadership profiles assembled by Beer, "Social Class of Ethnic Activists," pp. 143–58.

are quite prepared to welcome atypical, acculturated leaders. Secondly, the dimension of social typicality—even where it is a public-relations asset—tells us nothing about the likely political conduct of ethnic leaders. Thus, it cannot be demonstrated that socially typical leaders are more or less democratically responsive to their ethnic constituents, more or less effective on behalf of those constituents, or more or less militant in their policies than atypical leaders. Here, at any rate, linkage appears to be, at best, problematic, if not altogether absent.

Indeed, a respected, albeit conservative, tradition in political theory argues that there exists a kind of negative linkage between the social typicality of leaders of subordinate social categories and their capacity to represent effectively the true interests of their constituents. Though originally developed as a commentary on class politics, it may also be relevant to ethnic politics. It alleges that the socially typical leaders of subordinates tend to overvalue the sheer fact of their formal access to, or their admittance into, the councils of the dominants and hence are liable to being neutralized and coopted there. Subordinate constituents would be more effectively served, it is claimed, by socially atypical leaders—either acculturates from their own camp or even defectors from the dominant ranks—who do not suffer from such residual psychological vulnerabilities vis-à-vis dominants and hence are less likely to be "bought off" by them.[10]

In effect, this tradition also finds wanting a second, often claimed, linkage dear to the hearts of radical democrats: that is, between the responsiveness of leaders to their constituents and their effectiveness on behalf of those constituents. More precisely, it implicitly distinguishes between two kinds of respon-

[10] See, for example, Machiavelli's comments on the Roman plebeians and their Tribunate in his *Discourses on the First Ten Books of Titus Livius* (1531), Book I, Chapter 47. Other theorists of this school of subordinate representation are Edmund Burke and Walter Bagehot.

siveness: (1) responsiveness to the expressed wishes of constituents—which it distrusts as boding an abdication of real leadership and as self-defeating, for it simply invites challengers to outflank incumbent leaders with demagogic flattery and promises; and (2) responsiveness to the real interests of constituents—which it endorses while simultaneously suggesting that those real interests are likely to be unperceived by the subordinate masses and discerned only by astute and secure leaders.

One does not have to be a conservative or an adherent to this tradition in political theory to acknowledge that it has put its finger on a genuine problem relevant to this study. Ethnic leaders may invest so much political energy in trying to retain their leadership by being responsive to the current demands of their followers that they fail to serve effectively the true long-run interests of their groups. Or their effectiveness may be blunted by repudiation at the hands of the dominants. Alternatively, the dominants may coopt them, subtly encourage them to seem to be (spuriously) responsive to their constituents but actually effective only on behalf of their own ambitions and interests—and, by extension, the interests of the dominants. The arena of ethnopolitics is strewn with the careers of *soi-disant* ethnic leaders whose political effectiveness on behalf of the real interests of their groups was stunted by one or another of these distortions and by the fetishism for social typicality.

These caveats apply both to those situations where the long-run interest of the ethnic subordinates suggests a negotiated restructuring of their relations with the dominants so as to achieve better political integration, but the leadership-candidates try to outbid each other by pandering to and exacerbating their followers' secessionist alienation or revolutionary rage, and to the reverse situations, where ethnic militancy might indeed be rational and best serve the subordinates' interest, but their leaders engage in self-serving collusion with the dominants to deflect and smother their followers' political energies. Either way, the role of leaders in ethnic politics is critical, and the calculations impacting on their conduct are convoluted.

Candidates for leadership of subordinate ethnic groups compete in seeking to convert their prospective constituencies to diverse goals and strategies, which correlate, to an extent, with the various judgments on the desirability of integration (chapter 4, section 2); with the "crossed" versus "convergent" variants in the location of a state's political, economic, and cultural cores (chapter 2, section 6); and with the different types of available ethnic careers—"passer," broker, militant (section 1 of this chapter).

A survey spectrum of such potential goals and strategies must include the following:

1. Hypothetically, some would-be leaders may recommend multidimensional integration to the point of full assimilation, that is, of liquidating their group's elemental ethnocentrism. Politically unlikely to be heeded in the current era of heightened ethnic consciousness, such a recommendation would also seem to contain an ironic contradiction between its intended thrust and the leadership ambitions of the recommender, since its acceptance would deprive him of his prospective social and organizational base. In other words, since massive assimilation would entail the eventual dissolution of the group, it does not appear to be a rational political policy, though individual assimilation may be perceived as a rational personal stratagem. Nevertheless, in some historical situations, aspirants to leadership of immigrant ethnic groups have occasionally recommended assimilation to their groups as collectivities. A somewhat attenuated version of this stance occurs when assimilated individuals with leadership potential organize themselves and seek to mobilize their erstwhile fellow ethnics to protest residual dominant exclusionist discrimination against themselves. They remonstrate that this discrimination not only violates the dom-

inants' own regulative rules and values but also demeans the ethnic group. Nevertheless, even this exercise in tentative ethnic mobilization for the goal of subelite assimilation poses operational dilemmas. At a minimum, the means (mobilization) may nullify the ends (assimilation).

2. Ethnic leaders may recommend to their constituents and to the dominants a pluralistic goal of full political and life-chances integration (to be facilitated, if necessary, by Affirmative Action types of redress and other compensatory subsidies to reverse secular impairments), combined, however, with publicly guaranteed and officially protected cultural autonomy. This combination, they argue, would allow the members to rise socially and politically and to extend their economic activities as individuals without impairing the group's ethnic vitality. Belgium and, less formally, the United States may serve as examples of states where this formula has won substantial acceptance.

3. Alternatively, ethnic leaders may insist that cultural autonomy alone would be precarious, and therefore the group's ultimate survival jeopardized, unless buttressed by political-territorial autonomy, for example, by the state's federalization along ethnic lines, as in contemporary Yugoslavia and Czechoslovakia; or by its ethnohistorical "devolution," as proposed for the United Kingdom; or by its cantonization, as in Switzerland. Such territorial-autonomy formulae are, of course, feasible only for states where the ethnic groups are so distributed and concentrated as to form the local majorities in their respective regions. In practice, this usually means where they are autochthonous rather than immigrant groups. Nevertheless, functional politico-communal self-government without territorial autonomy has in past times occasionally been granted to "pariah" immigrant groups and even to geographically discontinuous autochthonous groups—as to the Jews in the old Polish-Lithuanian Commonwealth and to the several religious *millets* in the former Ottoman Empire. But modern states tend to shun

this device of nonterritorialized political autonomy as a derogation of their sovereignty.

An interpolation is in order here before I proceed with this itemization of ethnic leaders' diverse goals and strategies. Dominants accustomed to ruling via centralized institutions are often as unreceptive to ethnic appeals for cultural autonomy as to more radical demands for political autonomy. They fear that the former merely screen a hidden agenda for the latter, that "the appetite grows while eating," and that subordinates would simply exploit cultural autonomy, if it were granted, as a base from which to press on to political autonomy and possibly even to secession.[11] The other side of this coin—almost a case of antagonistic collusion—is the suspicion of militant aspirants to subordinate-group leadership that "mere" cultural autonomy might function as a preemptive sop, deflecting their subordinate group from the further pursuit of more substantial political goals. The appropriate proverb for this apprehension is that "the [supposed] good is the enemy of the best." It can serve here as a bridge to the final pair of strategic aims that may be pressed by the leaders of ethnic subordinates, to wit:

4. Secession to full political independence, and

5. Domination, or reversing the power relations within the extant state.

The ethnic dominants usually, but not always, resist these two radical subordinate strategies. On rare occasions, to preserve their own social and political systems, they may prudentially permit subordinate secession, as the Swedes acceded to inde-

[11] Different sets of dominants and different regimes are also nervous about different aspects of subordinate cultural expression. For example, French and Spanish governments have traditionally been unreceptive toward subordinate petitions that languages other than French (for example, Breton, Flemish, Occitan) and Castilian (for example, Basque, Catalan, Galician) be taught, preserved, and subsidized by the state, whereas the Soviet and Indian regimes, *per contra*, accept such ethnolinguistic demands but view the religious expression of ethnocultures with a jaundiced eye. Cf. chapter 3, section 5.

pendence for the Norwegians in 1905 (thereby possibly sparing themselves an "Irish" problem) and as interwar Yugoslavia's Serbian King Alexander offered (perhaps not altogether sincerely) independence to the Croatians in 1928. On other rare occasions a subordinate ethnic group secedes as a community but without its territorial base, by physically and collectively removing itself from the jurisdiction of the dominants' state and migrating to a new, external, territorial home—as the South African Boer "trekkers" did in the 1830s and the American Mormons in the 1840s. If the dominants sense that the last-itemized subordinate strategy of reversing the power relations is gaining the upper hand—either as the flow of the political tide in the state as a whole or only as the endorsed policy within the subordinate camp—they may themselves opt for a kind of sociopolitical secessionism or federalization or the restructuring of the state toward the model of parallel segmentation—witness the current enclave maneuvers of Lebanese Maronite leaders, or the earlier movement of the American White middle classes out of the central cities, or the Israeli government's autonomy proposal for the Palestinians in the so-called administered areas. But the more usual dominant response to subordinate bids for secession or reverse domination is mirror-image resistance and repression.

A subordinate ethnic group may be conducted through several of the itemized strategies successively, either by the same or by different leaders. In interwar Czechoslovakia, for example, the German community was initially led by secessionists on the morrow of World War I. Then, in the 1920s, its leadership devolved to moderate pluralists who professed to be satisfied with cultural autonomy. But during the 1930s yet another set of leaders escalated its goals and strategies—first to political autonomy, then to secession, and ultimately, during World War II, to domination even in core Bohemia and Moravia. No wonder that the Czechs, in retrospect, concluded that this last had all along been the true, albeit screened, target of this third generation of local German leaders despite their occasional earlier recourse to more moderate formulae. Similarly, one of the reasons why the Arab-Israel dispute is so recalcitrant grows out of the Jewish fear that the Palestinian leadership really intends to achieve domination in the entire area of the former British Mandate, even when it occasionally uses the veiled language of West Bank-Gaza separatism or tri-religious pluralism.

A subordinate ethnic group may pursue any of the above-listed goals in alliance with other subordinate groups or in strictly bilateral engagement with the dominants. This choice may entail a serious political dilemma. For example, some Scottish nationalist leaders propose cooperation with the Welsh to apply leverage on London, while others recommend negotiating with the English on an exclusive basis of "historic kingdom to historic kingdom." In Canada, the Francophone Québécois have emphatically—and understandably—chosen the second strategy by insisting that they are one of the two "founding nations" (the other being "the British") who must renegotiate the country's political structure with each other on a one-to-one basis. To share this political niche with additional ethnic groups such as Canada's Ukrainians, Poles, Italians, Jews, Germans, Inuits, Amerindians, and others, would—the Québécois fear—gratuitously dilute their own historico-moral status. Alternatively, Jewish activists in the Soviet Union still debate whether to ally themselves with other ethnic and political dissidents in a joint effort to change the Soviet system or to extract the regime's assent to their own group's emigration only. Similarly, in interwar Poland, some Jewish leaders recommended a minorities coalition with the local Belorussians, Ukrainians, and Germans, whereas others warned that the Jews could not rationally share these groups' goal of fragmenting the Polish state, and urged political aloofness from them, while advocating, instead, a direct Jewish understanding with the dominant Poles. In both interwar and contemporary Yugoslavia, again, Croatian leaders have pondered whether to organize a broad ethnic coalition to restrain real or alleged Serbian hegemony or whether to bid for bilateral balance with the Serbs. American ethnic groups confront analogous quandaries. Needless to stress, these strategic dilemmas of subordinates (or self-perceived subordinates) open up opportunities for maneuvering to dominants who may thus neutralize an incipient subordinate coalition by satisfying some of its prospective members at the expense of others. These dilemmas and opportunities are, of course, experienced most keenly in states approximating the pattern of a dominant central core versus an aggregation of ethnic political peripheries (chapter 3, section 2). Their resolution and exploitation is characteristically a function of perceived situational context.

In addition to the just-mentioned strategy of divide and rule, ethnic dominants and central governmental elites may opt for other policies vis-à-vis their ethnic subordinates—policies that may be applied singly or in combination and that may be directed differentially toward different ethnic groups in the same state. Their spectrum includes the following:

1. Genocide—for which, in modern times, Armenians, Gypsies, and Jews have been targeted by, respectively, Turks and Germans. This programmatic genocide as a policy should be distinguished from episodic interethnic massacres, such as those, for example, which the Hutu and Tutsi peoples of Burundi and Rwanda inflicted on each other in the 1960s and early 1970s. For the Nazis, indeed, the genocide of the Jews was even more than a policy; rather, it was a central ideological imperative, no matter how irrational its cost to their war effort.

2. Expulsion—which implies that the target group is perceived by the dominants as either marginal or, more likely, as incorrigibly inimical to their general goals. It was the lot of the Volksdeutsche (Germans) from East Central Europe after World

War II and of Uganda's Asians in 1972. The Palestine refugee problem, in turn, stems from a combination of flight and unofficial expulsion in 1948, just as Jews, too, were ejected and fled from the Arab countries shortly thereafter. An analogous fate befell many overseas Chinese from Indonesia during the 1960s (although many more remained). Two governments may agree reciprocally to expel and receive each other's ethnic subordinates, as in the Greek-Turkish population exchange of the 1920s or in the Indian-Sri Lankan agreements of 1964 and 1974 to repatriate about three-fifths of the million Indian Tamils of Sri Lanka to India and grant Sri Lankan citizenship to the rest.

Though mass expulsion, like genocide, is today generally viewed as violating civilized society's regulative values and hence as beyond the margins of legitimate ethnic political conduct, it periodically tempts dominants and central governmental elites because it appears to "work" by irrevocably and quickly changing the ethnic profile of the state's population in a direction that they define as necessary and urgent. In other words, though admittedly harsh and even cruel, expulsion seems to promise a definitive solution to an otherwise festering problem—much as the surgical amputation of a limb "cures" its gangrene.

A variant on expulsion out of the state is the forcible relocation of an ethnic group from its ancestral lands to other sites within the same state. Here the ethnic group is usually technologically unskilled but its territory is economically valuable. Moreover, the political power gap between the subordinates and the dominants is here so wide, and the dominants' self-confidence in their legitimacy so firm, that the latter generally impose the relocation without consultation or negotiation—often, indeed, without seriously considering the needs of the displaced subordinates. This has occurred, not only in explicitly colonial confrontations in primitive habitats, but also in several urban renewal programs in advanced societies, where ethnic neighborhoods were flattened to provide space for dominant business and residential needs.

3. Compulsory assimilation—such as the regimes of pre-World War I Hungary and Tsarist Russia sought to impose on several of their ethnic groups. This, too, has come to be regarded as illegitimate. Moreover, in today's era of heightened ethnopolitical assertiveness, it is likely to fail. Or, to state this point both more precisely and more conjecturally, attempts to enforce the assimilation of one (subordinate) ethnic group into another (dominant) one are both normatively and politically dubious. However, magnetization toward a supraethnic identity may be somewhat more promising. Thus, Croatians, Ukrainians, and Welshmen cannot be coerced or enticed into becoming, respectively, Serbians, Russians, and Englishmen. But a regime might have greater success in attempting to persuade Croatians and Serbians to supplement those identifications with a Yugoslav one; Ukrainians and Russians, with a Soviet one; Welshmen and Englishmen, with a British one. As always, the responses of ethnic leaders to such regime endeavors are crucial.

4. Uncoerced acculturation through cross-patterned reticulation, permitting and even encouraging the members of subordinate groups as individuals to improve their social status, economic lot, educational attainments, and the exercise of their civil rights and liberties. While this policy may be touted by the dominants as (and may indeed be) a significant accommodation—particularly to the aspirations of upwardly mobile ethnic subelites—it does not usually portend a major redistribution of power from dominants to subordinates. It may readily be accompanied by dominant recognition of cultural pluralism or even of cultural autonomy for the subordinate group(s), as well as by dominant support for the political roles and activities of ethnic brokers. Some of these brokers may even be given

patronage support to organize their groups into satrapies of a dominant political party or leader. The United States can serve as an example of this strategy.

5. Structural federalization, or cantonization, or devolution, to furnish a territorial base and territorial reassurance for ethnic political and cultural aspirations and anxieties. As such, this strategy is intended to preempt the appeal of would-be secessionist leaders. Furthermore, as was suggested in the earlier discussion of Swiss institutions (chapter 3, section 2), it often has the welcome effect of easing the burden of troublesome ethnic issues on the agenda of the central government—which is one of the reasons why it was adopted after World War II by Yugoslavia and India and is now being considered by several West European governments. Dominants conventionally hope to thwart any centrifugal secessionist dangers that might emanate from federalization through institutions that cross-cut the federal or cantonal units, such as supraethnic political parties and interest-group structures, and through central retention of key functions, such as defense, monetary, fiscal, and development policy.

6. A "machiavellian" version of otherwise benevolent, structural federalization occurs when dominants press it to the point of institutionally fragmenting a large extant, or latent, ethnic group and proliferating smaller new ones. As such, this strategy is a subspecies of divide and rule. In Soviet Central Asia, for example, Stalin and his successors sought to dismember a feared potential pan-Turkic or pan-Islamic phalanx by subsidizing and, in a sense, structurally creating, smaller linguistic ethnic groups, such as the Kazakhs, Kirgiz, Turkmens, Uzbeks, and others, through the institutions of Soviet federalism. Earlier references to the British midwifing the separation of Sikhs from Hindus in India and of Greeks from Turks on Cyprus are also relevant to this point. It illustrates that, for dominants, too, strategy

selection and situational context impact on each other reciprocally; each shapes and reshapes the other.

7. Deliberate neglect of ethnic political demands and more or less subtle belittlement of "backward" ethnic cultures—on the calculation that this will hasten their supposedly inevitable withering away. In a sense, this is the dominants' complement to the hypothetical recommendation of some subordinate leaders that their ethnic groups opt for full assimilation. Again, recent history strongly suggests that in the contemporary era such strategies are unrealistic and likely to backfire. Ethnic subordinates respond by revaluing their disparaged cultures and ideologizing them into weapons of delegitimation and challenge. (See chapter 2, section 6, and chapter 4, section 4.)[12]

A glance over all the itemized subordinate and dominant strategies and goals indicates that not one of them is universally workable and that several of them are so radical and hence so likely to be violently resisted by the other party (and condemned by the international audience) that the effort to implement them may well prove to be prohibitively costly in terms of lives, goods, and repute, and hence impractical. These are the following: total and enforced assimilation, categorical reversal of dominant/subordinate power relations (except in decolonialization), genocide, and neglect. Note that these are unilateral strategies, not entailing mutual bargaining or reciprocal concessions. Secession and expulsion are also unilateral imperatives, but for the reasons suggested above, they are, in certain marginal situations (perhaps in a shrinking arena of such situations), still perceived as cost-beneficial and feasible. Note also that these several strategies and goals imply a refusal, either by the subordinate or by

[12] These several possible dominant strategies are the specific expressions of the broad range of dominant attitudinal stances and defensive postures that was sketched as a coda to the earlier discussion of internal colonialism (chapter 2, section 6).

the dominant leaders, to accept multiethnicity (at any rate, multiethnicity along the particular marker-criterion of the controversy) as the permanent, tolerable condition of the given state or habitat. On the other hand, all the remaining strategies—acculturation with residual pluralism, guaranteed cultural autonomy, politico-territorial federalization, political and cultural satrapies for ethnic leaders—acknowledge the permanence and the legitimacy of several ethnic groups in potential or actual conflict with each other and hence also accept the need for continuous accommodative management of the resultant ethnic tensions and frictions. This again emphasizes the centrality of leadership—the leadership, respectively, of the subordinate ethnic groups, of the dominant ones, and of the central government.

3 · If the leaders of dominant and of subordinate ethnic groups accept as permanent their state's multiethnic condition and if they impute at least partial legitimacy to its structuring, then a number of political motives may prompt them to develop certain techniques and mechanisms to manage and regulate their several groups' interethnic conflicts and frictions. Among such motives are the following:[13] (1) A wish to avoid violence, with its risk of escalation. This motive may be particularly salient in a country with still vivid memories of a relatively recent civil war, such as Spain, Yugoslavia, and Nigeria. And yet, it may also wane as such memories recede and may therefore be relatively low in a country with no recent "learning experience" of that kind. (2) A wish to avoid jeopardizing the socioeconomic welfare of the ethnic groups and of the society as a whole. This motive is expected to be strong among the leaders of categorically dominant groups, of eco-

[13] Cf. Nordlinger, *Conflict Regulation in Divided Societies*, pp. 42–55.

nomically dominant but politically subordinate groups in the bipolar pattern of ethnic stratification, and of "pariah" minorities (chapter 3, section 2). It may also sway the leaders of subordinate groups that deem nonpolitical goods and values to be more important than political ones or that fatalistically assume that any change will leave them even worse off than they are currently. (3) A wish on the part of the several ethnic leaders to retain power and avoid the risk of being outflanked by more militant challengers from within their respective groups. (4) A wish to avoid supplying a hostile foreign foe with an alibi or opportunity to conquer, weaken, truncate, or partition the state. However, if interethnic alienation within the given state has passed beyond a certain threshold of intensity, this motive lapses—as, for example, when the Slovak and Croatian leaderships colluded with the Nazi German attacks on their countries in 1939 and 1941.

In short, the operational applicability, and even the presence, of these motives to manage and contain interethnic conflict peacefully is always a contingent matter and cannot be simply postulated. Other motives pull leaders in other directions. The temptation to achieve or to consolidate ethnic leadership by aggravating conflict and appealing to violence may appear easier, swifter, and surer, particularly if the political culture of an ethnic group or of the society as a whole derogates compromise as faintly disreputable. On the other hand, it must be conceded that, where ethnic stratification is so rigid and so inegalitarian and life-chances integration so deficient as to amount to blatant injustice, there peaceful conflict-management motives on the part of subordinate ethnic leaders may be considered suspect and militant challenge deemed morally more appropriate.

If, however, irenic motives to manage and contain interethnic conflict nonviolently are present, operative, and situationally appropriate, then these motives may prompt the respective ethnic leaders to design and to hone certain regulatory political mechanisms and techniques. These are analytically distinct from, though instrumentally related to, those previously enumerated strategies and goals (section 2 of this chapter) that acknowledge the permanence and the legitimacy of a given state's multiethnic condition. Among them are the following:[14]

1. The deliberate depoliticization of issues that could, if they were politicized, take on an ethnically divisive cutting edge. This is how Israeli leaders try to handle the current socioeconomic life-chances gap between Ashkenazim and Sephardim, as they simultaneously work to narrow that gap. This technique can be facilitated by authorizing prestigious and supposedly ethnically neutral leaders of functional and public interest groups to give to the political leadership policy-advice that purports to be objective, scientific, and nonpolitical.

2. Akin to purposive depoliticization are constitutional or institutional arrangements designed to keep potentially disruptive or divisive ethnic issues off the central government's political agenda and resolve them at other decision-making levels. Federalization and cantonization, as in Switzerland, Yugoslavia, India, and elsewhere, have already been mentioned as examples. In Lebanon, too, analogous arrangements, albeit not explicitly federalistic, functioned reasonably well until that country's domestic political system was overloaded and overwhelmed by the external intrusion of the Palestinian problem.

3. Advance agreement by the several ethnic leaderships to persist with coalition governments no matter what the outcome of elections or the oscillation of public moods. And if, despite the intent of such an arrangement, militant challengers appear to be successfully outflanking and leapfrogging the incumbent ethnic leaders, an attempt is made to coopt them, too, into the

[14] Cf. Ibid., pp. 21–29; and Levine, "Institution Design," pp. 60–63.

interethnic coalition. Belgium and Malaysia may serve as examples of such implicit or explicit understandings.

4. Related to the permanent coalition arrangement is the mutual veto, known in American political history as the Calhounian doctrine of the concurrent majority. This is intended to assure a relatively smaller yet important ethnic or regional group that it will not be relegated to political impotence, or possibly destroyed, by the operations of Lockeian "winner take all" majoritarianism. By giving the leaders of such a group a formalized, structured veto over policies that they genuinely perceive to be endangering the vital interests or even the survival of their group and by, in effect, thus guaranteeing them a disproportionate impact on the state's policy-process, it is hoped to dissuade them from desperate remedies, such as secession or violence, and from sterile legalistic-parliamentary obstructionism, to which their sense of demographic and historical beleaguerment ("relative deprivation") might otherwise drive them. Contemporary Belgium and, more tacitly, Yugoslavia again furnish examples of this mechanism.

5 and 6. Proportional representation as a mechanism and prudential dominant self-restraint as a technique are similarly intended to assuage the anxieties of the leaders of smaller, weaker, or subordinate ethnic groups and politically integrate them into the state's macrosystem. Pre-civil war Lebanon and contemporary Czechoslovakia may serve as respective examples of these two devices. Note that they may be operative in personnel staffing procedures, as well as in electoral arrangements and general policy definition.

7. Wrapping several controversial issues and recalcitrant problems together into a single package of reciprocal trade-offs, such that "everybody gets something, nobody gets everything, nobody gets nothing" (in the rhetoric of the operational code of Chicago's Daley machine), is sometimes the most feasible way for the political leaders of the several groups to defuse ethnic

tension and thaw out a confrontational situation in which different kinds of high-salience demands have been pressed on the political agenda by different groups.

All these conflict-containing mechanisms and procedures are, for better or worse, elitist in the sense that they require politically secure ethnic leaders and brokers, immune to being outbid by more militant challengers or ousted by grassroots revulsion against the compromises that these devices necessarily entail. Politically insecure leaders are apt to protect themselves by taking rigid and aggressive stances and nevertheless end without credibility in the eyes of their opposite numbers to make stick the compromise arrangements to which they might eventually assent. The leaders must also be psychologically secure in the sense of being ready to override the currently expressed wishes of their constituents for the sake of serving their groups' true long-range interests—interests that, again, are supposedly best served by compromises and that the leaders alone claim to discern. Psychologically insecure leaders are anxious, suspicious, easily distracted from this main task, and liable to misjudge their opposite numbers and misinterpret the situational context of the problem. There is a pervasive implication in all these mechanisms and techniques that ethnopolitical issues are too delicate and too explosive to be left to the democratic, referendal, competitive, majoritarian political process with its supposed premium on polarizing demagoguery. And it is, after all, true that the collapse of these regulative arrangements and the eruption of interethnic conflict are more frequently the consequence of an intraethnic repudiation of (or disaffection from) a leader by his constituency than of a falling-out among the leaders of the several groups.

Furthermore, the several itemized (and other) conflict-management mechanisms and techniques are also elitist in the more diluted sense that they require astute timing in their institutionalization. If a suitable opportunity to implement one or several of them is allowed to slip away, history may not give the ethnic leaders another chance, because the situational context will not stand still. For example, as was suggested in the preceding chapter's brief closing review of the competition for leadership within the Croatian group in interwar Yugoslavia, by the eve of World War II it was too late for that group to invest credence and confidence in tardy Serbian gestures toward institutional bipolarity, permanent coalitions, and dominant self-restraint. So, too, in contemporary Canada, it appears that Pierre Elliott Trudeau's policy of mandatory transfederal bilingualism, which might have been a successful conflict-mitigating technique if it had been effected at an earlier stage, has now been overtaken by changing Francophone and Anglophone perceptions of the cutting edge of Canada's interethnic conflict. In each of these two countries relatively moderate leaders were outflanked and the situational context was radicalized to a point where the very existence of the state, rather than its regulatory political instruments, became the central agenda-issue.

In addition to their implicit elitism, the enumerated conflict-regulating mechanisms and techniques also embed other potential liabilities. They may function so well technically and procedurally as to lead to immobility, while unacknowledged and untreated substantive grievances accumulate until they either boil over themselves or are ignited by a sudden externally injected overload—as in Lebanon. Less dramatically, the very success of these devices may enervate the capacity of the political system to innovate and may disillusion the electorate about the instrumental utility of supposedly democratic elections—as in Belgium. This, in turn, may induce in the electorate either a kind of indifferent dissociation from politics—as in the Netherlands—or a kind of suspicious orneriness toward the policies and proposals of its inveterate leaders—as in Switzerland. After all, the itemized conflict-regulating procedures are explicitly or implicitly designed to slow change; to preserve an extant structural balance; to encourage ethnic groups to organize themselves as collective, corporate entities; to give at least a suspensive if not an absolute veto to small and/or conservative groups; and to protect incumbent leaders and brokers from allegedly demagogic pressure and ouster, while at the same time discouraging any leader from bidding for transethnic, statewide, support beyond his own group. Thus they may blur the fine line between necessary compromise and lazy sellout, between historically responsible leadership and shallow, self-serving cronyism. Finally, several of these devices are grossly expensive and even deliberately inefficient in cost-accounting terms. Hence, they might become "part of the [interethnic] problem, instead of part of the solution" during an economic recession. Whether these several liabilities outweigh the benefits is a political value-judgment that cannot be rendered as a universal generalization.[15]

For the benefits are, after all, also very real. Not only are violence and fragmentation contained or averted—which may be in the interest of subordinates as well as of dominants—but a broader political and intellectual lesson is taught, to wit: political leadership and its institutions can shape events and are not merely the dependent functions of secular socioeconomic trends, inherited ethnocultural segmentations, or blind historic forces. Machiavelli's dialectic of *virtù* and *fortuna* is operative in the problematics of the multiethnic state. Political stability can here be achieved by astute leaders and calibrated procedures even in an initially unfavorable environment and absent a reservoir of homogeneity, consensus, and social trust. Leaders may aggravate or attenuate interethnic conflict; may bid for

[15] Dahl, *Polyarchy*, pp. 120–21; Steiner and Obler, "Consociational Theory," pp. 339–42; Zolberg, "Splitting the Difference," pp 104–06, 126–42; Hudson, "Democracy and Social Mobilization in Lebanese Politics," pp. 252–62; Heisler, "Managing Ethnic Conflict in Belgium," pp. 44–46; Heisler and Peters, *Implications of Scarcity*, pp. 13–14; Daalder, "The Netherlands," pp. 232–36; Glass, "Consensus and Opposition in Switzerland," pp. 361–72.

compromise or rupture; may press integrationist, autonomist, secessionist, or revolutionary strategies; may succeed or fail in any of them. But they, and their political arena, do make a decisive difference. The lesson is both optimistic and sobering.[16]

4 · Having proceeded from typologizing the optional goals and strategies of ethnic leaders through their possible motives and on to their operational mechanisms and techniques, the discussion has now reached the point where some comments about their range of tactics are appropriate. In this realm of tactics, leaders of both dominant and subordinate groups have available the traditional Aristotelian triad of force, rewards, and education, or some combination thereof. In modern political science rhetoric, Aristotle's itemization would be termed coercive, utilitarian, and normative means for eliciting compliance.

That dominants and central elites generally apply punishments, rewards, persuasion, education, and cooptation in some combination is well known and is more or less taken for granted by subordinates. Only the education and cooptation tactics of the dominants elicit intense political and moral controversy within the subordinate camp about whether they are intended to initiate authentic life-chances and political integration or merely to decapitate the subordinates of their prospective leadership and keep the bulk of the subordinates underprivileged and underrepresented. In turn, can subordinate subelites who respond positively to this pair of dominant overtures be expected to press for the expansion of opportunities for their fellow ethnics or are they to be suspected of incipient ethnic defection? Some aspects of these judgmental dilemmas and of

[16] See the Foreword by Samuel P. Huntington to Nordlinger, *Conflict Regulation in Divided Societies*. See also Huntington's essay "Political Development and Political Decay," pp. 386–430.

the differential responses to them by different types of ethnic groups were discussed in section 1 of this chapter. Here it remains only to mention that revolutionaries and ethnic militants denounce both authentic (integrative) and spurious cooptation ("tokenism") as liable to thwart their desired goals of secession from, of power-reversal within, or structural overhaul of, the state.

The same triad of coercive, utilitarian, and normative tactical means is also available to the ethnic subordinates. That is, they may riot and revolt (coercion); they may offer their votes or other services to one or another dominant leader or party in exchange for relief, favors, or concessions (utilitarian trade); or they may shame the dominants into observing their own regulative rules and values by playing on the dominants' sense of propriety, guilt, sympathy, and the like (normative devices). Some subordinates, of course, may reject collective politics and opt for individual "passing." Which of these tactical options is selected by the subordinates is a function of a number of variables, including the nature and quality of their leadership, the width of the power gap between themselves and the dominants, the degree of solidarity within the subordinate group, and the subordinates' perception of the dominants' cohesion, sense of self-legitimacy, and likely receptivity to subordinate petitions and demands. These (and other) contextual variables, as well as their behavioral implications, were sketched in chapter 4, section 1. Here, by way of supplementation, one may note that, the less trust the subordinates have in the dominants' readiness to abide by their own regulative rules and the more irredeemably hostile the dominants appear to be, the greater the subordinate temptation to resort to coercive tactics—for both rational and irrational reasons.[17]

[17] Katznelson, *Black Men, White Cities*, pp. 204–05; Etzioni, *Comparative Analysis of Complex Organizations*, chs. 1 and 5.

An interesting mode of subordinate tactical challenge, combining coercive, utilitarian, and normative cutting edges, is the so-called protest movement.[18] Adapted by American Blacks in the 1950s and 1960s from a tactical cluster innovated by Gandhi several decades earlier and later adopted by other subordinate ethnic leaders in other countries, the protest movement is a form of unconventional but noninsurrectionary politics, intended to disrupt the instrumental functioning of macrosystemic institutions that the dominants control and regard as indispensable. It requires a finely synchronized application of force short of violence, of economic sanction, and of moral shaming such as to induce significant defections from the ranks of the dominants and to elicit strategic pressure upon the dominants from important, legitimating and delegitimating, reference publics. Marches, processions, sit-ins, civil disobedience, boycotts of certain commodities and/or services, refusal to communicate in or to heed dominant instructions in "alien" languages, tax strikes, work strikes, voluntary closing of one's shop or business, fasting, and resignation of offices and titles are some of the possible tactical components of the protest movement. It implies a power gap too wide to render feasible either a direct violent challenge or a direct bilateral bargain-offer by the subordinates to the dominants, because at the time the subordinates lack the resources to render these devices credible or enticing to the dominants. So the subordinate leaders devise a package of protest tactics designed to be indirectly effective: injuring the dominants sufficiently to prompt them to seek relief but not so critically as to provoke them into massive, violent retaliation, while simultaneously stimulating third parties who have economic, political, or moral leverage on the dominants to enter the arena in a direction favorable to the subordinate protesters.

[18] The next three paragraphs draw on Lipsky, "Protest as Political Resource," pp. 1144–58, and Bondurant, *Conquest of Violence*, ch. 3.

These third parties may be important or prestigious defectors from the dominant camp whose sense of its legitimacy has frayed or relative outsiders. They cannot realistically be defined as allies of the protesters—except in the most immediate short-run sense—because their own political goals and cultural values are likely to diverge substantially from those of the protesters. But they are, for the moment, morally and materially impressed by the subordinates' case and particularly by the protesters' readiness to incur risks and sacrifices. Hence these third parties are ready to intervene as reference publics to press, coax, and shame the dominants into concessions.

The reference publics, of course, seek to exact certain conditions for performing this interventionist function—conditions that may constrain the protest leaders into a dilemma between them and the expectations of their own followers. Thus, the reference publics may insist that the protesters be "reasonable," "responsible," nonviolent, and compromising in rhetoric and action. The dominants, aware of this fastidiousness of the reference publics, often seek to turn it to their own advantage. Thus they may seek to delegitimate the leaders of the protest movement in the eyes of the reference publics by depicting these leaders as apolitical bandits and criminal rioters, or as noisy demagogues without a credible following, or (in the Soviet Union) as certifiably insane. Another dominant tactic may be to deflect and neutralize the reference publics, whose attention span is presumed to be short and volatile, by symbolically vivid but substantively hollow acts, such as the appointment of prestigious panels to study the immediate problem that has evoked the subordinates' protests, or expressions of understanding, or even the cooptation of some protest leaders into some new agencies that the dominants establish to defuse the protest-issue. Such tactics are intended to satisfy the reference publics without making serious concessions to the protesters, while severing the ties between them.

Alternatively, dominants may signal their contempt of reference publics by exiling, jailing, or even assassinating the leaders of a subordinate ethnic protest movement. But if—as is often the case—the monitoring and intervention of the reference publics inhibit the dominants, then the relative political efficacy of relatively weak but normatively self-confident subordinate groups is demonstrated, and the protest movement's triadic, indirect approach is validated.

In the contemporary era, reference publics are often international and staggered. For example, South African Black protesters against apartheid stimulate American Blacks to press American White liberals to urge American bankers to impose a credit squeeze on the Pretoria government. The assumption here is that this government will be more responsive to external bankers than to its own Black subjects. Jewish (and other ethnic) dissidents in the Soviet Union similarly try to activate a multiplier-effect of reference-public leverage on the Kremlin far beyond the limited effectiveness of their own direct pressure by mobilizing for their cause the American political system via the American Jewish electorate. The Palestinians, in turn, have been singularly successful in activating international actors as their reference publics and even as more reliable auxiliaries and allies in their campaign against Israel.

* * *

With the preceding allusion to the international character of reference-public pressure in many domestic interethnic confrontations, my analysis reaches the point of assessing in general the interstate factors and actors in interethnic relations.

Chapter Six

THE INTERSTATE IMPACT OF POLITICIZED ETHNICITY

1 · Because most contemporary states are multiethnic and because many ethnic groups are distributed through two or more states, politicized ethnicity has become a major aspect and issue of interstate relations. Furthermore, the emotionally most intense type of "international" solidarity is today anchored in ethnic, rather than in class or in formal ideological, affinities (though, as indicated in chapter 2, section 6, these are not necessarily mutually exclusive and may, indeed, overlap). This concatenation of circumstances and developments has resulted in much political ambivalence and inconsistency in the "international" behavior of states relative to ethnopolitical issues. On the one hand, reasons of expediency and pressures of public sentiment tempt the rulers of states to capitalize on the weaknesses or embarrassments accruing from the multiethnic condition of other states—in the professed name of the principle of self-determination of peoples and in their own claimed capacity as appellate international reference publics. On the other hand, the vulnerability—current or potential—of virtually all states to such ethnopolitical destabilization prompts rulers to appreciate the utility of the alternative principles of sovereignty and noninterference in the internal affairs of states.

The resultant policy-making dilemmas frequently blur the traditional formal distinction between domestic and foreign politics. At a minimum, no government—not even of a Great Power—can any longer pretend that its treatment of its state's ethnic groups is exclusively its own internal, sovereign affair; nor can it deny that, in weighing its foreign policy options, it considers their anticipated differential effects on its domestic ethnic support-base. The near-universal contemporary consciousness of ethnicity, the large number of ethnic irredentas and diasporas (recently increased by massive interstate migrations of laborers), and the reemergence of long dormant and supposedly resolved ethnopolitical tensions even in the classic and supposedly homogeneous "nation-states" of Western Europe (not to stress here the newer and more familiarly multiethnic states of other world regions) all ensure an acute sensitivity on the part of governments and elites to the reciprocal ethnopolitical implications and interactions of their internal and external policies, reputes, supports, and security. Even the Soviet Union and the United States carefully monitor foreign reactions to their treatments of, say, Jews and Blacks and domestic reactions to their Middle Eastern and African foreign policies.

Historically, the notion that a government's treatment of the population under its rule can be the legitimate concern of another government in another state was initially directed toward the legal nationals (subjects, citizens) of the second state who happened to be residents of, or migrants into, the host state. As such, the notion remains of primary interest to states that "export" their citizens for labor in other states. In time, the class of potential beneficiaries of such interstate interventions was broadened from conationals (in the juridical sense) to coreligionists (in the sense of formal belief doctrines) as Christian states, for example, would make representations at the Sublime Porte of the Ottoman Empire on behalf of that empire's own Christian subjects and citizens. Eventually, coethnics were added to coreligionists and conationals as the objects of such legitimate and recognized interstate concern, intercession, and intervention. Both the Weimar and the Nazi governments of Germany, for example, sought (though in different ways and styles) to provide such protection for the ethnic German Volksdeutsche communities of interwar East Central Europe, and Fifth Republican France today manifests a lively politico-cultural interest in the Francophone Québécois of Canada.

But since the beneficiaries of such interstate intervention and concern—that is, the parties supposedly aggrieved by the host state's activities, and hence the objects of the second state's solicitude—are individuals and social groups, whereas the intervening actors are governments and states operating in a system of states, it is inevitable that the latter anticipatorily calculate the costs and benefits to themselves of intervening with another government and state on behalf of even the most closely akin ethnic or religious or juridical brethren. Even the racial imperialist Hitler temporarily turned a deaf ear to the ethnic Germans of Pomerania and Southern Tyrol when the overall requirements of his foreign policy dictated cordial relations with their host states of Poland and Italy during the middle 1930s. *A fortiori*, rulers with greater respect for the interstate system may well be understandably cautious and reluctant to take steps that might subvert, destabilize, or offend its members and eventually ricochet upon themselves and their allies. But their hand may be forced by irredentist domestic ethnofraternal constraints. Such cross-pressures are another example of the intersecting of internal developments with the external environment and another reason for that chronic ambivalence in the "international" behavior of states relative to ethnopolitical issues, to which allusion was made in this chapter's opening paragraph.

The League of Nations had sought to alleviate this ambivalence during the interwar era by regulating its causes through the Minorities Protection Treaties of 1919, which were intended to guarantee ethnic group rights short of secession. Though this was not the first time that such protective clauses were incorporated into peace treaties, it was the most ambitious and extensive effort of the kind. Reflecting the then widespread view that the multiethnic character (and, supposedly therefore, the authoritarian nature) of the defeated continental empires had been a major source of international instability and war, the arrangements of 1919 were intended to eliminate this alleged source of strife by (1) granting independent statehood to several East Central European ethnic groups (for example, the Poles, Czechs, and Lithuanians) and (2) assuring guaranteed international protection to others who were deemed to be too small, scattered, primitive, or awkwardly located to render either independent statehood or incorporation into their respective ethnocultural "mother countries" feasible (for example, the Belorussians, Jews, and Germans and Magyars severed by new frontiers from Germany and Hungary).

Though brave and optimistic, this experiment of 1919 soon proved to be abortive and disappointing. Since (1) the victorious Allied Powers simply imposed the Minorities Protection Treaties on the new and restored states of East Central Europe without committing themselves to the same obligations toward their own substantial ethnic minorities, and since (2) Weimar Germany and Trianon Hungary exploited these treaties to chronically put Poland and Romania in the dock of international opinion, and since (3) the League lacked enforcement teeth, the upshot was that the supposedly protected minorities became cynical, the East Central European governments were embittered, and the governments of other states were not relieved of their policy-making dilemmas on the issue of whether and how to react to interethnic tensions in the targeted states.

The United Nations has learned something from this unhappy experience of its predecessor. It tries to involve itself less in the protection of ethnic groups—an involvement that member states tend to resent as implicitly denigrating their sovereignty and as explicitly interfering with their internal affairs—and concerns itself more with the universal human rights of individuals. The theoretical rationalization here is that the full assurance of human rights would *ipso facto* eliminate ethnic repression and grievances. But this UN stance entails two difficulties. First of all, it cuts against the prevailing contemporary tendency for aggregates of sharers of ethnic criteria and markers to bond and politicize themselves into self-conscious ethnic groups, demanding recognition, rights, and entitlements as groups. Second, it still leaves the UN and its member states entrapped in its dual commitment to, on the one hand, the sovereignty, integrity, and inviolability of the internal jurisdiction of *states* (to whom alone UN membership is available) and, on the other hand, the principle of self-determination of *peoples*. In practice, UN majorities have wriggled off the hook of this contradiction by (1) recognizing as prior and absolute the right to self-determination when a colonial people seeks political independence from a metropolis from which it is geographically separated by a wide and deep body of water and (2) sidestepping the issue when it arises within contiguous territories—unless the confrontation is structured along the Black/White racial criterion, as in southern Africa, in which case the Black struggle is supported.

Though somewhat inconsistent (if, say, the Namibian and Zimbabwan movements merit principled UN support, why not also the Biafran and Kurdish ones?) this double standard of UN majorities is pragmatically understandable. The number of overseas colonies being limited, whereas the number of contiguous ethnic groups is vast, endorsing the self-determination aspirations of the former does not open up the Pandora's box of possibly limitless regress, inflicting intolerable strains on the state-system per se, that blanket support for the same aspirations of the latter would entail. There is also, of course, the consideration that the current governments of most UN member states are historically conditioned to be particularly sensitive to the White/Nonwhite racial criterion, which was at issue in the now largely fulfilled struggle to end European overseas political colonialism.

Indeed, above and beyond the pragmatism and/or hypocrisy of UN majorities, a principled argument could be made that, since the unit, the "self," in the phrase "self-determination of peoples" is unspecified, the concept expressed by this phrase would become politically unmanageable if it were interpreted as conferring a blanket legal right upon social entities that are not identifiable in advance, without regard to the interests of extant states or of world order. Antidemocratic and terroristic groups would be given an incentive to advance spurious claims to being ethnically oppressed and seeking self-determination; new minorities would become entrapped within new—and often infirm and quarreling—states; old core states would be truncated and impoverished; regional and global balances of power and of peace would be disturbed; and the ongoing domino/demonstration effect might provoke universal instability and chaos, eventually inviting a strong actor to engage in imperialistic aggression, as Hitler once capitalized on the ethnofidelic "Balkanization" and residual irredentisms of interwar East Central Europe to divide and conquer it. Hence the reluctance of the world's state-system to concretize and extend the self-determination formula from a general political principle putting governments on notice that their treatment of their ethnic groups is subject to international monitoring and will play a role in determining their generalized legitimacy in the eyes of other governments and publics, into a stipulated legal right of potentially atomistic groups against their current states.[1]

2. But this understandable and valid reluctance of international bodies to bridge this gap between political principle and legal right returns the policy problem, with its attendant dilemmas and ambiguities, to the individual states and governments. Now it would be an exaggeration and an error to infer from the preceding discussion—phrased, as it was, in somewhat formal and abstract terms—that this problem always confronts states and governments in starkly polarized, "worst-case scenario" terms, that is, as a choice between turning a blind eye to even the most naked ethnic oppression in another state or supporting the most revolutionary and/or secessionist ethnic demands against such a state. The reader will recall from the preceding chapter that both ethnic subordinates and ethnic dominants (and central governmental elites) may select from a wide spectrum of optional goals, strategies, mechanisms, techniques, and tactics. Hence, external reference publics also usually enjoy a corresponding range of graduated choices in determining their reactions and policies toward the ethnopolitical problems of an afflicted state.

It stands to reason that ethnic dominants and central govern-

[1] Buchheit, *Secession*, chs. 1, 2, 4. Another author has summed up the current global positions as follows: the Western countries prefer to define human rights in civil libertarian terms, the Communist ones concentrate on socioeconomic aspects, those of the third world focus on the anti-colonial struggle but vehemently oppose "tribalistic," that is, contiguous, secessions. No political bloc of states endorses or even defines any universal rights of ethnic groups. Duchacek, "Antagonistic Cooperation," p. 27. See also Van Dyke, "Individual, State, and Ethnic Communities," pp. 343–69, and Thornberry, "Minority Rights," pp. 249–63. The political liabilities of the ethnic mosaic of interwar East Central Europe are itemized by Rothschild, *East Central Europe* pp. 4–14.

ments who have confidence in their own and their system's legitimacy should seek to exclude—or, at any rate, to limit—most external involvement in their domestic interethnic problems. But even subordinate subelites often have good reason to refrain from inviting external intervention in their own ethnic group's support. If they view their state as legitimate, and if their goal is the reallocation of political power and/or the redistribution of socioeconomic power within that state rather than secession from it (chapter 5, section 2), and if they have selected political negotiatory rather than violent revolutionary mechanisms and techniques (chapter 5, section 3), then it would be irrational and probably counterproductive for them to solicit external intervention. At a minimum, this would tend to cast doubt on the bona fides of their professed goals within, and legitimacy-imputations to, their state. At a maximum, the prospective intervenor might have predatory intentions and sponsor an alternative, more militantly radical, set of subordinate leadership-candidates. Either way, the intensity of the interethnic conflict would be heated beyond the interests of the initial subordinate subelite. Only if they are seeking friendly mediation and can be confident that their prospective patron harbors no exploitative ambitions, or if they are simply seeking to neutralize the foreign support-linkages of their dominant competitors, might it be sound politics for such moderate subordinate subelites to mobilize external support.[2] Thus, for example, Catalan and Walloon leaders will not invite French political intervention on their behalf against their own Spanish and Belgian states, but they may lobby with officials of the European Community at Brussels and Strasbourg for greater benevolence toward their ethnoregional interests.

In the contingency just sketched, the external states are clearly

[2] Suhrke and Noble, "Introduction" to their coedited volume, *Ethnic Conflict in International Relations*, pp. 3, 12.

not confronted with a polarized emergency dilemma between impassivity and intervention. But even if a troubled state's interethnic conflict is intense and violent, with its ethnic subordinates explicitly repudiating its systemic legitimacy, external states and governments usually have substantial time and range to determine their responses. First of all, time is provided by the fact that most such violent ethnopolitical conflicts tend to be prolonged. Second, while the revolutionary or secessionist ethnic subordinates do, of course, try to shape world opinion and the stances of external reference publics into directions that impair and drain the dominants' capacity and will, they are often quite cautious about soliciting explicit external intervention even by an ethnically fraternal state. They are reluctant to risk losing control over their own decisions and becoming mere pawns in a game played between or among states, with the ultimate hazard of betrayal in the interest of their patron's *raison d'état*—as happened to the Iraqi Kurdish ethnic rebels at the hands of the Shah of Iran in 1975. Note, for example, how carefully the PLO leadership maneuvers along a tightrope between soliciting the support of the Arab states for its Palestinian cause but shunning their control over its activities and how chary the Catholic leadership in Ulster has been about urging Dublin's political intervention there. A frequent additional dampening consideration is that the militant ethnic subelite in the afflicted state perceives the government and society of the potential intervening state as overly conservative, despite the ethnic bonds between them. Hence, in general, even revolutionary ethnic subelites who perceive their current state as illegitimate tend to avoid or postpone inviting decisive external intervention unless or until they are either *in extremis* (militarily and politically) or they experience the interstate frontier that separates them from their ethnic "mother country" as such an intolerable trauma that they are indifferent to questions of control, autonomy, socioeconomic ideology, and the like, and care only to be "redeemed" through secession from their current state and incorporation into the intervening one. The leaders of the ethnic Germans of interwar Czechoslovakia came close to this last-mentioned stance in the late 1930s, though even they appear to have expected less drastic *Gleichschaltung* with the Reich's institutions and more generous solicitude for their ethnoregion's particularities than eventually were applied by Berlin. Moreover, it is noteworthy that, as a group, Czechoslovakia's Germans had not experienced the frontier severing them from their ethnic brethren as quite such an intolerable trauma during most of the 1920s, when Germany was economically troubled but Czechoslovakia prosperous; and this suggests that utilitarian-prudential considerations impact on even the most intense ethnofraternal sentiments and that the enthusiasm for "redemption" of all but the most fervid ethnosecessionists is affected by cost/benefit expectations.

The preceding mention of interwar Czechoslovakia serves to place on the agenda an additional complication, operative as well in today's universe of ethnopolitics. If a state incorporates more than two ethnic groups—that is, if it can be subsumed under the structural patterns of either a dominant majority versus several subordinate minorities or of a dominant central core versus an aggregation of peripheral ethnic segments (chapter 3, section 2)—and if its political integration is low or incomplete, and if, finally, one of its subordinate, peripheral ethnic groups bids for external intervention, then the other subordinate groups, though not initially revolutionary or secessionist, may nevertheless "hedge their bets" by "putting on ice" or keeping tentative their loyalty to the state, or at any rate to its political system, regime, and authorities.[3] This is what happened in Czechoslovakia and Yugoslavia in 1939 and 1941, respectively, and appears to be happening currently in Pakistan

[3] Weiner, "The Macedonian Syndrome," pp. 679–80.

after the loss of Bangladesh, in Israel with respect to the changing political attitudes of the younger generation of her Druze, and even in Ethiopia among the Galla, Tigre, and other ethnic groups despite the vivid Soviet-Cuban counterintervention of 1978 in support of the central Amhara-dominated government against the Somali- and Arab-supported secessionists of the Ogaden and Eritrea.

If, on the other hand, political integration and legitimacy are above, and the intensity of conflict is below, certain thresholds, then one or more of the previously listed conflict-regulating motives come into play (chapter 5, section 3), and other ethnic subelites rally to the state, repudiating the alienated group's bid for external intervention. The stances of Israel's Sephardim and Beduin, of contemporary Yugoslavia's Macedonians and Czechoslovakia's Slovaks in the face of occasional Soviet efforts to fish in those two countries' ethnic waters, of Canada's other ethnic groups in response to some recent Québécois efforts to involve France in their quarrel with the federal government, and, apparently, of China's other ethnic minorities in reaction to occasional episodes of Kazakh-Uighur secessionist collusion with the Soviet Union in Xinjiang might serve here as examples of this generalization. Now, since integration and legitimacy are not static conditions but mutable processes ever subject to erosion and to regeneration, one must expect ethnic subordinates to move in either direction between these two described modes of behavior in the situation here stipulated.

What if the prospectively or potentially interventionist state is itself also multiethnic—as is quite likely given the overwhelming statistical preponderance of multiethnic states in the world? Clearly, not all the ethnic constituents of such a state will be equally enthusiastic at the prospect of incurring costs and risks on behalf of the ethnic brethren of only one of them. Thus, the Slovenes of Yugoslavia may be concerned about the real or supposed deprivations inflicted on the Slovene minorities of

Austria and Italy, but Yugoslavia's other ethnic groups are less so; the Malays of Malaysia may care deeply about Thailand's treatment of its Malay minority, but the Chinese of Malaysia do not; during the crisis that eventuated in the secession of Bangladesh from Pakistan in 1971, the Bengalis of India were far more ardently interventionist on behalf of their fellow Bengalis of then East Pakistan than India's other ethnic components were. Such differentiated domestic attitudes are assessed by the central governmental elite of such a multiethnic state as one of the important inputs into its overall (internal and external) cost/benefit calculations as it decides whether or not, and how, to intervene in the problems of another multiethnic state.

The just-cited examples indicate that the decision may be for or against intervention, depending on the total situational context. Powerful considerations, temptations, constraints, emotions, and principles push and pull in both directions, as follows:

1. For intervention: the ethnic group urging intervention upon the government of the potential intervening state may be strong, perhaps even dominant, and the government domestically dependent on it; the treatment being inflicted on its ethnic kin in the prospective target state is (or can be depicted as) so brutal or neglectful that it tends to delegitimate and isolate that state's regime internationally; the central governmental elite of the potential intervening state perceives intervention as likely to enhance its international esteem and "clout"; it perceives intervention abroad as likely to enhance its domestic repute and popularity and possibly even to rescue it from imminent repudiation; intervention, and possibly subsequent annexation of ethnoregional irredenta, are perceived as righting an historic injustice and/or as permitting the acquisition of control over valuable human and material resources. Finally, one additional consideration that does not focus specifically on the ethnic aspect but nevertheless may impinge on it occasionally presses

for intervention, to wit: the dominant elites of states subscribing to the same grand ideology, such as Marxism-Leninism or Islam, claim greater warrant for intervening in each other's internal affairs in the name of ensuring doctrinal orthodoxy (for example, the so-called Brezhnev Doctrine of 1968) than in the affairs of states outside their particular ideological universe.

2. Against intervention: most states being multiethnic, they share a common interest in not roiling each other's ethnic waters, an interest whose violation by any one of them renders it vulnerable to *tu-quoque* charges and to possible retribution along the same criteria and allegations as it has used to justify and rationalize its own interference; similarly, the fact that the vast majority of states is multiethnic tends today to feed a generalized bias among central elites and governments against ethnically propelled frontier revisions—a bias whose forcible breach by any one of them entails some international and domestic risks. (Such considerations probably account for the apparently reciprocal decisions of the governments of Indonesia, Malaysia, and the Philippines, after some earlier experimentation with interference and irredentism, to refrain from exploiting each other's ethnic vulnerabilities and of France and Spain not to play the Basque card against each other.)[4] Intervention abroad may be domestically controversial, costly, and possibly destabilizing for the government of a multiethnic state that bases itself on some degree of domestic interethnic consensus; the ethnic brethren in the other state may be so poor and backward as to be a prospective burden for the potentially intervening state; alternatively, these ethnic brethren in the other state may endorse political or socioeconomic ideologies

[4] A possible historical analogy was the refusal of the Habsburg, Tsarist, and German imperial regimes before World War I to capitalize on each other's vulnerable Polish ethnic flanks. During the war, however, they did so with a vengeance, and this illustrates how the balance of such decisional considerations changes with changing situational contexts.

that are apprehended as radical and subversive by the governmental elite of the potential intervening state. (This is the other side of the coin of the above-mentioned frequent reluctance of a militant ethnic subelite to solicit the intervention of a conservative, albeit ethnically fraternal, state. Thus, for example, the governments of most Arab countries and of the Republic of Ireland reciprocate the ideological suspicions harbored toward them by the Palestinian PLO and Ulster IRA leaderships.)[5]

As one examines historically and politically how central governmental authorities of potentially intervening states have weighed these sets of antithetical considerations, temptations, constraints, emotions, principles, pushes, and pulls in the balance of their decision-making apparatus, one comes to the following rough statistical conclusion. No government ever acts exclusively from affective ethnofraternal considerations in resolving its dilemma, though it may sometimes give them decisive priority. It always weighs those considerations against utilitarian, instrumental-prudential ones—strategic, economic, domestic, and the like. If the total balance of all these considerations appears to be even doubtful, let alone negative, the utilitarian ones outweigh the affective ones—as when Athens concluded that the interstate calculus (that is, the Turkish-Greek military balance) obliged it to jettison the Cypriote Greeks in 1974, or when Dublin determines that the domestic calculus (that is, it wants neither intractable Protestants nor seditious IRA terrorists under its jurisdiction) militates against intervention in Ulster.[6] Only if the utilitarian considerations clearly seem to reinforce, rather than to crosscut, the affective ethnofraternal ones and

[5] Again, an analogous historical example: in the late 1930s, the conservative Horthy-Teleki government of revisionist Hungary was more enthusiastic about the prospects of "redeeming" the also conservative fellow-Magyars of Romania than the right-radical Magyars of Czechoslovakia.

[6] Suhrke and Noble, "Spread or Containment," in their coedited volume, *Ethnic Conflict in International Relations*, pp. 222–28.

intervention appears to be relatively low cost—as in the calculations that interwar Berlin made about supporting the irredentism of the ethnic German Volksdeutsche against the states of East Central Europe, or New Delhi in 1971 about assisting the Bangladeshi (Bengali) secession from Pakistan—will such intervention be selected. The second situational context, that is, governmental and elite perceptions of mutually reinforcing utilitarian and affective considerations, is rarer than the first, that is, perceptions of contradiction and of a negative or doubtful balance. The cost of a miscalculation can be harsh—as with Bulgaria's repeated, abortive efforts of 1913, 1915–18, and 1941–45 to "redeem" the Macedonians of Serbia, Yugoslavia, and Greece and with Somalia's efforts of the mid-1970s on behalf of her fellow ethnics in neighboring Ethiopia.

Governments always make these calculations and take their decisions in the context of a prevailing interstate systemic environment, as well as in the context of domestic political pressures, opportunities, and risks. And here the following generalization—admittedly very broad—would appear to have merit: the interwar systemic environment was, on balance, more receptive to political-territorial irredentism and hence to interventionist decisions than the systemic environment of the first three decades after World War II has been. Whether the second half of this comparison will remain valid into the last quarter of this century and beyond will bear scrutiny. Of course, governments—as well as politicized ethnic groups—always test and probe and do not merely register and accept the prevailing interstate systemic environment.

Occasionally, a government supports a refractory ethnic group in another state for purely instrumental-utilitarian reasons, without any initial affective-ethnofraternal considerations being engaged at all. Such was the case, for example, when the Soviet Union endorsed Pashtun and Baluchi restiveness against Pakistan; or when Israel subsidized Kurdish, Southern Anyanya, and Maronite Christian insurrections against, respectively, the central governments of Iraq, Sudan, and Lebanon; or when interwar Italy supported the Croatian and Macedonian secessionist subelites against Yugoslavia. In such cases, ethnic bonds between the intervenor and the intended beneficiary of the intervention are absent, but the target state and its government are perceived by both as inimical.

At other times, when an ethnically troubled state is perceived as friendly, such purely instrumental-utilitarian, ethnically neutral considerations tend to point in the opposite direction, toward other states supporting that state's integrity and central government. For example, the NATO allies of Canada, Belgium, and Great Britain (and, by analogy, the Warsaw Treaty allies of Czechoslovakia), without prejudice to the merit of the claims and grievances lodged against the governments of these multiethnic states by their several restive ethnoregional groups, must nevertheless be concerned—to phrase it conservatively and mildly—lest such ethnopolitical issues (1) weaken these states, (2) exercise a domino/demonstration impact on potentially similar fault-lines in other allied states, and thereby (3) destabilize the alliance as a whole. While the overt conduct of the allies of a troubled multiethnic state in such a situation is usually reticent and screened—so as not to aggravate the problem—their covert hopes and sympathies lie with its continuing viability. This is all the more so if the wayward ethnic group harbors reservations toward the alliance policy and the general foreign policy of the central government—as some current Québécois leaders, for example, appear to do, albeit enigmatically and obliquely.

Furthermore, quite apart from alliance considerations, utilitarian-prudential reflection tends to render central governments concerned lest ethnopolitical effervescence in any one state exercise a demonstration effect upon other states. In a world in which the state is still perceived as the normative and principal international actor, and in which all but a handful of states are multiethnic, their governments are bound to perceive a revolutionary or secessionist ethnopolitical challenge to any one fellow-state as potentially more than a purely domestic matter within that state (though, for the overt record, they may make this disclaimer). Except for those directly interested central governments and dominant elites in other states who calculate that the total balance of their stakes—affective and utilitarian—clearly points toward support of the ethnopolitical challengers, most noninvolved governments and dominants tend to see their self-interest to lie in containing, isolating, or possibly mediating challenges to the legitimacy and integrity of another state in the universe of states.[7] The more intense and violent the interethnic conflict in the afflicted state, the greater these concerns and these inclinations within the governments of other states. If, however, the ethnopolitical challenge is directed not so much against the integrity of the afflicted state as at the legitimacy of its political system and regime, and if that system and regime are widely perceived as blatantly unjust by significant external reference publics—as in the case of South African apartheid—then these sympathetic inclinations of noninvolved external governments toward the afflicted state are likely to be neutralized.

3 · Do the "natural" interests, solidarities, and inclinations of challenging, secessionist, or revolutionary ethnic groups lie in a direction opposite to those just described for central governments and dominants? Do they have rational, aprioristic reasons to support each other across frontiers against their several states and against the prevailing system of states as such? Here the analysis is even more difficult and the answers even more speculative than in the case of governments.

[7] Suhrke and Noble, "Introduction," in ibid., pp. 5, 12.

Let us dispose, first of all, of those ethnic groups, albeit subordinate or "pariah" minority ones, whose leaders perceive their current state and its political system as basically legitimate and seek only redistributions of power within it through nonviolent processes. As was suggested toward the beginning of the preceding section of this chapter, it would be implausible for them to solicit paramilitary or direct political assistance from abroad, lest they mar their reputation for loyalty and render themselves vulnerable to governmental retribution. But they do often invite and accept moral, financial, and cultural aid, not only from their own ethnic brethren—such as, for example, Jewish, Armenian, and overseas Chinese communities extend to each other across state frontiers—but also from sympathetic international reference publics. Occasionally the parties extending such aid fall somewhere between the categories of ethnic brethren and nonfraternal reference publics, as, for example, when Francophone Walloons of Belgium and Québécois of Canada support the quest of Swiss Jurassiens for a Francophone canton of their own. Although this last-mentioned case was marred by some violence in the mid-1970s, clearly all these examples are members of the general set of issues where the state and its political system are perceived as basically legitimate, and there is no question of generalized transfrontier support by ethnopolitical movements against their several states and the prevailing system of states.

The problem becomes more complicated and even enigmatic when the ethnic subelites are unabashedly secessionist and/or revolutionary vis-à-vis states and political systems whose control over their groups they deem to be illegitimate. Here the issue may manifest itself in the following modes:

1. An ethnonational group finds itself partitioned among several states—as the Poles were partitioned throughout the nineteenth century among the Habsburg, Tsarist Russian, and Prussian-German empires; the Kurds find themselves today

partitioned among Iraq, Iran, Syria, Turkey, and the USSR; the Baluchis among Afghanistan, Iran, and Pakistan; and the Basques have historically been partitioned between Spain and France. If the group is sufficently self-conscious and so politicized as to experience this partition as a trauma and an injustice (which is not always the case), then its leadership must decide whether all the partitioning states are to be adjudged as equally inimical and hence equally the targets of secessionist aspirations and activities, or if one of them is to be regarded as its potential ally against the others.[8] In the former case, independent statehood is clearly the goal; in the latter case, association with the favored state—in which the said ethnonational group hopes to become a major political actor—is the indicated policy. But in the latter eventuality, the previously cited risk of becoming a mere pawn in an interstate game comes into play. (Hardly ever will such a partitioned ethnonational group see itself as a goodwill bridge between its partitioners.) The debate over these two options is likely to be intense and to invoke the difficult problem of defining the particular ethnonational group's essen-

[8] Before and during World War I, many Polish leaders regarded the Habsburg Empire—a Roman Catholic state that treated its Polish population with relative political generosity—as their potential associate against the other two partitioning empires. Others scoffed that the Habsburgs had forfeited such a role through their alliance with Prussia-Germany, whose eastward demographic and cultural pressure ("Drang nach Osten") was deemed the major threat to the Polish nation, and reluctantly recommended a Polish-Russian understanding against the Teutonic menace. Still others concluded that all such hopes of playing the three partitioning empires off against each other were illusory short of a general European war that would have to erupt over other issues, since the three shared a common interest in keeping Poland partitioned and off the map of European states. In the event of such a war—the last group urged—Poland must resurrect herself at the expense of all three partitioning empires. In this process, it might accept temporary tactical association with, but not a principled commitment to, one or another of them. During the nineteenth century there had been occasional, always abortive, Polish insurrections directed seriatim against all three partitioners—the Polish leadership never having resolved these divergent analyses and prescriptions.

tial character, identity, and affinity (if any) with the ethnic dominants in the prospective favored partitioning state (if one is selected). Yet both options allow and, in theory, mandate, cross-border cooperation and mutual assistance by the divided segments of the partitioned ethnonation in revolutionary and secessionist activity against one or more states whose "occupation" and rule are deemed illegitimate.

2. The mode in which the issue manifests itself may be that of a "pan" movement—such as the pan-Germanic, pan-Slavic, pan-Turkic, pan-Arabic, pan-Islamic, and pan-African ones. These seek to appeal, in near-messianic terms, to the multitudinous population of a supposed unitary ethnocultural universe for political unity, over the heads and, if necessary, against the very existence of the particularistic states and governments that are alleged to be selfishly and illegitimately fragmenting it. No "pan" movement has ever been politically successful in forming the overarching state that its ideology implies.

3. The issue may manifest itself in the mode of a diaspora-redemption movement, propagating the return of an exiled and scattered ethnic group to its claimed historic homeland. Jews, Armenians, and Blacks have, at various times, generated such movements. But they do not present really serious or even intended challenges to the states in which these diasporas currently find themselves. The fact of exile, not the country of exile, is deemed illegitimate; the movement calls for secession through human emigration, not through frontier revisionism; the irredenta to be redeemed is one of past (and future), not of current, settlement; and no territorial, political, or military challenge to the states of current residence is contemplated.

4. A really serious and intended challenge to extant states, their central governments, their ethnic dominants, and even to the prevailing system of states occurs when explicitly secessionist and/or revolutionary ethnic subelites give each other significant political and paramilitary assistance even in the absence of

ethnic bonds between them—as in the case of IRA and PLO collaboration. (Here the respective ethnic groups may be partitioned or may each be incorporated within the frontiers of but one state.) This mode of the problem's manifestation might be seen as the converse of the utilitarian-prudential inclinations that the central governments of states have to be sympathetic toward each other's ethnopolitical problems (see the close of section 2 of this chapter). Here, indeed, the several cooperating ethnic subelites appear to believe that they have rational, aprioristic reasons to support each other across frontiers against several states and—if they also purport to be ideological as well as ethnonational revolutionaries—against the prevailing system of states as such.

But not entirely. Even here there are ambiguities, complications, and countervailing rationales. Since such secessionist and/or revolutionary ethnopolitical subelites, unlike nonethnically specific sheer terrorist movements, do, after all, hope to achieve statehood for their groups and/or to attain governmental authority within states—which implies an eventual need for some kind of international recognition and acceptance—they cannot, in utilitarian prudence, afford to persist in behavior that violates all international norms or offends the entire community of states and governments as such. This is a standing dilemma, in the realm of internationally resonant behavior, facing such militant ethnopolitical movements that challenge the legitimacy of some states and governments. And the closer these movements come to success (or seem to do so) the more this dilemma intensifies and the greater the constraints on them to behave "responsibly."[9]

On balance, therefore, one may provisionally conclude that,

[9] Anthony D. Smith, "Introduction" to his edited volume, *Nationalist Movements*, pp. 4, 28.

while politicized ethnicity has indeed become a keenly honed edge of interstate conflict, and while the emotionally most intense type of "international" solidarity is today indeed anchored in ethnic, rather than in class or formal ideological affinities, nevertheless the persisting power of states and the resiliency of the world's system of states pose serious resistances to the full actualization of the ethnopolitical idea and ideal in the interstate dimensions of political life. Not only are these resistances direct, but they also secondarily oblige even militant ethnopolitical leaders—both those in and out of power—to phase and to temper their strategies, procedures, and tactics in accordance with the utilitarian-prudential calculations that the stubborn tenacity of the state-system imposes on them.

Note, however, that these resistances, which the state as an institution and the world's network of states pose to the unleashing, at the interstate level, of the full potential energy and thrust of the ethnopolitical idea, are resistances that operate through and upon elites—governmental, dominant, and even subordinate elites. Thus we have here a confirmation and a reinforcement, in the interstate dimension, of the generalization made earlier apropos of domestic, intrastate politics to the effect that secure elites are decisive for conflict-management, conflict-containment, and conflict-resolution (chapter 5, section 3). How are we then to account for the fact that in today's world most mass political violence—interstate as well as intrastate—has an ethnic cutting edge? One school offers the following explanation. As political activation and activity move downward from the elite to the mass level, the prospective balance between utilitarian-prudential and affective-ethnofidelic evaluations tilts toward the latter; ethnic masses (like other types of masses) are volatile and more prone than their leaders to emotion-driven violence and less capable or likely to engage in cost/benefit calculations; therefore, if and when interethnic violence erupts—whether it is in the intrastate or the interstate arena—elites have lost control over masses.[10]

This explanation is insufficiently nuanced. While it is true that the ethnofidelic allegiance of ethnic masses and lower classes to their groups has a highly affective and expressive component, and while their xenophobia is often emotional, unreflective, stereotypical, and potentially explosive, it is emphatically not true that they are incapable of rationally calculating their prospective losses and gains from recourse to violence and militancy. In Quebec, for example, the Francophone lower classes are very rationally concerned about the costs to themselves of separation from the rest of Canada; it is a part of their elite that is stirring up their ethnofidelic emotionality for instrumental-utilitarian reasons of its own. Analogous statements could be made about the Palestinians, the Basques, the Catalans, the Croatians, the Ibos, the contending ethnolinguistic and ethnoreligious groups of the Indian subcontinent, and many others. What has happened and is happening in many situations of interethnic violence is not that volatile and emotional ethnic masses slip out of the restraining leash of rational elites but that outbidding and outflanking counterelites seek to tap this mass emotional potential by inciting ethnopolitical radicalization. Even incumbent ethnic elites may have to tap it once violence erupts and they are obliged to mobilize mass support or to protect their flanks. Thus the critical, often negative, factor is not the emotionality or unreflective xenophobia of ethnic masses per se, but the manner of its political activation by ethnic elites or counterelites. And on the reverse, positive tack, note how relatively speedily such elites

[10] Nordlinger, *Conflict Regulation in Divided Societies*, pp. 39–41, 74–78; Shibutani and Kwan, *Ethnic Stratification*, pp. 391–401; William Kornhauser, *The Politics of Mass Society* (New York: Free Press, 1959), passim.

can usually regain control over mass emotion-driven activism and curb interethnic violence when they choose to do so.

Where both of these explanatory paradigms agree is in seeing the ethnic emotion (and its attendant stereotypes) as potentially the most intense and most readily activated mass political emotion of the contemporary era. Hence mass political violence—between and within states—can readily be directed toward ethnic cleavages despite the institutional resistances of the state and the world system of states to the unfolding of the ethnopolitical idea at the interstate level. Among the many tragic recent examples that could be cited in confirmation are the mass bloodshed, destruction, flights, and expulsions that accompanied and followed the end of the British Mandate in Palestine; the simultaneous partition of British India into the successor states of India and Pakistan; the later ethnosecession of Bangladesh from Pakistan; the failed would-be ethnosecession of Biafra from Nigeria; the communal conflicts in Ulster, Cyprus, Lebanon, Sudan, Burundi, Rwanda, and Indonesia; and the earlier genocidal assaults on the Armenians of Asia Minor and the Gypsies and Jews of Europe, as well as the interethnic civil war within World War II in Yugoslavia, and the vast numbers of ethnic refugees generated by most wars in this century. But note again that in all these cases the mass violence was initiated and halted by leaders and elites.

4 · It remains now to sketch the characteristic domestic responses of ethnic dominants and central governments whose states and political systems are under externally supported ethnopolitical assault. They may, of course, respond with an effort to reearn and regenerate their own and their state's legitimacy by initiating one or more of the several conflict-regulating mechanisms and techniques itemized in chapter 5, section 3. And they may do this even without explicitly conceding

that their rule has been ethnically structured and biased—protesting, instead, that it was based on universalistic, modernizing, and hence potentially open and accessible norms and values. Or they may concede past, ethnically based structural bias and now offer redressive innovations. Or, fearing that what is being demanded are not finite concessions but open-ended risks to their (and their state's) ultimate survival, they may respond with mirror-image countermilitancy and redoubled repression (chapter 2, section 6). Often they may try to move in all three directions at once: accelerating integrationist programs while denying that there exists a political problem, cultivating those ethnic subelites who would exchange gestures of loyalty in return for corrective compensations, and nevertheless also intensifying surveillance and controls over the refractory subordinate ethnic population.

Often there are sharp disputes within the dominant and governmental ranks over the right tilt—ameliorative, suspicious, or tough—of these several options and their mix. Sometimes this results in a fitful, spasmodic series of policy oscillations in response to the initiatives of the unruly ethnic subordinates and their external supporters; sometimes in a consistent, subtly calibrated, judiciously administered, and ultimately successful effort to defuse the challenge and achieve political integration and legitimacy for the challenged multiethnic system. On the whole, it appears plausible to expect and to suggest that the higher the degree of external intervention in support of the militant (secessionist and/or revolutionary) ethnopolitical subordinates, the greater the likelihood that the dominants will be politically grudging and skittish toward them.

Indeed, the dominants may even try to cut the Gordian knot of their domestic problem through a direct confrontation—political or even military—with the external party that is providing assistance, incitement, and sanctuary to their militant subordinate challengers, as with the Ethiopian warning of 1978 to Somalia to cease its aid to the Ogaden insurrectionists or the more fateful and famous Austro-Hungarian ultimatum to Serbia in 1914, which precipitated World War I. However, if this external party is perceived as overwhelmingly powerful and menacing, the dominants of the target state may have to tack course and appease it, as with the reluctant and apprehensive concessions that most East Central European governments made to their German ethnic groups on the eve of, and during, World War II to propitiate the Nazi Reich.

Somewhat parallel developments often occur in the domestic political stances of a state whose regime has decided, for converging affective-ethnofraternal and instrumental-utilitarian reasons, to engage in irredentist intervention in the ethnopolitical problems of another state. Not only does such a regime do its best to hamper the efforts of the target state's dominants and government to achieve political integration and regenerate legitimacy, but it also tries to impose internal "discipline" and cohesion on its own population in the alleged interest of its "sacred" revisionist, irredentist external goals. Priorities are reordered; internal evolution is harnessed to the external strategy; dissent from the irredentist-revisionist fervor may be labeled as appeasement, cowardice, or disloyalty; and free and rational political discourse may fall victim to an oppressive and fevered conformity. The momentum of such developments can become obsessive and occasionally plunges the regime and its state into miscalculated military adventures—as in the above-mentioned cases of Bulgaria in 1913, 1915, and 1941 and of Egypt and Jordan in 1967. Usually, however, more prudent elements within the regime, recalculating the balance between their ethnofraternal affections and their utilitarian interests, intervene at the precipice of disaster to brake this myopic process—as when the Bulgarian army itself suppressed the too recklessly irredentist-revisionist (anti-Yugoslav and anti-Greek) Internal Macedonian Revolutionary Organization (IMRO) in

1934, and when King Hussein of Jordan defeated and expelled the PLO in 1970 lest it drag his country into yet another unpropitious war with Israel and subvert his own regime.

5 · It would be an error to assume that the interstate impact of politicized ethnicity always and necessarily manifests itself in the form of such drastic irredentist-revisionist or even disintegrative assaults on (some) states as were discussed in the three preceding sections. Often it manifests itself as a would-be policy-input by the ethnic groups of a multiethnic state into its foreign-policy formulation—an input that is, of course, intended to have an interstate impact but not necessarily one that is programmed to truncate or dismember another state or the would-be inputters' own state. This can occur in countries of historic immigration, whose ethnic groups may seek to influence their governments' policies in favor of "the old country" (or the country of current emotional cathexis)—as when America's Black, Chinese, Greek, Jewish, and Polish ethnic organizations seek to cultivate the foreign policy of the United States into desired directions in Africa, the Far East, the Eastern Mediterranean, the Middle East, and East Central Europe.[11] It can also occur in states whose ethnic groups are autochthonous—as when Croatian leaders recommended a less Francophile Yugoslav foreign policy during the interwar era or when Lebanese Christians press for a less pan-Arabic orientation by their country today, or when Belgium's Walloon politicians urge that

[11] In this type of situation, the authorities of the once ancestral "mother country" (for example, China, Greece, Israel) can often influence the competition for leadership within the "daughter" ethnic group in the current host country through the selective distribution of affective and instrumental recognitions and rewards. They can also use such instrumentalities in a more general way to try to preserve the ethnic group's sense of cultural distinctiveness and offset the assimilationist pressures and temptations (where present) of the host society. McBeath, "Political Behavior of Ethnic Leaders," p. 407.

the country's air force be equipped with French fighter planes while the Flemish push for American ones.

As these examples suggest, the intended thrust of such attempted foreign-policy inputs by ethnic groups may be fairly parochial or quite sweeping—occasionally so sweeping, indeed, as to imply, if successful, a revolution in the diplomatic posture of the country and, if repudiated, rather dire domestic consequences. For example, until the spring of 1938, the militant leaders of Czechoslovakia's German ethnic community repeatedly hinted at a readiness to halt their autonomist and secessionist agitation in return for a reversal of Czechoslovakia's pro-French foreign policy and its synchronization with Nazi Germany's.[12] Given the nature of Nazism, for the Prague government to have acceded would have involved even more than a diplomatic revolution—drastic as that would have been. Eventually, domestic and ideological coordination to Hitlerian totalitarianism would have been a required corollary to such a *volte-face* in foreign policy. Therefore, the democratic pre-Munich government eventually decided—not without some criticism from aspiring counterelites within the dominant Czech ethnic camp—that this was too high a price to pay for those improved relations with the German Reich and with the local German ethnic group that it otherwise seriously sought.

Sometimes the government of a multiethnic state tries to preempt and neutralize these potentially conflicting ethnic inputs into the foreign-policy-making process—as, for example, in the case of the standing Swiss policy of international neutrality, which, as mentioned earlier (chapter 3, section 2), is in large part predicated on a desire to avoid foreign-policy dilem-

[12] Ironically, there was a curious echo here of the pre-1914 insistence of certain Czech leaders (Karel Kramář et al) that the Habsburg imperial regime could appease its Czech subjects only by exchanging its alliance with Germany for a rapprochement to Russia.

mas that could prove to be ethnically divisive domestically. Similarly, India's aprioristic pro-Arab approach to the Arab-Israeli quarrel is largely a domestic strategy to anticipate and thereby blunt a potential bid by her huge Muslim minority for a foreign-policy input. At other times and in other places, the government of a multiethnic state fails to decide on any consistent posture and allows its so-called foreign policy (in effect, a nonpolicy) to fall hostage to discordant and shifting domestic oscillations and balances. Yugoslavia's diplomatic maneuverings of 1939–41, for example, were less a rationally calculated quest for external security than a frantic scramble to forestall interethnic disintegration and civil war.

But these late interwar Czechoslovak and Yugoslav situations were extreme examples of the marginal, limiting case. On the whole, ethnic groups do not find it easy to formulate, let alone press, coherent foreign-policy options upon legitimate governments. Among the obstacles that often confront and baffle them are the following:

1. The professional diplomatic guardians of the purportedly comprehensive, objective, supraethnic "national interest" are usually as resilient and resistant to political ethnicity in the concrete policy-making process as the state and the world's system of states are to the actualization of the ethnopolitical idea in its more general sense.

2. This is doubly true when the policy preferences of these diplomats are endorsed, or even prompted, by important functional, nonethnic interests such as the energy industry, the armaments industry, various branches of the armed forces, the trade union movement, or multinational corporations. While ethnic groups and leaders may receive a sympathetic hearing in legislatures, this entente of professional diplomats plus functional power blocs is likely to be solidly entrenched in the executive corridors of government. (Of course, when it suits them, the functional interests and power blocs can turn around

and play the game of ethnicity with a vengeance as, for example, when military establishments focus their support and their recruitment drives toward "traditionally martial" ethnic categories or when multinational corporations site their investments so as to find their labor supply among "traditionally docile" ones.)

3. The ethnic groups within a particular state are often indifferent or even opposed to each other's efforts in the realm of foreign-policy inputs. Thus, instead of coordinating and adding their limited assets, they frequently compound their weaknesses and fail to bring a critical mass to bear on the policy process. For example, American Jewish and Polish ethnic groups are both generally anti-Soviet. But whereas the former presses the American government to extract more emigration from the Soviet Union, the latter would prefer it to emphasize the desatellization of East Central Europe. Thus their general agreement fails to result in specific coordination. In an earlier era, American Black and Italian ethnic leaders had canceled out each other's intended inputs into America's policy response to Mussolini's invasion of Ethiopia in 1935.[13]

4. Not all ethnic groups are committed with equal intensity to their foreign-policy preferences. Half a century ago, Irish-American ethnics would press their anti-British foreign-policy choices with great passion, while Jewish-Americans articulated their pro-Zionist ones much more faintly. Today, this asymmetry is reversed.

5. Even those foreign-policy problems that are of direct interest to an ethnic group may be too complex and controversial to permit it to develop a clear position on the issues, and thus its leaders are prevented from pressing a cohesive policy rec-

[13] For further elaboration, see Irving Louis Horowitz, "Ethnic Politics and U.S. Foreign Policy," pp. 175–80, and Snetsinger, "Ethnicity and Foreign Policy," pp. 322–29.

ommendation on the government. For example, overseas Chinese ethnic communities in many Southeast Asian and Pacific countries were baffled and split by the problem of mainland China versus Taiwan. Similarly, Black Americans were politically confounded by Black-versus-Black conflicts such as the Biafran civil war in Nigeria.

6. In this area, too, utilitarian cost/benefit considerations once again come into play. The resources and energies of ethnic groups and ethnic leaderships being limited, they ordinarily cannot afford to mobilize and direct these resources and energies en masse away from group-maintenance and domestic politics into foreign-policy pressures.[14]

All in all, therefore, it can be affirmed at this point that the efforts of ethnic groups to influence the foreign policies of the governments of their multiethnic states are now conceded to be legitimate in principle and are no longer *a priori* repudiated with insinuations of double (and dubious) loyalty—at any rate, not in democratic and politically integrated multiethnic states. (Albeit the dominants and central elites may still complain about the allegedly debilitating effects of these attempted ethnic engagements in foreign-policy formulation.) But it is not possible to claim that these ethnic efforts are likely to achieve their intended policy impact except in the indirect, though important, sense that a central government, in weighing its foreign-policy options from its central perspective, considers their anticipated differential effects on its domestic support base. In other words, governmental elites, dominant elites, and subordinate subelites remain in control, but they temper the exercise of that control

[14] An exception is American Jewry, which, by activating itself for massive support of Israel after 1967, found itself thereby gaining new and hitherto unsuspected resources and energies for internal group maintenance and cultural renewal. Here, in other words, its investment in a particular foreign policy had a multiplier, rather than a subtractive, effect on the group's total assets for at least a decade. Whether this effect can be maintained remains to be seen.

in the light of their assessments of popular responses and—at the margin—of possible popular repudiations and even delegitimations of their authority. Hence ethnic groups with significant electoral or other political strength and with skilled leaders are more likely to elicit this "tempering" anticipatory response from governments and central elites than groups are that lack such assets—even if the latter's case is just.

To gain a hearing and even to avert and disarm insinuations of double (or dubious) loyalty, an ethnic group's leaders seeking to influence the policy-making process of the government must depict their group's policy desires as congruent with the public values, ideology, and interests of the state as a whole—provided that the group perceives this state as indeed legitimate. In the above-mentioned Walloon/Flemish debate over which type of aircraft was most suitable for the Belgian armed forces, each side characterized its own preference as particularly consonant with Belgium's general commitment to help "construct Europe" and, respectively, to affirm NATO.[15] In the United States, Polish-American, Jewish-American, and—more recently—Afro-American subelites have, at varying times, been quite adept at dovetailing and rationalizing their policy interventions with stipulated American values and declared American interests. The Polish-American anti-Communist and anti-Soviet "captive nations" pressures of the immediate post-World War II years, followed by the Jewish-American portrayal of Israel as a democratic, pioneering, innovative western society that was making the desert bloom after centuries of "feudal" Arab neglect, and then the subsequent Afro-American championing of Black African liberation against the abominated systems of apartheid and colonialism—all meshed well in their times with the values and goals of the general American public, which also felt aroused against Soviet expansionism during the Cold War,

[15] Zolberg, "Splitting the Difference," pp. 103–04.

which saw itself as the heirs of pioneers who had tamed a continental wilderness, which had recently professedly rededicated itself to ethnic equality and human rights.[16]

Of course, such claims of a fundamental harmony between the foreign-policy recommendations of an ethnic group and the putative general state interest and general public ideology may become thin or fall on deaf ears. With the thawing of the Cold War and the initiation of detente, the Polish-American ethnic community lost much of its earlier resonance with American foreign-policy makers—as did the "China (Taiwan) lobby" of the 1950s and 1960s when the United States became fascinated with "playing the (mainland) China card" in the 1970s. So, too, the Jewish-American effort on behalf of Israel has become more difficult with America's increasingly vivid dependence on the oil of the Arab states. Afro-American interventions to give a Black direction to American foreign policy in Africa were for long impeded by a previously prevailing judgment that general American economic and strategic interests dictated otherwise. The Helleno-American community has also found it difficult to persuade both the general public and the foreign-policy Establishment that a confrontational posture against Turkey (such as it recommends) is in the general American interest.

It goes without saying that the political persuasiveness (or its waning) of such ethnic-group assertions of a congruence between their own foreign-policy preferences and the general political interest is not only a function of the intellectual or analytical plausibility of such claims but is emphatically also a product of the ethnic group's effective domestic political "clout," for example, the potency of its electoral leverage, its lobbying apparatus, and its leaders' access to the inner sanctums of central elites.

[16] Weil, "Can Blacks Do for Africa?" pp. 121–22.

6 · It would not be proper to close a chapter with this title without a discussion—albeit brief—of the problem of divided nations and an assessment of the relative weights of politicized ethnicity and of other factors in determining the chances for an eventual reunification of these nations. In a sense, the divided nation is the converse of the multiethnic state. The latter is a political-legal entity incorporating several ethnonations within its jurisdiction. The former is a single ethnonation divided between two (or, hypothetically, more) states, in each of which it is the dominant—perhaps the only—ethnic group. This dominant status renders divided nations analytically distinct from partitioned nations, for example, the Poles in the nineteenth century, the contemporary Basques, Kurds, Baluchis, and others, who are subordinate fractions in the states among which they are distributed (see section 3 of this chapter). It also distinguishes them from the more conventional manifestations of the irredentist issue wherein the dominants of one state may seek to reclaim a fraction of their ethnonation that happens to reside within the jurisdiction of another state, where it is relegated to a subordinate niche.

The divided nations of today's world are the two Germanies (on the assumption—one that is no longer as likely to be challenged as it formerly might have been—that by now the Austrians are a nation distinct from the Germans to their north and do not constitute a third Germany), the two Koreas, the two Chinas (the mainland and Taiwan), and, arguably, the two Yemens. Should the Irish also be added to this list of divided nations? IRA sympathizers respond with an emphatic affirmative, but Ulster Protestants insist vehemently that they are ethnonationally different (British) from the Irish Catholics and hence deny that the two communities constitute a single, albeit divided, nation. Without taking prescriptive sides, all of this study's earlier allusions to the problems of Ulster have assessed them as expressing an interethnic conflict whose protagonists are discrete ethnic groups. Hence, without prejudging the desirability of alternative political and constitutional scenarios for Ulster, the Republic of Ireland, and the border that currently separates them, we continue with that assessment and, for analytic purposes, here omit the Irish from the class of divided nations.

Also omitted from the following discussion are the two Yemens because, at the time the border was drawn between them by an Anglo-Ottoman Boundary Commission early in the twentieth century, these were tribal areas without a sense of single nationhood, and even today, operative ethnopolitical allegiances among their populations are still fluid. Do their people's "terminal" allegiances belong to the clan, the tribe, the sect, southern or northern Yemen, the concept of a unitary Yemen, the pan-Arab community, the pan-Islamic idea? Indeed, some would suggest that the basic question here is not so much whether the Yemenis are a single ethnonation divided between two states but, rather, whether the Arabs are a single people divided among a score of states. Therefore, with this decision to omit the Irish and Yemeni cases, the following discussion attempts to generalize some questions and tentative answers from the examples of the currently divided German, Korean, and Chinese ethnonations.

In the general context of this study, the crucial question is the one posed above in chapter 3, section 4, to wit: can different states, different political institutions, shape populations that were originally a single ethnic category into separate and distinct ethnopolitical nations? In other words, the issue is not only—as the present chapter's title implies—what is the impact of politicized ethnicity on states and on the interstate system but also the reverse: what is the feedback of state institutions and the interstate system in shaping and directing ethnonational formations? Note that the divisions of Germany, Korea, and China in the 1940s were initially the contingent, perhaps even accidental, residues of how World War II and the Chinese civil war ended and were then rigidified by the decisions and vetoes of the Great Powers implementing their own perceived interests. In other words, the divisions were not initially the product of free choice by the divided nations themselves and were, indeed, resented by them. The question that now poses itself against that historical background is: what is the balance—presumably a changing balance—over time between latent or active ethnonational pressure for reunification on the one hand and, on the other hand, newer pressures and trends to invest a kind of neoethnic political allegiance and legitimation in the current pairs of separate states—East and West Germany, North and South Korea, mainland China and Taiwan?

In each of these three exemplary pairs, the first-mentioned state is Communist, the second, anti-Communist in ideology and political practice. And the second, anti-Communist state in each pair is the more productive and prosperous one, its population enjoying the higher living standard. Though this advantage may render the non-Communist state into an economic reference line for the aspirations of the citizens of the Communist half of the divided nation and thereby indirectly fuel the pressure for reunification, it has not so far been sufficiently magnetic to lead to any generalized political delegitimation of the three Communist states. Even if we set aside for the moment the vetoes that other powers (the Soviet Union, France, Japan, China, the United States) would presumably cast against a reunification of Germany, Korea, and China through the absorption of the economically weaker by the stronger state,[17] the available evidence suggests that each half has now sufficient indigenous reserves of legitimacy, leadership skills,

[17] In the case of the two Chinese states, the anti-Communist one (Taiwan) is economically stronger only on a per capita basis, not in aggregate terms. In the two Germanies and Koreas, the anti-Communist state is economically stronger by virtually all scales and measures.

administrative competence, public socialization to its ideology, and military effectiveness to hold its own against the other politically, as a state, even without Great Power patronage.

Korea is here a paradigmatic test case. Unlike the German nation, which has been divided among several states for almost all of its history, and unlike the Chinese, whose historical experience has been one of chronic oscillation between a centralized state and its fragmentation into local warlordism, the Korean ethnonation had been united in a highly centralized polity virtually uninterruptedly for well over a millenium, from 668 until its "accidental" division into two zones of occupation and then two states in 1945. And not only had Korean political history been thus characterized by constant and intense unity but also in the ethnocultural dimension Korea was highly homogeneous. Here, in short, the experience of being a divided nation since 1945 is unprecedented and hence particularly traumatic. One might, therefore, expect Korean pressure for reunification to be particularly strong and persistent. Furthermore, the presumption of a supposedly inevitable external veto against such reunification is today less warranted apropos of Korea than of the two Germanies and Chinas, for no other power has reason to fear or oppose a reunited Korea. In sum, therefore, here one might reasonably expect the balance between ethnonational and other pressures to tilt decisively toward Korean reunification.

Such an expectation is not, however, borne out by recent history. Indeed, human, personal contacts between the two Koreas are fewer, and political contacts between their governments are more hostile, than between the two Germanies. No family reunifications, no mail flow, no private telephonic or telegraphic communications have crossed the border dividing this once paradigmatically united nation since 1945. It is as though a paradoxical dialectic were at work: the very history of ethnonational unity, centralization, and homogeneity has prompted the two Korean regimes to redouble the levels of estrangement and enmity to counteract the "natural" centripetal tendencies toward reunification and to protect their vested political and bureaucratic stakes in maintaining the division. And in the course of this "antagonistic collusion," the two regimes and the two sets of elites have generated new particularistic allegiances and legitimations on each side of the dividing border and new psychological alienations across it.[18]

In the two Germanies and the two Chinas separate *Staatsgefühle* have also developed over time. East Germans no longer view themselves as residents of a Soviet-occupied zone of Germany but as citizens of a distinct state—German and socialist in character—with its own concrete achievements and expressive symbols. And they appear unwilling to let these achievements and symbols—these "German socialist accomplishments"—be dissolved and submerged in any foreseeable scenario of reunification, even if there were no external systemic prohibition against such reunification. West German identifications and allegiances are moving in a reciprocally centrifugal direction. Thus each of the two Germanies is developing its own distinctive national consciousness and pride—politically, culturally, and socioeconomically—while operative all-German identification weakens.[19]

Though cultural differentiation between the two Chinas is more difficult to measure and to judge than between the two Germanies, and though both Chinese regimes continue to insist emphatically on the ideological and ethnonational norm of one,

[18] Henderson, "Korea," and Soon Sung Cho, "Changing Pattern," both in *Journal of International Affairs* 27, no. 2 (1973): 204–12 and 213–31; Kihl, "International Integration Theories," pp. 55–66.

[19] Hanhardt, "Socialization and Integration Strategies," pp. 40–54; Remak, "Two Germanies—and Then?" pp. 175–86; Starrels, "Nationalism in the German Democratic Republic," pp. 23–37; Ludz, "The SED's Concept of Nation," pp. 206–24; Schweigler, *National Consciousness in Divided Germany*, passim.

and only one, China (the question being, which regime is the legitimate government of that one China), it is nevertheless also here true that—pending some future realization of that unity which both profess in the name of Chinese ethnonational destiny—each regime energetically proceeds to render its part of China into a viable polity and to legitimate itself and its state by socializing the population under its control to its particular ideological, political, and structural system.[20]

Do the recent histories of these three divided nations furnish answers to the general question first posed in chapter 3, section 4, and then repeated at the beginning of this discussion? That is: have different state structures, different political institutions, shaped populations that were originally a single ethnonational category into separate and distinct North and South Korean, East and West German, mainland and Taiwanese Chinese ethnonations? In other words, have the divided nations been forged into separate nations by the political institutions of separate states, whose effects are buttressed by an interstate system that incorporates these very divisions as a structural feature of its own status quo? Not as of today. Are the trends in such a direction? It is too early to say. The consummated examples of analogous processes cited in chapter 3, section 4, and in chapter 5, section 2, that is, the creation by political, state institutions of ethnopolitically self-conscious and distinct Macedonian, Swiss-German, Guatemalan, Honduran, Kazakh, Kirgiz, Turkmen, Uzbek, and other nations, are here possible but not necessarily indicative precedents. Those forgings of new nations by states occurred at a time when identifications and allegiances were more amorphous and therefore, presumably, more malleable than is the case with the currently divided Korean, German, and Chinese nations. Yet, if the several stalemates that now preserve the political and institutional clefts

[20] Wei, "Unification or Confrontation," pp. 67–79.

sundering these three nations were to persist for a long time, then we might yet witness another demonstration of the structural power of states and of the interstate system to mold distinctive new national entities out of the dominant populations that fall within the political jurisdictions of the divided nations' pairs of states. Precisely because these populations are the ethnic dominants, it might prove easier to socialize them into imputing legitimacy to these states (as distinct from their governments) than if they were the subordinates, for they need not perceive, and normatively reject, these states as controlled and directed by ethnic aliens, occupiers, and oppressors.

* * *

This chapter's discussion of the interaction between politicized ethnicity and the state in the latter's capacity as an actor in, and product of, the interstate arena invites a more proliferated analysis of additional interactions between ethnic groups and the state in some of its other institutionalized capacities, roles, and agencies. The next chapter turns to that broader discussion.

Chapter Seven

ETHNICITY AND THE STATE

1 · So far, this study may have conveyed to readers an implicit assumption that multiethnic states are more complicated and difficult to rule than uniethnic states are. Indeed, readers may also have inferred a secondary assumption to the effect that the fact of multiethnicity is always a problem and a liability, and never an opportunity and an asset, from the perspective of central governmental elites. Whatever the validity of the first assumption, that is, that multiethnic states are *ipso facto* politically more problematic to govern than uniethnic ones are, this chapter seeks (together with certain other goals and tasks) to correct and to balance the secondary corollary by indicating some situations and circumstances in which the fact of a multiethnic population may serve as a resource and a policy lever to rulers and central elites.

Hidden in this secondary, overdrawn corollary is a tertiary and even more erroneous misperception of central elites as supposedly always representing rational, state-wide, long-run, and even cosmopolitan political perspectives, whereas ethnic groups and their leaders are allegedly prone to emotional, parochial, peripheral, and even marginal political myopias. Hence arises the supposedly valid and understandable tendency of the former to look with a jaundiced and impatient eye on the latter, seeing them as dysfunctional liabilities, not as helpful assets, in the governance of the state. But not only do central elites and governments themselves have ethnic commitments and specific ethnic constituencies of their own (generally politically dominant ones); they also frequently welcome and exploit the multiethnic character of the population under their control as a veritable toolbox for regime-maintenance and governance. Here are some structural and situational examples:

1. One functional field in which the fact of a population's multiethnicity can at times serve as a policy lever to a state's central government—admittedly within serious limits and constraints—was discussed in the preceding chapter. This is the field of foreign policy, where a government opting to pursue an irredentist, interventionist, or generally aggressive policy toward another state may use and exploit the ethnic links between a sector of its population and a sector of the target state's population to try to penetrate that target state and destabilize its government and political system (chapter 6, section 2). It is not necessary to dwell further on that functional field in this chapter, except to mention the other side of the coin, namely, that when a government wishes to pursue a supportive rather than an aggressive and destabilizing policy toward another state's political system and regime or simply wishes to influence the other state's policy, it may then also exploit the ethnic links between a sector of its population and the other state's. Thus, for example, American governments used to utilize Italo-Americans to influence electoral behavior in Italy in favor of the Christian Democratic governments and against their Communist challengers during the late 1940s and the 1950s. Today they try to persuade Jewish-American leaders to urge forbearance from unwelcome policies and actions on Israeli governments. An analogous but more problematic exploitation of ethnic linkages may be seen in the Soviet Union's efforts since 1978 to prop up the Communist regime in Af-

ghanistan. Initially, the availability to the Soviet regime of Tadzhik, Uzbek, and other cadres who could speak the languages and dialects of the peoples of Afghanistan was an asset in the pursuit of this Soviet policy. Nevertheless, these very same ethnic linkages appear eventually to have had the reverse effect of "contaminating" some of these Soviet cadres of Muslim origin with ethnofidelic politicization.

2. We turn, then, from the conduct of foreign policy to another, albeit somewhat related and also "machiavellian," area of politics where the multiethnic character of a state's population may serve the central government and elite as an asset—the area of the recruitment of personnel into sensitive agencies of the state apparatus, for example, the armed forces and police forces, so as to ensure these organs' institutional reliability. In Weberian ideal-type theory, of course, impersonal standards of functional competence and formal constitutional allegiance are alone supposed to govern the recruitment and promotion of such personnel and to ensure the loyalty of their agencies to the political authorities. In practice, however, central elites often judge exclusive reliance on such purely rational-legal, institutional, impersonal standards of competence, obedience, and loyalty to be politically risky—especially in the case of army and police forces, which inevitably command equipment that could be diverted from their assigned missions to an attack or an ultimatum against the central government itself. Hence the frequent tendency of governments and central elites, in their endless quest for political loyalty and reliability on the part of the state's institutional arms and agencies, to supplement (occasionally even to replace) the impersonal criteria of functional competence with ethnic criteria in the recruitment and promotion of personnel.[1]

[1] Mill, *Considerations on Representative Government*, p. 288; Adekson, "Ethnicity and Army Recruitment," pp. 152–57.

The preferred ethnic group is often, but not always, the political and governmental elite's own. The first variant is exemplified by the overwhelming preponderance given to the dynasty's and the political elite's fellow Serbs in the officer corps of interwar royal Yugoslavia, by President Assad's current reliance on his fraternal 'Alawi officers to hold Syria's armed forces loyal to himself, and by ex-President Idi Amin's use of his Muslim Nubian coethnics to achieve the same effect in Uganda. The alternative variant, in which the favored ethnic group is not the elite's own, is illustrated by the quasi-praetorian role played by the Latvian Riflemen in the defense of Soviet Russia's infant Bolshevik regime on the morrow of its seizure of power and during its initial civil war ordeal and by the prolonged favoritism shown by Morocco's King Hassan toward socially underprivileged and therefore supposedly faithful Berber officers. Particular "ethnic attention" may be devoted to recruitment for those subbranches of the state apparatus that the government regards as especially sensitive for its own security, such as the intelligence branches of the defense and interior ministries, the riot-suppression gendarmerie, the counterinsurgency units of the armed forces, and the like. Here, even a professedly transethnic and supraethnic regime may engage in deliberate ethnic "skewing" in its recruitment policies. One recalls the disproportionate concentration of Jews and Poles in the Cheka and its successor emanations of the political police apparatus in the Soviet Union and an analogous favoritism toward Serbs in Titoist Yugoslavia's equivalent institution, the UDBa.

All in all, therefore, the functional professionalization and the relatively high technological profiles that may characterize the security agencies of the state apparatus do not contradict the possibility—indeed, the likelihood—that their personnel may be selected, promoted, and deployed on the basis of ethnic criteria so as to optimize the central elite's sense of control.

Nemesis may, however, eventually exact a price for such deliberate ethnicization in the staffing of the agencies of state. First of all, the original reliability rationale may backfire against the central elites and governments as favored ethnic groups come to take a proprietary view of their traditional overrepresentation, or even monopoly position, in "their" particular branches of the state apparatus and come to regard them as their groups' reserved and privileged fiefdoms. Second, they may go further and act out this perception through resistance and challenge to a central government seeking to reassert its control over them and/or seeking to diversify its ethnic recruitment policy. Third, when such ethnically skewed military, police, or administrative agencies are deployed by the central government to help it cope with a serious domestic interethnic conflict (or, indeed, any kind of domestic crisis), they will not be accepted by the contending dominant and subordinate groups as the neutral instruments of some supraethnic *raison d'état* but will be perceived as ethnic participants, reflecting prevailing ethnopolitical stratification, with an ethnic stake of their own in the mode and shape of the conflict's prosecution and resolution.[2] Indeed, in the Lebanese civil war of the mid-1970s, the ethnically skewed (that is, overly Christian) army was, ironically, rendered useless to the government at the moment of its greatest need precisely because of this universal perception of that army as being already ethnically committed and biased. An analogous situation and perception has stigmatized the overly Protestant Royal Ulster Constabulary in the interethnic violence that has plagued Northern Ireland since the late 1960s. In other words—and to respecify a point made more generally at an earlier stage of this study (chapter 4, section 3)—the overethnicization of important, and in theory neutral, institutions of the state may compromise their legitimacy and discredit

[2] Enloe, "Police and Military," pp. 138–40.

their acceptability as supposedly impartial executors of the society's transcendent regulative rules and values.

However, short of such extreme, and hence limiting, situations as interethnic civil war, selective and judicious ethnicization in the staffing of the state's administrative arms often serves governments as a useful tool. They have found that it becomes a politically salient and controversial issue only at relatively infrequent intervals. Particularly in the case of the military and police institutions, governments have learned that controlled and undemonstrative ethnic skewing in recruitment policies is generally accepted by the multiethnic society as a whole—and proves to be a resource and an asset to the government—provided that these agencies be seen as professionally competent and not blatantly overpoliticized and as not so expensive as to drastically deplete allocations for social, educational, and various ameliorative programs. Indeed, the issue may be partially defused if the favored ethnic group for personnel recruitment is also the one that might be expected to be most insistent in demanding such compensatory socioeconomic programs—as with the Malays of multiethnic Malaysia—for this ethnic group is then less likely to regard funds allocated to the military and police as being diverted from its own needs to subsidize a rival ethnic group's fiefdoms.[3] In Lebanon and Ulster, alas, this happy equation was missing. There, the army's and the constabulary's highly visible and long-standing interethnic salience and controversiality arose in part from the fact that the poorer Muslim (Lebanon) and Catholic (Ulster) communities most in need of social programs had traditionally—even before the respective civil wars—resented expenditures on the "Christian" and "Protestant" security apparatuses, staffed, as these were, by their more prosperous ethnic rivals with lesser claims for publicly financed socioeconomic, ameliorative programs. The

[3] Enloe, "Military-Ethnic Connection," pp. 275–76, 282.

civil violence then aggravated and accelerated these polarizations in the ethnocommunal reputations of the military and the constabulary. In Lebanon, the polarization ultimately resulted in the neutralization and disintegration of the army.

Because the perimeters of the spectrum within which the ethnic skewing of personnel recruitment are accepted as politically tolerable are imprecise and occasionally volatile perimeters, most governments—particularly governments of developed states—are reluctant to concede openly that they engage in such skewing as a deliberate recruitment policy. Rather, they pretend that it accrues from allegedly unplanned and natural contingencies, such as the tendency of ethnic groups with a "martial tradition" and/or those characterized by economic marginality to take up soldiering and state-service as careers promising esteem and upward mobility.[4] Whereas these sociohistorical tropisms undoubtedly do exist, they supplement but do not really contradict the observation that governments of multiethnic states, their disclaimers to the contrary notwithstanding, have traditionally and frequently found the deliberate exploitation of ethnicity as a recruitment policy in the staffing of the state apparatus to be a useful *arcanum dominationis*.

3. A third, quite unedifying, but, alas, all too common stratagem by which central elites and governments exploit the multiethnicity of the state's population as a lever for regime-maintenance consists of deflecting social frustrations, angers,

[4] Ibid., p. 268. It is interesting to note here Machiavelli's scorn for the traditionalist claim that some groups are "naturally" endowed with martial prowess, and others not. Four-and-a-half centuries ago, he insisted that "Good discipline and exercise will make good soldiers in any country, and the defects of nature may be supplied by art and industry—which in this case is more effective than nature itself. . . . Good order makes men bold. . . . Neither the Greeks nor the Romans were remarkable for their natural ferocity. . . ; they were obliged to resort to good discipline. . . . Few men are brave by nature, but good discipline and experience makes them so." Niccolò Machiavelli, *The Art of War* (1521) (Indianapolis: Bobbs-Merrill, 1965), pp. 25, 61, 169, 202.

and antagonisms away from the government and onto certain vulnerable "scapegoat" groups. "Scapegoat" is not altogether the *mot juste* here, for it implies that the substitute target is altogether innocent and selected at random—which is not necessarily the case in the type of situation here being discussed. What is meant is that political and social outrage and aggression can be, and often are, deflected from "rational" targets that are primarily responsible for the experienced frustrations of the public onto displacement targets, whose antecedent historical or stereotypical roles and qualities render them eligible and vulnerable to be assigned this unfortunate role. While they are not the primary frustrators of the population's aspirations and expectations, these displacement targets may be secondary frustrators; hence they become the seemingly plausible, but actually inappropriate, objects of the cumulative, stored-up, and overdetermined—primary and secondary—frustrations, angers, antagonisms, and resentments of the population.

In politics, such displacement is frequent because the primary frustrators are often too powerful, inacccessible, remote, unidentifiable ("the system"), taboo-protected, or otherwise inhibiting to be attacked by the frustrated population. "Pariah" ethnic minorities, being conspicuous, rich, vulnerable, and nonindigenous (chapter 3, section 2), are especially liable to be indicated for this role of displacement target by governments and elites needing alibis for their own failures. Indeed, they are sometimes historically institutionalized in this role—witness the repetitive fate of Jews in Europe, overseas Chinese in Southeast Asia, Indians in South and East Africa, and so forth.[5]

One might, parenthetically, hazard here the suggestion that one of the explanations of why lower socioeconomic strata consistently show higher levels of ethnic xenophobia and jin-

[5] Donald L. Horowitz, "Direct, Displaced, Cumulative Ethnic Aggression," pp. 1–16.

goism than the upper classes do lies precisely in the fact that "their own" ethnic in-group superiors, that is, these very same upper classes, though often the primary frustrators of the lower classes, arrange to seem to be too strong and inhibiting to be attacked and succeed in displacing lower-class resentment onto ethnic outgroups. This process is facilitated by and, in turn, greases the previously discussed "Greshamite" flow-gradient of stereotypes from social-role to ethnic image patterns (chapter 2, section 7). And it helps to account for the historical generalization that potential class conflict within an ethnic group is often and easily transformed into actual interethnic antagonism between ethnic groups, whereas the reverse dynamic is rare and difficult. In short, the exploitation of interethnic animosities through the displacement process does double service for elites and upper classes by mitigating felt vertical and hierarchical strains within groups and systems.[6]

4. More positive and productive use by the central elites of the population's multiethnic character occurs when the ethnic groups are identified as the administrative units for development planning. This strategy is most feasible where the ethnic units are regionally concentrated and autochthonous—as in China and Yugoslavia. Note, however, that this is not a sufficient condition for their use in this manner. The Soviet regime, for example—and for transparent reasons—deliberately shuns rendering its planning units structurally congruent with its ethnofederal units, lest the latter thereby acquire centrifugal leverage. Rhetorically, at any rate, South Africa's Bantustans are also examples of ethnic groups used as economic planning units by the central government. In New York and some other American multiethnic metropolitan centers, various governmental social-service and poverty agencies try to render their

[6] LeVine and Campbell, *Ethnocentrism*, pp. 117–39.

activities manageable by structuring them upon and around ethnic groups.

5. More generally, in this era of the capitalist welfare state, of the would-be socialist state, and of the directed-development state, governments find that ethnic groups are more serviceable units than socioeconomic classes are for organizing the distribution of the benefits that the state allocates and for managing the tensions that accrue from this distribution. Classes are too large, too amorphous, too general in their expectations (for example, "halt inflation"), and politically too ungrateful to be propitiated with (probably evanescent) allocative awards. Provided the state and the regime enjoy an adequate reservoir of legitimacy, it is easier, cheaper, and politically more effective for a government to "give something" to, say, the Slovaks or the Catalans or the Blacks than to "do something" for the working class or the middle class or the poor in general. Thus a circle is drawn: ethnic groups learn that organization is a necessary condition for achieving political recognition and extracting socioeconomic awards; governments, in turn, find that this ethnic-group consolidation facilitates the performance of their distributive and allocative responsibilities, and hence they reinforce it with their political and administrative decisions and procedures. Thus both governments and ethnic groups develop an interest in using ethnicity as an organizational principle and as a social category to elevate the ethnic group into the principal unit of political participation and the leading transmission belt for political mobilization in the modern multiethnic polity.[7] And, in addition to this dual interest-instrumentality, ethnicity currently carries the further advantage of serving as a stronger

[7] Glazer and Moynihan, "Why Ethnicity?" pp. 33–39. Note, for example, the irony in the dialectic of the United States' Civil Rights Act of 1964, which was supposed to render the federal government color blind and yet led directly to a proliferation of ethnic categories in that government's distributive practices and accountability requirements.

affective bond than socioeconomic class does (chapter 2, section 7).

Given these advantages to using ethnicity as a fulcrum and ethnic groups as levers for policy and administration, it seems unlikely that governments will let themselves be deflected from this route by the consideration that, if judged by the norms of a rational-legal merit system, a certain degree of ethnic-communal "corruption" is likely to ensue. In both the area of recruitment of personnel discussed under item 2 of this section, and in this area of governmental allocations and distributions, the central government is simultaneously trying to solve its own functional problems and to attend to the expectations of ethnic groups and the claims of their subelites. That the ethnic personnel recruited into powerful organs of the state apparatus or placed in charge of allocational subdistributions favor, in turn, their own groups is "corrupt" only by the standards of a rational-legal system blind to ethnic communalism; it is "correct" and efficacious by the norms of ethnic-communal obligation. The only kind of behavior that would indeed be corrupt by both sets of norms would be sheer market behavior for private advantage, that is, the sale of state services—appointive or distributive—to the highest bidder regardless of both merit and of ethnic solidarity. This would be perceived and, presumably, punished as systemically subversive by both central elites and ethnic subelites. But ethnic-communal patronage (in contrast to such private, entrepreneurial, market behavior) might readily be tolerated by central elites as an expediential, even if not optimal, way to cope with some of their functional governmental problems and responsibilities by exploiting multiethnicity as a lever and an opportunity.

6. Ethnicity is also usable as an asset in the formation and consolidation of political parties. This can be done very explicitly—as with the Parti Québécois in Canada—or more subtly—as with the Liberal Party in Canada, both being dependent on

Francophone votes and support. The Democratic Party in the United States has, in the twentieth century, rebuilt itself on the support of—and for service to—ethnic groups. Related to this process of using ethnicity for party building is the obverse strategy whereby political parties manipulate ethnic anxieties to win or keep office. They warn their traditional and their prospective ethnic supporters that the electoral victory of an alternative party would entail the ascendancy of rival ethnic groups or at least of a political elite indifferent to their clients' particular ethnic needs and aspirations. Not only are the party politics of ethnically polarized societies such as Guyana and Malaysia predicated on such manipulation of ethnic anxiety, but it is also a conventional stratagem in more diffuse political systems as well. In the American presidential election of 1948, for example, the Democratic Party indicated to the Black electorate that if it now failed to support the reelection of President Truman and instead defected to Henry Wallace's Progressive candidacy after Truman had stood up to and faced down the Dixiecrat secession of Senator Thurmond, then a long time might elapse before any future Democratic presidential candidate would again accept the political risk of defying the South to champion Black rights.[8]

7. The central elites of a multiethnic state may find it useful to select a particular ethnic group—not necessarily the largest or most powerful one—as the supplier of the state's would-be integrative identity symbols. For example, the modern Indian elite, prevented by its secularist ideology and by the exigencies of Hindu-Muslim tensions and of the caste problem from appropriating either explicitly Hindu, or Muslim, or caste-

[8] Lubell, *Future of American Politics,* p. 222. For some European examples of similar mobilization and anxiety manipulation of ethnicity both by system-wide parties and by ethnically specific parties, see Rudolph, "Ethnonational Parties and Political Change," pp. 401–26.

resonant cultural-historical emblems to express its political integrationist hopes for the state, chose instead to resurrect and to celebrate the symbol of the consolidator-emperor Ashoka—a Buddhist and hence free of Hindu, Muslim, and caste identity. (Ashoka's wheel was then superimposed on the middle white stripe of the country's flag, which also contains upper saffron and lower green stripes in integrationist acknowledgement of the huge Hindu and Muslim segments of India's population.) Analogous considerations prompted the choice of the Bahasa Indonesia tongue—rather than Javanese or Sundanese—as the official, integrative, national language of multiethnic Indonesia. Or again, the mestizo elite of Mexico goes out of its way to celebrate the cultural patrimony of the politically and socio-economically subordinate Amerindians as the supplier of the country's symbols of statehood, of legitimation, and of political integration. As these examples indicate, while the ethnic group selected to be the furnisher of these symbols need not be the central elite's own group, it must be an autochthonous group, for indigeneity appears to be a moral-psychological and political requirement for this role. Thus the European-descended Afrikaner Boers go to considerable lengths to claim a kind of autochthony for themselves by insisting that, upon their ancestors' arrival in South Africa in the seventeeth century, the land was empty and they thus became its original inhabitants. If pressed, they even define themselves as a sort of white native tribe and label the Anglophones alone as European colonialists and immigrants—a semantic exercise intended to prevent the latter group from functioning as the supplier of the state's symbols of legitimation.

The current Soviet elite finds this problem of selecting the rhetoric and the apparatus for the symbolic legitimation and integration of its multiethnic state to be difficult and controversial. It seeks to straddle and to link both supraethnic Soviet and specifically Russian symbolism—and may, in fact, be falling between two stools. On the one hand, the effort to sit in part on the Soviet stool affronts the nationalists of the dominant Russian group, who feel that it profanes their holy Russia on behalf of a cold, abstract, nonemotive, and unsatisfying formula; simultaneously it fails to attenuate or to satisfy the grievances, aspirations, and pride of the country's other ethnonations. On the other hand, ideological as well as political imperatives preclude a decision to sit fully on the Russian stool and abandon the supraethnic Soviet-Marxist one. The regime's relations with its Russian ethnic constituency have thus come to resemble the predicament of the proverbial lady riding a tiger, who could neither stay on nor get off without incurring prohibitive risks. Russian nationalism cannot be spurned lest the Russians disown the regime and the non-Russians perceive such a gesture as more a signal of ideological and political desperation than of integrative confidence. But neither can Russian nationalism be openly and explicitly adopted or be permitted an uncontrolled life of its own lest the other ethnonations be repelled and the Russians themselves perceive such developments as symptomatic of weakness and retreat on the part of the regime. Nor, finally, can the elite realistically hope to revitalize the rhetoric and the apparatus of Sovietism as an authentic conferrer of symbolic legitimation and integration upon the state. The attempted resolution of this dilemma is the language of supraethnic Sovietism and the real policy of flattering the Russians as the supposedly most progressive, productive, and leading ethnodemographic component ("the elder brother") of the Soviet state. But this hybrid stance only irritates the non-Russians without fully satisfying the Russians and fails to extract the regime from its degenerative, symbolic-legitimation vortex.

The ethnonational problem is currently being managed and contained in the Soviet Union at a level below that of a crisis, thanks largely to an upward mobility escalator for most nonpolitical ethnic elites and professionals, as well as to the regime's toleration toward ethnic aspirations that are marginal to the system's essential core and structure. Yet the interaction of this ethnonational problem with still other structural problems, policy dilemmas, socioeconomic constraints, and ideological impasses may yet render it incendiary in the coming decade and/or insoluble within the prevailing political system. Or, to state this point more analytically and more dialectically, the ethnonational problem complicates the many other problems—political, economic, administrative, and the like—that the Soviet elite faces and tends to stifle innovative and rational approaches to their possible solution. All such approaches point to greater decentralization—but this is precisely what the central elite fears as entailing the risk of centrifugal ethnic particularism and jeopardizing its own control over the entire Soviet system. Yet without such innovations the system drifts toward both stagnation and possible combustion. Meanwhile, the unresolved ethnonational problem, even at its current subcritical level, aggravates the tensions between Russians and other ethnonations—and between all of them seriatim and the regime. It thus poses a serious liability—substantive and symbolic—to the legitimacy of the Soviet system and the integration of Soviet society.[9]

2 · From these important but mundane (and not always successful) methods whereby central elites and governments may try to turn to their own instrumental utility the fact

[9] "The polarization of the Soviet peoples along ethnic lines is increasing faster than their identification with, and consciousness of, a new Soviet nationhood, and it is nourished both by tradition and by socioeconomic progress." Bialer, "Soviet Political Elite," p. 44. The dissident Soviet mathematician Igor Shafarevich also warns that, "Of all the urgent problems that have accumulated in our life, the most painful seems to be that concerning relations between the various nationalities of the USSR. No other question arouses such explosions of resentment, malice and pain—neither material inequality, nor lack of spiritual freedom, nor even the persecution of religion." Shafarevich, "Separation or Reconciliation?" p. 88.

of a given state's multiethnicity, we now raise our focus to a more theoretical level. In doing so, we note again that, while on the one hand the mere existence of a given state in no way guarantees that it will be, or will become, its population's main referent for identity, identification, and "terminal" loyalty (chapter 1, section 1 and chapter 2, sections 4 and 5), yet, on the other hand, the state does command integrative resources that have enabled it, in a number of historic cases, to mold the demographic raw material of its populations into authentic, organic political and cultural communities, that is, into nations (chapter 3, section 4, item 7; chapter 6, section 6). Thus states on the one hand, and ethnic groups on the other, may be competitive, harmonious, or reciprocally indifferent in their respective psychological, cultural, and political mobilization efforts. The conventional rhetoric expressing this dialectic describes a state apparatus that achieves or approaches success in the cultural as well as the political and life-chances dimensions of integration (and whose efforts in this direction come to be accepted as legitimate by its originally disparate or prepolitical ethnic publics) as either an accomplished "nation-state" or as a state still engaged in "nation building," whereas a state that fails to achieve or does not even seek to achieve these comprehensive integrative goals is labeled an "empire"—that is, an apparatus imposing political order but indifferent to or accepting of ethnosocial and ethnocultural heterogeneity.[10] Empires are

[10] Hechter, *Internal Colonialism*, p. 60, and McNeill, "On National Frontiers," pp. 207–19. The term *empire* became conventional on the strength of Old World and colonial institutions and experiences. It is somewhat awkward when transported to label, say, Latin American states that indeed (as the description above puts it) also seek to impose political order but are indifferent to the ethnocultural heterogeneity of their populations. One does not customarily think of Bolivia and Peru, for example, as empires. And yet, the policies of their regimes toward their Amerindian subjects has indeed been, and remains, "imperial" precisely in the political sense stated above. Hence, my retention of the label *empire* to convey this specific meaning appears generally valid even if fractionally awkward.

usually, therefore, assignable to either the vertical-hierarchical or the parallel-segmental models of ethnic stratification, but only rarely to the cross-patterned reticulate one (chapter 3, section 3).

A multiethnic empire (in the sense of this noun as used above) poses no intentional threat to the separate ethnocultures of its subject populations. And a premodern, relatively primitive state apparatus of low technological and administrative competence poses no effective threat to them, regardless of its intentions. But unintentionally, a modernizing empire, improving, innovating, and concentrating the state's capabilities in communication, transporation, and administration, is likely to shatter the former relative isolation of its several ethnic populations. It may therefore come to be perceived by them as conveying such a threat to their ethnocultures and thereby stimulate their reactive, secessionist, anti-imperial-state ethnonationalism. Even more menacing to subordinate ethnic groups is the intentional, comprehensively integrationist program of a would-be nation-state. Thus the political salience of ethnic cultures and the quality of allegiance to them change across historical time and across the spectrum of types of states.

This point may be illustrated by comparing the political ambience of East Central Europe in the Habsburg imperial era with the interwar, *soi-disant* nation-state era. Thus, the Czechs, Poles, Slovenes, and others, of the old Habsburg Empire had not been obliged to view themselves as ethnic subordinates in an explicitly German state. Though they felt themselves ethnically aggrieved at particular and various times, they could always quite realistically anticipate a future imperial government's reversal of a current schedule of ethnic favoritism. Even the more consistently excluded ethnic subordinates of the empire's Hungarian half awaited a change with the next royal sucession. But in the interwar era of the so-called successor nation-states to the destroyed empire, an ethnic minority seemed fated, short of a war and a redrawing of frontiers, to remain a subordinate minority forever—not simply in a neutral statistical sense but also in terms of political, economic, cultural, and often even civil-legal deprivations. The central elites of the new or restored interwar states, unlike those of the Austrian half of the former empire, regarded themselves as the custodians of explicit and specific nation-states, each bearing and enhancing an explicit and specific ethnonational culture.[11] Impatient with the fact of their states' multiethnicity, that is, with the fact that these were not then true nation-states, they disdained accommodative, mutual-bargaining strategies vis-à-vis ethnic subordinates and failed to cultivate conflict-assuaging political mechanisms and techniques (such as those analyzed in chapter 5, sections 2 and 3). For example, they imposed land reforms, expropriations, and redistributions in which the effective operative criterion was less the agricultural proficiency than the ethnonationality of the old and new owners. By thus rendering property rights and other individual rights subject to purely political considerations, the hypernationalistic dominants of the interwar era eroded the very concept of assured, guaranteed, transpolitical rights—unintentionally preparing the way for their Communist successors' even greater scorn for individual human rights.

Thus the lot of East Central Europe's many (and usually large) subordinate ethnic minorities became emotionally more

[11] Governments of de facto multiethnic states who wish to feign them as nation-states often engage in census manipulation, not merely in the form of pressure applied on respondents, but also by way of "statistical" ethnocide and ethnogenesis through redefinitions of subordinate ethnic categories—sometimes even defining them out of existence, and at other times fragmenting a relatively large and formidable subordinate group into several smaller and weaker ones. Such artifices were neither confined to, nor even practiced most egregiously in, interwar East Central Europe. Thus, from 1890 on, the census of Germany sought to reduce the statistical weight of her subordinate Polish population by designating the Kashubians and Mazurians as separate categories; the Soviet Union divides the potentially solid bloc of her Central Asian Muslim population into several ethnoliguistic nations; India has used the census to withdraw official acknowledgment of the very existence of certain tribal peoples.

demeaning and politically more desperate in the interwar era of *soi-disant* nation-states than it had formerly been in the imperial era. Their own subelites, in turn, often locked themselves into a vicious cycle of antagonistic collusion with the central elites by contesting the new states' legitimacy and pursuing subversive strategies against them. Each side's political behavior thus tended to confirm the other's suspicion of its bona fides. As a result, the pretended nation-states of interwar East Central Europe were crippled by domestic and external maladies stemming from these reciprocal refusals to accept their multiethnicity as a base from which to work and on which to build.

It thus appears that a central elite or government determined to press comprehensively integrationist "nation building" (not just "state building") goals on reluctant or resisting ethnic groups is least likely to make constructive or benevolent use of either the methods itemized in the preceding section for capitalizing on multiethnicity as an asset and a resource to rulers of states or the conflict-assuaging techniques and mechanisms discussed in chapter 5, section 3. And its program is, furthermore, most likely to prove counterproductive for the stability, progress, and legitimacy of its own state. From the perspective of the ethnic objects of a state's integrationist activities, one might phrase this point, which was introduced above with the claim that the political salience of ethnicity and the quality of allegiance to it change across historical time and across the spectrum of types of states, as follows: traditionalist ethnic categories, living in a world of little change and with no systematically effective, state-supported challenge to their ethnic cultures, experience their ethnic allegiance less politically, though perhaps with greater psychological serenity, than they would, and do, in modern conditions of rapid, sustained change and of state-directed, integration-targeted mobilization efforts. Indeed, the ethnocentrism of traditional man is often akin to a kind of apolitical solipsism, ignoring and psychologically denying the world outside, whereas the ethnonationalism of transitional and of modern man strives for power over, or for autonomy from, outsiders. Hence the latter attitude has an explicit and conscious political dimension, entailing an active stance—affirmative or challenging, as the case might be—toward the extant state in which a modern or a transitional ethnic group finds itself. And this is as true of dominant as of subordinate ethnic groups. (See also, in this connection, the more extended discussion of the modalities of integration in chapter 4, section 2, and the earlier critique of the "primordialist" theory of ethnicity in chapter 1, section 4.)

In sum, the state has become the decisive political vehicle and political arena for ethnic groups—dominant and subordinate—in modern conditions of rapid change in which it redistributes ever higher proportions of its citizens' and subjects' general income and assets. To protect and articulate their social, cultural, and economic interests, grievances, claims, anxieties, and aspirations, ethnic groups must enter the political arena—that is, they must add the quality of becoming conflict groups to their previous qualities of being status groups, interest groups, cultural groups, and the like. In the present historical era, this means, in effect, that they must bid for exclusive or participant political control over and/or in a state. Without some such political leverage through a state apparatus, even their cultural and socioeconomic, let alone their political, interests are jeopardized. And if an ethnic group's bid for an adequate share of political power and control within an extant multiethnic state proves unproductive, is repudiated as nonnegotiable, or the like, it may then well make a secessionist bid for a state of its own—driven by interest, as well as emotion. After all, even in this age of the world economy, of multinational corporations, of cosmopolitan vogues, a state of its own—albeit a relatively small one—can nevertheless still offer some palpable protection and enhancement to the cultural, economic, and sheer demographic interests and goals of an ethnic group.[12]

Another way to formulate this point is to note that, since the modern, mobilizing state's redistributive performance is often either inefficient or perceived as biased, or both, certain categories of its citizens and subjects are likely to be alienated by and from it. If these alienated categories regard and organize themselves as ethnic groups, and if their discontent is sufficiently deep and systemic, they may challenge the very structure or boundaries and domain of their current state and either assay civil war or bid for an alternative state of "their own" (unaware or heedless of the prognosis that such a state, too, will not spare them frustrations and disappointments).

This secessionist option is, of course, available only to regionally concentrated, autochthonous, ethnic groups. Other types of ethnic groups—and also these autochthonous, concentrated ones—have other, additional political options vis-à-vis their current multiethnic states. As it becomes apparent that economic development, industrialization, and modernization do not automatically eliminate the socioeconomic disadvantages and inequities suffered by the ethnic subordinates (and, indeed, may initially even aggravate them, as was demonstrated in the discussion of the theory of "internal colonialism," chapter 2, section 6), these ethnic subordinates demand that the state

[12] The converse of this point has also been confirmed historically. For example, Ireland's full incorporation into the United Kingdom and her loss of all shreds of sovereign statehood in 1801 was followed by the destruction of her small nascent industry and the interruption of her incipient economic diversification. Deprived of the potential protective capacity of their own state, the Irish were thereupon reduced to a more rural, more agricultural, and far poorer economic lot. Hechter, *Internal Colonialism*, pp. 92, 95.

The argument in the text above to the effect that ethnic groups increasingly tend to perceive state power and the state apparatus as instrumentally decisive for their needs, grievances, and claims does not contradict the earlier assessment (chapter 2, section 4) of a generalized decline in the affective respect and awe in which modern men formerly held the authority of the state.

engage in political intervention to supply political redress for the failure of market forces and of historic trends to bring them parity or equity. And here many contemporary states, with their universal suffrage—albeit sometimes plebiscitary—and other professions of democratic openness—albeit often spurious—are more vulnerable to such pressures than they were in former eras when avenues of access and participation were more restricted. In other words, whereas limited or nonexistent suffrage once allowed ethnic dominants and central elites to use the state to consolidate de jure their de facto socioeconomic, cultural, and political advantages and headstarts, today's greater accessibility of the state apparatus furnishes potential compensatory leverage to the subordinates and thereby incipiently narrows the power gap between them and the dominants and/or central state elites. Furthermore, this very accessibility of the state and this narrowing of the gap render subordinate challenge to received arrangements more rational and realistic; thus they encourage ethnopolitical assertiveness and stimulate interethnic conflict. These secular changes in the accessibility of states to the political leverage of subordinates may help to account for the fact that, whereas Europe's first Industrial Revolution (which occurred in an era of restricted or nonexistent suffrage and of low subordinate access to the state apparatus) tended to depress ethnopolitical assertiveness, the massive economic developments of the post-World War II era (coming in an environment of far greater political participation) have everywhere—in Europe and throughout the world—spurred ethnopolitical allegiance, organization, assertiveness, and competition. And the resultant politicization of ethnicity poses challenges—potentially even delegitimating challenges—to the extant state in the realm of its sovereignty (for example, secessionism, federalization, devolution) and/or in the domain of its socioeconomic stability.[13]

[13] Mughan, "Modernization, Deprivation, and Distribution," pp. 361–64; Birch, "Minority Nationalist Movements," p. 337; Grant and Wellhofer, "Introduction" to their edited volume *Ethno-Nationalism*, p. 2.

It is as though the modern participationist, redistributive state—be its mode Keynesian, socialist, or developing—virtually invites and facilitates ethnic demands upon itself. In contrast to the so-called laissez-faire state of classic nineteenth- and early twentieth-century capitalism, which sought to disconnect economic grievances directed against landed nobilities and entrepreneurial bourgeoisies from political demands made upon itself, this contemporary state declares itself to be the valid and responsible target for both the socioeconomic and the political expectations of its citizens and subjects.[14] And since ethnic groups harbor a mix of both these types of expectations, they are thereby presented with a politico-organizational premium over entities with primarily economic or primarily political demands—for example, classes or "grand" ideological movements—as well as with a powerful incentive to organize and politicize themselves as ethnic groups vis-à-vis the state. Thus the posture and the structure, as well as the programs and goals, of the contemporary multiethnic state furnish resources, motivations, and (unintentionally) grievances to regionally concentrated, as well as to geographically dispersed, ethnic groups. Its increasing rate and level of intervention in the economy and the society render it ever more the focus of social discontent (replacing here private-sector employers) and of organizational targeting—as ethnic groups and their leaders become correspondingly increasingly confident that not only can the very aims of the state be exploited to extract policy concessions from it but also that it can even be obliged or persuaded to base and to funnel the implementation of its aims and policies on and through ethnic groups. This assessment—or, rather, differential confidence in the validity of this assessment—in turn, brings into play the previously discussed competition between brokers and militants for ethnic-group leadership (chapter 5, sections

[14] Ronen, *Quest for Self-Determination*, p. 14. See also Berger, "Politics and Antipolitics," p. 30.

1 and 2). Earlier in the present chapter the seductions of this scenario from the perspective of the central state elites were discussed (section 1, items 4 and 5).

None of this means that ethnic dominants and central state elites have been disarmed or necessarily demoralized. After all, while universal suffrage and the other current avenues of openness to the contemporary state do give hitherto unavailable political opportunities to subordinates, they are not one-way streets, nor is traffic on them restricted to subordinates. They are potential compensators, not automatic equalizers, for the subordinates' disabilities and disadvantages. Ethnic dominants and central state elites, respectively, still have available the triptych of possible moral-historical justifications to hone their own ethnopolitical identity (chapter 2, section 6), the seven-item spectrum of dominant goals and strategies (chapter 5, section 2), the seven various conflict-regulating mechanisms and techniques (chapter 5, section 3), and Aristotle's three modes of influencing the behavior of others toward directions desired by oneself (chapter 5, section 4). Moreover, they can exploit the long-ignored (and even denied) fact that, within definite but wide limits, modern economic development and industrial institutions are contextually malleable and can be adapted to, and nestled within, highly inegalitarian ethnosocial stratifications and restrictive political systems. These stratifications and systems can be sustained (or challenged) by political power; they are not automatically—and certainly not quickly—responsive to, still less disintegrated by, so-called long-run, secular trends, nor by the allegedly inevitable, "rational," imperatives of industrialization.[15] In short, the political weapon of assertive and even

[15] Blumer, "Industrialisation and Race Relations," pp. 220–53. The extreme, perhaps limiting example is the extent to which South African industry adapts itself to the constraints of apartheid. Overreliance on secular trends and "rational" production imperatives and underestimation of political intervention and leverage limit the otherwise impressive analysis of Deutsch, *Nationalism and Social Communication*.

militant ethnonationalism is as realistically available to ethnic dominants as to subordinates, and the central state elites also have considerable space for maneuver in their engagement with either and with both of them.

3. As ethnic groups—dominant and subordinate—transform and organize themselves into political conflict groups to protect their perceived interests through exclusive or participant control over and in a state, the emotional intensity of their internal ethnic cohesion rises. This intensification may be accelerated if the members of the ethnic group also perceive themselves as sharing a common economic lot and destiny. In other words, ethnic group allegiance today is likely to correlate with the degree to which the group's political and socioeconomic history has been experienced as setting it apart, as assigning its members to a special condition and fate. Such intensified ethnic-group allegiance and cohesion also impacts on the group's relationship to its cultural patrimony—but in convoluted and differentiated ways about which it is difficult to generalize. Nevertheless, a tentative attempt to do so is here hazarded.

While it is true (as argued in chapter 4, section 4) that in tandem with, or in preparation for, its emergence into politicized assertiveness, an ethnic group reappropriates its own history and reaffirms its own cultural heritage, this cultural face of the group's revitalization is not always integral or substantive. It may be only symbolic or even merely nostalgic[16]—without,

[16] "Not least among the marks of a twilight period is nostalgia, which is the rust of memory. Nostalgia flourishes in the absence of ritual, or, rather, in the conditions left by the erosion of ritual. Ritual binds past and present, and it is when ritual breaks down or ceases to seem relevant to human needs that past and present become separated, and traditional respect for the past tends to become supplanted by nostalgia." Robert Nisbet, reviewing William Manchester, *The Glory and the Dream* (Boston: Little, Brown, 1974), in the *Columbia Spectator* 99, no. 74 (February 18, 1975), "Connection" Supplement, p. 1.

however, attenuating or compromising the group's political punch. Thus, for example, the modern Catalans, Flemings, Jews, Ukrainians, Welsh, and others, on the one hand, have invested substantial effort and resources in the successful revival, elevation, and preservation of their ancient languages—in the belief that only through such a substantive linguistic-cultural commitment could they ensure their groups' historical survival and political enhancement. In other words, their language-loyalty is to them an act of revolutionary cultural affirmation and of political challenge, not merely of traditional, conservative practice. And they often link it to "internal colonialist" analyses of their historic conditions. On the other hand, the current Basque, Scottish, and Irish ethnonational movements appear in practice to be reconciled to the waning of their Euskara, Gaelic, and Erse tongues as conventional vehicles of communication—apparently confident that their groups' political cohesion, historical pride, and future momentum can be sustained even without an instrumentally effective linguistic-cultural base and buttress. In the Breton movement, indeed, it is now sometimes even suggested that its former preoccupation with language revival may have been a political mistake, for it resonated only in the western part of the Armorican Peninsula and hence divided and thus weakened the potential political expression of Breton ethnonational grievances and aspirations. Of course, even the ethnonational movements of this latter type are not utterly indifferent to the ancestral languages. They treasure the ethnic tongue as an affective symbol even as they accept its ebbing in usage. And they perceive themselves as posing no less serious, no less radical, and no less intentional a challenge to their several multiethnic states and the central elites of these states than the language-committed groups do.[17]

[17] Anderson, "Renaissance of Territorial Minorities," pp. 133–36; Reece, "Internal Colonialism," p. 276.

Both types seek to reappropriate their histories and to gain control of their futures—albeit by using different genres of symbols.

Pursuing this point from the linguistic into the religious dimension of cultural heritage and cultural/political interface, one notes that it is most unlikely—indeed, it is literally incredible—that all the militant partisans in the ethnoreligious civil wars of Ulster and Lebanon, for example, are authentic believers in the religions that putatively are the crux of these conflicts. But again, the point here is that such attenuation in the vitality of the cultural (religious or linguistic or other) content of a group's ethnic patrimony and heritage does not correlate in any general or predictable way with either the political salience of felt ethnic issues or the allegiance of individuals to their ethnic groups as conflict groups. Hence agnostics and atheists fight in Ulster and Lebanon on behalf of religiously identified ethnic groups out of a sense of political commitment, while relegating and transforming their "specifically" religious attachments into externally symbolic or merely nostalgic expressions—in a sense, transferring a kind of religious value to the ethnic community that has been the historic vessel of the religious doctrines they have abandoned. This allows them to "return" to their people without necessarily practicing or believing all the tenets of its religion. Furthermore, the converse of this point also holds: the intrinsic, substantive content of the cultural heritages to which ethnic groups subscribe does not ordinarily require them to engage in interethnic conflict, nor does it explain the often fierce intensity of their conflicts. Thus the theological doctrines per se of Roman Catholicism and of Protestantism, or of Christianity and Islam, do not account for the violence of the ethnoreligiously structured civil wars of Ulster and Lebanon.[18]

[18] Cf. Anthony D. Smith, *Theories of Nationalism*, pp. 249–51; Cross, "Colonialism and Ethnicity," p. 39.

Here again the evidence suggests that, while the political momentum of ethnopolitics is never totally severed from its stipulated cultural base, it nevertheless often becomes the propelling variable.

Finally, also in the historiographical dimension of an ethnic group's cultural patrimony and of cultural/political interface, politics is generally the active shaper and energizer. Though the content of a group's historical memories and the intensity with which it holds them do color its political expectations and stances, they are not "objective" or constant; rather, they are interpreted and fashioned by and for political purposes. In short, once ethnicity has been brought into the political arena, thenceforth politics per se—more specifically, the political urge for participant, autonomous, or independent power in a state—becomes the engine of ethnic allegiance, ethnic salience, and ethnic competition. Politics harnesses cultural and socioeconomic symbols, stereotypes, and ideologies to its drive, while itself functioning as the motor force of ethnic solidarity and interethnic conflict. Indeed, so powerful has this political motor become that it occasionally jeopardizes the necessary residual minimum of cultural reserve and of psychological distance vis-à-vis the state and the political process that must be maintained lest ethnicity be totally absorbed by politics and become only political and lest the qualitative difference between ethnic groups and purely instrumental interest groups vanish.

Hence many central state elites are now coming to recognize the futility of either seeking to suppress politicized ethnonationalism or of pretending to ignore it. Rather, they seek to accommodate it to the civic order and the interests of *raison d'état*—and vice versa. They do this partly out of sagacity, partly out of a pragmatic recognition that ethnic groups are today more readily politicized (for or against their extant state, as the case may be) than other types of groups are, and partly out of an historical appreciation that, unlike the central state elites of some earlier eras, they lack the moral authority and the political legitimacy to suppress ethnicity, to ignore it, or to purport to stand above it.

4 · At the other end of the political spectrum, leaders of would-be "grand," nonethnic ideological and/or class-based revolutionary movements against the state apparatus face, ironically, more or less the same problematics, opportunities, and constraints vis-à-vis politicized ethnic groups as the central state elites themselves do. But this fact is often initially screened from both the actors and observers. As class and ideological cleavages and interests intersect with, but do not displace, ethnic interests and interethnic cleavages, and as the salience of class does not covary inversely with that of ethnicity (their interplay not being a zero-sum game), and as several ethnonational movements (as well as most anticolonial movements) now tilt toward the general Left and a few have apparently come under authentic leftist leadership (for example, the Basque ETA, the Ulster IRA), it might at first glance appear as though the problematics of the relationship between "grand" ideological or class-based revolutionary movements and politicized ethnicity are close to being resolved and sublated.

Such an inference is, however, at best premature and probably erroneous. Despite—or, more accurately, because of—the just-cited conditions, trends, and developments, "grand" revolutionary movements still confront the dilemma of either attempting to harness politicized ethnicity to their own comprehensive goals—perhaps initially even to incite and foment it against an extant state apparatus—or of channeling their strategy so as to neutralize ethnicity and render it politically peripheral to the fate of the revolution. The first horn of this dilemma is tricky because it raises the question of "kto kogo," that is, who harnesses and penetrates whom for whose ultimate goals? Who might emerge as the tail wagging whose dog? Or, to phrase it in the Communist movement's own formal rhetoric, is class solidarity among workers of different ethnic segments the precondition for the elimination of structural ethnic inequality, or is the abolition of the latter the precondition for a classless society?[19] The second horn of the dilemma is rendered improbable by the consideration that, since "grand" revolutionary movements (for example, Marxism, Shi'ah Islam) are, by definition and by purpose, mobilization movements seeking a broad social base for the transformation of whole social systems and state apparatuses, as well as for the overthrow of regimes and governments, a would-be strategy of sidetracking and neutralizing such a telling force as politicized ethnicity appears *a priori* unpromising.

Though they are indeed potent and readily politicized—and hence are often an important component in the overall complex of a revolutionary situation—ethnic groups are, however, usually too bounded by exclusivity and hence insufficiently supple and elastic in the short run to form the directive core of a "grand," full-scale social revolution. Furthermore, their political aims are normally tangential to, rather than coterminous with, those of an overarching, social-system transforming, ideology-guided revolutionary movement. That is, their maximal goals—hypothetically maximal, but by no means inevitable—are either secession from the state or the reversal of the dominant/subordinate political relationship within the state (chapter 5, section 2), rather than total social revolution. While such goals are indeed politically drastic, radical, subversive, and delegitimating, they do not aim at the unraveling and reknitting of the entire

[19] The Communist movement's internal postwar debate over this issue is synopsized by Kuper, "Race, Class, and Power," pp. 404, 412–13. For a different judgment on the West European Communists' mode of apprehending this problem, see Anderson, "Renaissance of Territorial Minorities," p. 139.

social fabric. They are, at the outer margin, "civil war" goals rather than "social revolutionary" goals. And, in practice, ethnic groups do not often press even to these outer political margins.[20]

Occasionally, indeed, this noncongruence of goals compartmentalizes and mutually isolates two or more separate antisystem pressures, as each actor's aims and strategies are perceived as divisive and diversionary by the other(s) and a potentially revolutionary situation is aborted. Examples that could be cited here are the reciprocal suspicions dividing the ethnoregional from the Communist oppositions to the current French and Spanish political systems, the inability of most East Central European Marxist parties to comprehend or to harness that area's pent-up ethnopolitical energies during the interwar era, the failure of the Communist and Huk guerrillas in Malaysia and the Philippines to transcend ethnic cleavages and their own overidentification with single ethnic groups in these two states after World War II, or, possibly, the frustration of Che Guevara's revolutionary designs and efforts by the suspicions—ethnically and socially rooted—of the Amerindian peasants of Bolivia toward himself and his ideology (both alien in their eyes) in the mid-1960s.

Thus, while politicized ethnicity often erodes the legitimacy of a state and the effectiveness of the state's apparatus, and while it sometimes triggers or even spearheads antiregime and antigovernmental violence, it ordinarily does not supply the follow-through conceptual model for major, historic, systemic social revolutions. Furthermore, even on those occasions when a state apparatus and a regime have been toppled by a contingent, momentary synchronization of ethnopolitical and social-ideological revolutionary pressures, the leaders of the latter arm of this alliance generally decide that the consolidation of the revolution (in their understanding of its goals) requires the

[20] Cf. Enloe, *Ethnic Conflict and Political Development*, pp. 222–26.

reimposition of strong, statewide, centralized control on the morrow of victory—implicitly or explicitly at the expense of their quondam ethnic confederates. Such was the case in Soviet Russia in the 1920s and in Iran after the Shah's overthrow in 1979. Even in Yugoslavia, this was the initial policy of the revolutionary Titoist regime during its first two-and-a-half decades, though it subsequently felt sufficiently secure to make substantive concessions to ethnoregional aspirations—that is, to those segments who had supported its wartime struggle for power from ethnic rather than social-revolutionary motivations. (A much earlier, premodern, though nevertheless possibly apropos example of the more frequent evolution of this type of situation would be Cromwell's turning against his erstwhile Scottish allies in the second phase of the British civil war, after their joint defeat of the royal regime by 1648. His actions, too, stemmed from a perceived need to consolidate the revolution through political and administrative recentralization.)

Of course, the actual flow of historical events may deviate from this scenario of the revolution's consolidating its "grand" social-ideological goals via recentralization at the expense of its initial ethnic auxiliaries. The cost of first arousing ethnic expectations to mobilize disaffected ethnic groups into revolutionary momentum against an extant state apparatus and then reneging on these expectations can be high. Sometimes the repudiated and aggrieved ethnic energies and aspirations fester and feed on themselves below the surface, despite the revolutionary regime's claim to have solved the problem by reconciling all the state's ethnic groups to itself and to each other—as in the Soviet Union and earlier in France. Eventually they may reemerge above the surface—as is now indeed occurring in France with the resurgence of Breton, Corsican, Occitanian, Alsacian, and other manifestations of ethnoregional assertiveness two centuries after the supposed definitive triumph of Jacobin-republican revolutionary centralization. At other times nemesis strikes much more quickly. Thus in Iran and in the states of the Burma-Thailand-Cambodia-Laos-Vietnam region, current conflict among (1) the partisans of central social-ideological revolutionary regimes and movements, (2) affronted and politicized ethnic groups, and (3) the residual loyalists of old prerevolutionary regimes (a category now quiescent in Iran but active in the Southeast Asian states listed above) yields a generalized and apparently out-of-control complex of violence, stagnation, and political incapacity.[21]

In sum, the problematics of "ethnicity and the state" can be as troubling for revolutionary central state elites and for "grand" revolutionary movements as for status-quo central elites and conventional political leaders. Even within an ostensibly transnational and supraethnic ideological movement itself, these problematics are often corrosive. Thus East Central European and Chinese resentment against the Soviet Russian interpretation, appropriation, and domination of "proletarian and socialist internationalism" forced the partial desatellization and loosening of the Soviet bloc during the 1950s and 1960s. In the next decade, similar sentiments of ethnonational pride, particularism, and autonomy fueled the West European "Eurocommunist" challenge to Moscow's hegemony over and within the world Communist movement. And even within the USSR itself centrifugal ethnopolitical pressures strain against the central, *soi-disant* revolutionary system. Marxist internationalism remains as elusive as Christian or Muslim brotherhood and is subject to the same ethnopolitical stresses.

[21] Ibid., pp. 248–60.

Chapter Eight
CONCLUSION

1 · The focus of this study—a study intended to serve as a framework for further research and analysis—has been on the political dimension and the political-structural problematics of ethnicity. The psychological and cultural dimensions, though also intrinsically important and interesting, have here been introduced only when this was deemed necessary to help explain political allegiances and political processes. Thus, for example, it was conceded that, under contemporary conditions of rapid change, intrusive yet remote state apparatuses, weak functional-interest groups, and diluted political consensus, people often cleave to, or rediscover, or even invent, their ethnicity—putatively rooted in "primordial" bonds—for personal identification, emotional security, and communal anchorage. But our focus was never on such ethnic identities or ethnocultural loyalties per se but always on their possible (yet never inevitable) politicization into public issues and conflicts that require political adjustment and regulation or else eventuate in violence. Furthermore, this study has consistently specified that the parties and actors engaged in this politicization of ethnic solidarities and ethnic categories and in the resultant competition for the "terminal" loyalty of individuals are not only the

emblematic ethnic groups and their leaderships but also the central state apparatus and its elite. Indeed, the ethnic dimension of politics and the political dimension of ethnicity have become a major and nagging concern for the central elites of multiethnic states, who appreciate that sheer and mere pragmatic effectiveness in the mobilization and allocation of material resources does not suffice to earn legitimacy for their states and regimes unless they also come to ideological and institutional terms with politicized ethnicity.

Probing for the reasons why ethnicity can be so readily politicized, it was suggested that, in addition to the psychological and cultural sustenance that it supplies and on which it draws, ethnicity—or, more accurately, allegiance to organized ethnic groups—can be instrumentally advantageous in the competition and struggle for power, prestige, authority, position, wealth, and income. Thus, whereas ethnicity is not necessarily or inevitably politicized in all historical eras and under all social conditions, it is likely to become so (1) if the patterned correlation among ethnic categories, socioeconomic categories, and political-power distributions is such as to generate systems of structured interethnic inequality and (2) if those with a conscious interest in maintaining or changing these existing patterns, distributions, and structures determine that it would be instrumentally useful to them to mobilize ethnicity from a psychological or cultural or social datum into a political resource and lever of action. Transitional (modernizing) and modern multiethnic societies present optimal conditions for this translation of ethnicity into the political dimension.

It is therefore insufficient—though partially correct—to explain the persistence and even the revival of ethnicity into and in the modern era as reflecting a primal "need to belong" to supposedly more enduring, more nearly comprehensive, more organic, more supportive psycho-cultural collectivities than the admittedly secular, specific, functional, utilitarian ones generated in modern societies around the foci of profession, occupation, legal claim, and other rational interests. Such an explanation must be amplified and extended to incorporate also the perception that to politicize ethnicity is no less instrumental and rational a mode of interest-assertion than the organization of these other types of voluntary, albeit impersonal, groups and entities is. Indeed, precisely in this rational and instrumental component of politicized ethnicity lies the possibility of reconciling it with loyalty to a multiethnic state. This study has explored some institutional programs and negotiating practices that might achieve such a reconciliation and permit the coexistence of political allegiance to ethnic group on the one hand and to multiethnic state on the other, despite the strains and even conflicts generated by their respective claims. This is basically a difficult but not *a priori* insoluble problem of regulating competing interests, respecting different identities, and—hardest of all—adjusting political wills.

But the perception of interest may also suggest the opposite—a repudiation of reconciliation and the honing of ethnic militancy against an ostensibly oppressive state and its allegedly hostile dominant group. A newly emergent social stratum within a traditionally subordinate ethnic group may instrumentally serve its particular interests by radicalizing and politicizing the entire group toward such militantly resurgent ethnonationalism—as their freshly assertive, professionally educated, "new" middle classes and intelligentsias are currently attempting to do among the Québécois, the Welsh, the Scots, the several ethnoregions of France, and elsewhere.[1] And while this latter political stance is likely to be asserted in more emotionally resonant psycho-culturalist rhetorical images than is the former,

[1] Pious, "Canada and the Crisis of Quebec," pp. 55–58; Khleif, "Language as Identity," pp. 352–53; Esman, "Scottish Nationalism," and Beer, "Social Class of Ethnic Activists," both in Esman, ed., *Ethnic Conflict in the Western World*, respectively pp. 262–63 and 150–58; Weiner, *Sons of the Soil*, passim.

reconcilianist strategy, it is not necessarily any less rational or calculated a pursuit of perceived interest.

Neither the reconcilianist nor the militant strategy recommendation by an ethnic subelite or would-be subelite is a mere or a deliberate smokescreen of ethnic politics behind which and through which such a stratum pursues only its own narrower "class" interests. More likely and more frequently, such a subelite authentically believes its particular grievances and aspirations to be utterly congruent with those of its ethnic group as a whole. While it does not deny that it serves itself by pressing its preferred political strategy on the entire group and exhorting group solidarity behind its recommendations, it is also sincerely and plausibly confident that the group as a whole is thereby served best. After all, both the subelite stratum and the group as a whole would lose, in psychological, cultural, and political coinage, if the former were to pursue its particular interests by deserting the ethnic group; far better for both if the subelite raises itself through improving the group's general political and social position while simultaneously using, maintaining, and strengthening its links to the group. And the ethnic group's lower strata and classes are, indeed, often persuaded that their security, welfare, and expectations are better served and enhanced by such intraethnic cohesion than by transethnic class solidarity.

Even if and where this claimed commonality of an ethnic group's fate is statistically dubious, that is, even when socioeconomic change impacts quite differently and differentially on various strata and classes of an ethnic group, nevertheless the ideology of politicized ethnicity often succeeds in maintaining the political cohesiveness of the ethnic group—be it a dominant or a subordinate one. This is not to be explained simply as an example of "perceptions" outweighing "objective facts"[2] (though

[2] Kuper, "Theories of Revolution," pp. 57–58.

that is undoubtedly often the case) but of an "objectively" real political interest in ethnic-group solidarity having been forged by the politicization of ethnicity in the context of structured interethnic inequality in resource allocations and power distributions. Once this process of politicization has risen above a certain threshold, then the psychological, cultural, and social reservoirs on which it originally drew serve to redouble and to sustain it.

This does not mean that all ethnic groups politicize themselves to the same levels of intensity. Nor do they formulate their self-images with the same degree of ideological consciousness. (Nor, of course, do all individuals within an ethnic group identify themselves in equal measure with that group.) Politicized ethnicity is a matter of scaled degrees; it is a variable.[3] Some groups engage in secessionist guerrilla warfare; others only sponsor an annual ceremonial folk festival. Some groups have honed highly articulated theories of their several collective histories, cultural heritages, and political aspirations, while others are only tenuously and incipiently self-aware as groups. Occasional ethnic groups may be highly conscious and protective of their cultures and yet still eschew recourse to the overt political arena in defense and assertion of those cultures (for example, Hutterites in the United States, Tunisian Jews in Israel). Or the reverse situation may pertain: ethnic groups may be intensely politicized while their specific ethnocultural heritages evanesce (chapter 7, section 3). But, all these variations and degrees notwithstanding, the general and overall tendency of the current era is toward the politicization of ethnicity. And this tendency is universal in the sense that it manifests itself in all types of systems and states—modern and developing, capitalist, communist, and socialist, centralistic and federalistic, large and small, old and new.

[3] Abner Cohen, "Introduction," to his edited volume *Urban Ethnicity*, p. XIV; McKay and Lewins, "Ethnicity and Ethnic Group," pp. 420–22.

2 · Many observers and analysts regret this contemporary politicization of ethnicity. Some judge it to be a deplorable anachronism and a deceptive exercise in so-called false consciousness, in obscuring "objective facts" (that is, class) with manipulated "perceptions" (to recall a pair of terms from the preceding subsection). Others view it as the product of a massive failure of nerve by a disillusioned and deracinated intelligentsia fleeing from the secular, rationalistic, and therefore admittedly unsettling values of modernity to which it was formally educated back into a self-indulgent romanticism that falsely touts the putatively primordial ethnic group as supposedly more "authentic," "natural," and "supportive" than the allegedly depersonalized and homogenized contemporary mass society with its alien and bureaucratized state. By stipulating such a bogus dichotomy—these critics charge—the contemporary intelligentsia has once again committed *trahison des clercs* and pandered to our world's most atavistic, insular, unscientific, and chaotic tendencies.[4] Still other critics elaborate these indictments into an itemized charge-sheet of the reactionary developments that are allegedly nurtured by the current deliberate politicization of ethnicity in the developed world, to wit:

1. Under the cloak of its professedly egalitarian and democratic aims, politicized ethnicity feeds the regressive temptation to render invidious judgments about groups of people on the basis of their phenotypical, religious, and other cultural differences—differences that should be politically irrelevant but cannot be so in an atmosphere of overheated ethnic consciousness.

2. It blunts the search for the causes of class inequalities and the urge to correct them. Instead, it offers the spurious compensation of ethnic pride for poverty, low status, and powerlessness.

[4] Kedourie, *Nationalism*, passim.

3. By encouraging particularistic group values and solidarities, the politicization of ethnicity devalues universalistic norms and discourages a truly open and democratic opportunity-system.

4. Its ideologization of ethnic groups relegitimates ascription and delegitimates mobility based on individual achievement. This intimidates individuals of a tender ethnic conscience into premature identity foreclosure and resignation from mobility options and corrupts other, more ambitious ones into adopting calculated career strategies predicated on an opportunistic exploitation of ethnicity.

5. The claim by the politicizers of ethnicity that they are protecting and ensuring societal diversity is specious, for their insistence on diversity by descent groups actually subverts the democratically more desirable pattern of diversity by individual choice and free association. Furthermore, this claim probably screens a fear of natural attrition from the ethnic descent groups through defection by talented and mobile individuals. Finally, it refuses to face the uncomfortable fact that not all ethnic descent groups merit survival as groups; some of them encapsulate cultures that treat their members inhumanely or are irrelevant to the future.

6. Societal resources and energies being limited, those that are expended on subsidizing ethnic institutions and politicizing ethnic groups are deflected and subtracted from more rational, more scientific, more universalistic, and more progressive priorities.

7. The politicization of ethnicity generates, in style and substance, a politics of absolute, uncompromisable end-values that subverts civic order. Its rhetoric and its emotional tone are suffused with images of collective anxiety, moralism, and violence (for example, "defiled homeland," "historic deprivation," "stolen rights," "threat of annihilation," "genocide," "revenge").

Hence interethnic conflicts are more prone than other types of social-group conflicts to eventuate in actual, gratuitous physical violence.[5]

These normative strictures are overdrawn and unconvincing. Several are themselves vulnerable to the *tu-quoque* riposte of screening hidden agendas and postulating false dichotomies, such as they charge against the politicization of ethnicity. Thus, for example, norms that are purported to be rational, secular, and universalistic (in contradistinction to the supposedly parochial and particularistic ethnic ones) are often a value-screen legitimating the power and rationalizing the interests of the society's ethnic dominants. Furthermore, the inflated ideologization of individualism and of a supposedly utterly free individual choice mistakenly insinuates that individual autonomy is incompatible with group allegiance (including descent-group allegiance) and ignores the reality that even the most autonomous and free individual sustains his sense of personal identity, worth, survival, and continuity through belonging to meaningful social groups. There is no good reason why the Apollonian exhortation to the would-be rational and free man, "know thyself," should exclude knowledge of his ethnicity and identification with his ethnic group. And while there is indeed a contingent, but by no means inevitable, danger that the politicization and ideologization of ethnicity might obscure the analysis and correction of class inequalities, it is, after all, a historical fact that the preoccupation with economic classes and material production in classic social science either blindly rationalized or occasionally even deliberately celebrated the flattening of ethnic cultures and the exploitation or destruction of ethnic communities. Hence neither of these two traditions of theory-and-praxis

[5] Porter, "Ethnic Pluralism in Canadian Perspective," pp. 288–304; Patterson, *Ethnic Chauvinism*, passim, and, by the same author, "Hidden Dangers in the Ethnic Revival," *The New York Times*, February 20, 1978, Op-Ed page; Devereux, "Ethnic Identity," pp. 42–70.

can validly claim a monopoly on concern for correcting historic injustice in the world. And while both ethnic conflict and class conflict can degenerate into violence, both have also shown themselves to be manageable short of violence.

Beyond such retorts to specific charges levied against the politicization of ethnicity, one questions the critics' general indictment that the whole phenomenon is a sort of destructive hoax invented and inflicted on modern society by an intellectually lazy and morally cowardly intelligentsia. While this study has repeatedly indicated the crucial role of intellectual (as well as other) elites in mobilizing ethnic categories into politicized, self-conscious, assertive ethnic groups (for example, in chapters 1, 4, and 5), it has throughout balanced the significance of that volitional input with an emphasis on the historical, structural, and systemic factors that have of late come to facilitate the politicization of ethnicity even in developed states (in chapters 2, 3, and 7). Thus, to assign exclusive responsibility for resurgent politicized ethnicity in the modern world to the intelligentsia is to blame (or credit) it with too much. The charge erroneously implies that, but for this gratuitous volitional intervention, the natural systemic and structural tendency of modern historical development would be to erode ethnopolitical allegiances.

But no type of contemporary society, be it capitalist, socialist, or developing, supports this inference of an allegedly natural tendency for modernization to undermine ethnic identification and bonds. Nor does the proliferation of science, technology, and literacy do so with any sustained and consistent propensity. True, some local identities and loyalties are dissolved and fused into larger ones in the early stages of modernization, with its revolutionary productive, scientific, technological, cultural, psychological, and political impacts. But in subsequent stages, middle-level ethnic groups in all types of societies become increasingly resistant to further assimilative pressures, suspecting that the modernist, scientific, cosmopolitan images in which such pressures are garbed often really veil the interests and norms of the dominant ethnic groups, with headstart advantages, in their several states. And this resistance of the ethnic groups to such assimilative pressures is usually successful because, paradoxically, the very same modern state apparatus that is the vehicle for the pressure also supplies the instruments for resisting it (chapter 7, section 2). Hence the possibility and the challenge to devise political arrangements that might accommodate both the integrative requirements of states and the survivalist interests of ethnic groups.

Politicized ethnicity in the modern world is problematic and ambivalent. It has served as a vehicle for aggression, oppression, and imperialism, as well as a protective vessel against these hegemonial impulses. Ethnic groups that fear being overwhelmed by the forces of modernization and by dominant groups and central state apparatuses that embody those forces politicize themselves to resist, dialectically, the feared fate by harnessing the very forces that portend it. Politicized ethnicity therefore may appear to be a culturally conservative reaction against modernity and yet also promote structural change and redistribution of power. It can indeed be internally coercive toward individual members of the group and press or seduce them into a defensive constriction of their horizons, and yet it can also liberate them from a directionless anomie, expand their humaneness, and deepen their self-esteem. It can be suspicious and hostile or flexible and affirmative toward the "outside" world and other ethnic and nonethnic groups. It may enhance or restrict freedom and progress. It is potentially creative or destructive.

These moral and evaluational dilemmas impact on public policy-making in multiethnic states. Should state institutions sustain the claims of ethnic groups to a right to retain their members (and thus preserve their distinctiveness) through politico-administrative fiat and public organizational sanctions (as in Belgian and Québécois schooling policy)? Or is the state obliged to protect the freedom of individual choice (including the choice of forsaking the ethnic group) in such matters of sociocultural identification and affiliation? Or—intermediately—should the state provide incentives for continued individual affiliation to ethnic groups by subsidizing them (American Affirmative Action and "outreach" programs)? Should citizenship be held directly and individually or should it be juridically mediated through the citizen's ethnic group? Should the law be formally blind to ethnicity or take cognizance of it? Should public policy consciously aim at preserving or modifying prevailing structural distributions of power among the society's ethnic groups? How should the central state elite position the state apparatus vis-à-vis ethnic dominants and ethnic subordinates? (cf. chapter 3, section 2). Today, these questions pose themselves in an ambience where ethnic groups not only fear deliberately inimical policies by states and dominants (as was the situation before World War II) but also demand protection against the unplanned erosive effects of economic and historical trends upon their ethnic cultures and habitats.[6]

These, and similar, questions and issues ensure that the ethnic dimension of politics and the political dimension of ethnicity will be on the public-policy agenda of modern and modernizing states for some time to come. We need neither lament nor celebrate this projection—but should accept it and subsume it into our political analysis and planning for the intermediate future. And since politicized ethnicity can be shaped into a politics of interest-optimization and need not inevitably become a politics of uncompromisable absolute ends, it follows that

[6] Cf. Van Dyke, "Individual, State, and Ethnic Communities," pp. 343–69, and Thornberry, "Minority Rights," pp. 249–63.

many (though probably not all) conflictual claims of different ethnic groups vis-à-vis each other and vis-à-vis the state are adjustable and potentially compatible with civic order. The task of wise political leadership is to nurse this potentiality to fruition through astute selection and adaptation among the policy options that flow from this "rational" aspect of politicized ethnicity.

SELECTED BIBLIOGRAPHY

A. Books

Akzin, Benjamin. *State and Nation.* London: Hutchinson University Library, 1964.

Alcock, Antony E.; Taylor, Brian K.; Welton, John M., eds. *The Future of Cultural Minorities.* London: Macmillan, 1979.

Allardt, Erik. *Implications of the Ethnic Revival in Modern Industrialized Society.* Helsinki: Societas Scientiarum Fennica, 1979.

Barth, Fredrik, ed. *Ethnic Groups and Boundaries.* Boston: Little, Brown, 1969.

Bell, Wendell, and Freeman, Walter E., eds. *Ethnicity and Nation-Building.* Beverly Hills, Calif.: Sage, 1974.

Beqiraj, Mehmet. *Peasantry in Revolution.* Ithaca, N.Y.: Cornell Research Papers in International Studies, Vol. 5, 1966.

Bertelsen, Judy S., ed. *Nonstate Nations in International Politics: A Comparative System Analysis.* New York: Praeger, 1977.

Birch, Anthony H. *Political Integration and Disintegration in the British Isles.* London: George Allen and Unwin, 1977.

Bondurant, Joan V. *Conquest of Violence: The Gandhian Philosophy of Conflict.* rev. ed. Berkeley: University of California Press, 1969.

Brass, Paul R. *Language, Religion, and Politics in North India.* London: Cambridge University Press, 1974.

Buchheit, Lee C. *Secession: The Legitimacy of Self-Determination.* New Haven, Conn.: Yale University Press, 1978.

Cobban, Alfred. *The Nation State and National Self-Determination.* rev. ed. New York: Crowell, 1970.

Cohen, Abner, ed. *Urban Ethnicity.* London: Tavistock, 1974.

Coser, Lewis A., and Larsen, Otto N., eds. *The Uses of Controversy in Sociology.* New York: Free Press, 1976.

Dahl, Robert A. *Polyarchy: Participation and Opposition.* New Haven, Conn.: Yale University Press, 1971.

De Silva, K. M., ed. *Sri Lanka: A Survey.* Honolulu: University Press of Hawaii, 1971.

Despres, Leo A., ed. *Ethnicity and Resource Competition in Plural Societies.* The Hague: Mouton, 1975.

Deutsch, Karl W. *Nationalism and Social Communication.* 2nd ed. Cambridge, Mass.: MIT Press, 1966.

——. *Nationalism and Its Alternatives.* New York: Knopf, 1969.

Deutsch, Karl W., and Foltz, William J., eds. *Nation-Building.* New York: Atherton, 1966.

De Vos, George et al. *Socialization for Achievement: Essays on the Cultural Psychology of the Japanese.* Berkeley: University of California Press, 1973.

De Vos, George, and Romanucci-Ross, Lola, eds., *Ethnic Identity: Cultural Continuities and Change.* Palo Alto, Calif.: Mayfield, 1975.

Driedger, Leo, ed. *The Canadian Ethnic Mosaic: A Quest for Identity.* Toronto: McClelland and Stewart, 1978.

Eisenstadt, S. N., and Rokkan, Stein, eds. *Building States and Nations.* 2 vols. Beverly Hills, Calif.: Sage, 1973.

Elazar, Daniel J., ed. *Federalism and Political Integration.* Ramat Gan, Israel: Turtledove, 1979.

Emerson, Rupert. *From Empire to Nation: The Rise to Self-Assertion of Asian and African Peoples.* Cambridge, Mass.: Harvard University Press, 1960.

Enloe, Cynthia. *Ethnic Conflict and Political Development.* Boston: Little, Brown, 1973.

Esman, Milton J., ed. *Ethnic Conflict in the Western World.* Ithaca, N.Y.: Cornell University Press, 1977.

versity; Faculty of Political Science, Department of Sociology, doctoral dissertation, 1979.

Hechter, Michael. *Internal Colonialism.* Berkeley: University of California Press, 1975.

Heisler, Martin O., and Peters, B. Guy. *The Implications of Scarcity for the Management of Conflict in Multicultural Societies.* Glasgow: Centre for the Study of Public Policy of the University of Strathclyde, 1978.

Higham, John, ed. *Ethnic Leadership in America.* Baltimore: The Johns Hopkins University Press, 1978.

Hoetink, Harmannus. *Two Variants in Caribbean Race Relations.* London: Oxford University Press, 1967.

Holland, Stuart. *The Regional Problem.* London: Macmillan, 1976.

Inglehart, Ronald. *The Silent Revolution: Changing Values and Political Styles Among Western Publics.* Princeton, N.J.: Princeton University Press, 1977.

Isaacs, Harold R. *Idols of the Tribe: Group Identity and Political Change.* New York: Harper and Row, 1975.

——. *Power and Identity: Tribalism and World Politics.* New York: Foreign Policy Association; Headline Series, No. 246, October 1979.

Jackson, Robert. *Plural Societies and New States: A Conceptual Analysis.* Berkeley, Calif.: Institute of International Studies; Research Series, No. 30, 1977.

Jacobs, Jane. *The Question of Separatism: Quebec and the Struggle Over Sovereignty.* New York: Random House, 1980.

Johnston, Ray E., ed. *The Politics of Division, Partition, and Unification.* New York: Praeger, 1976.

Katz, Zev et al., eds. *Handbook of Major Soviet Nationalities.* New York: Free Press, 1975.

Katznelson, Ira. *Black Men, White Cities.* London: Oxford University Press, 1973.

Kedourie, Elie. *Nationalism.* London: Hutchinson University Library, 1960.

Kuper, Leo. *Race, Class, and Power.* Chicago: Aldine, 1975.

Kuper, Leo, ed. *Race, Science, and Society.* New York: Columbia University Press, 1975.

Etzioni, Amitai. *A Comparative Analysis of Complex Organiz* rev. and enl. ed. New York: Free Press, 1975.

Feldman, Elliot J., and Nevitte, Neil, eds. *The Future of America: Canada, the United States, and Quebec Nationalism.* bridge, Mass.: Harvard Studies in International Affair 42, 1979.

Fouques-Duparc, Jacques. *La Protection des minorites de r langue, et de religion.* Paris: Dalloz, 1922.

Francis, E. K. *Interethnic Relations: An Essay in Sociological* New York: Elsevier, 1976.

Geertz, Clifford, ed. *Old Societies and New States.* New Yorl Press, 1963.

——. *The Interpretation of Cultures.* New York: Basic Books

Gelfand, Donald E., and Lee, Russell D., eds. *Ethnic C and Power: A Cross-National Perspective.* New York: Wiley

Giles, Howard, ed. *Language, Ethnicity, and Intergroup R* London: Academic Press, 1977.

Glaser, Kurt, and Possony, Stefan T. *Victims of Politics: T of Human Rights.* New York: Columbia University Pres

Glazer, Nathan, and Moynihan, Daniel P., eds. *Ethnicit* bridge, Mass.: Harvard University Press, 1975.

Grant, Ronald M., and Wellhofer, E. Spencer, eds. *Nationalism, Multinational Corporations, and the Moder* Denver: University of Denver; Monograph Series in Affairs; Vol. 15, book 4, 1979.

Greeley, Andrew M. *Why Can't They Be Like Us?* Nev Dutton, 1971.

Grigulevich, I. R., and Kozlov, S. Y., eds. *Races and Contemporary Ethnic and Racial Problems.* Moscow: Publishers, 1974.

Grove, D. John. *The Race Vs. Ethnic Debate: A Cross- Analysis of Two Theoretical Approaches.* Denver: Univ Denver; Center on International Race Relations, 19

Hall, Raymond L., ed. *Ethnic Autonomy: Comparative* New York: Pergamon, 1979.

Halle, David. *America's "Working Man": Work, Home, an Among Blue-Collar Property Owners.* New York: Colun

Ladas, Stephen P. *The Exchange of Minorities: Bulgaria, Greece, and Turkey*. New York: Macmillan, 1932.

Lee, Danielle Juteau, ed. *Frontières ethniques en devenir*. Ottawa: Editions de l'Université d'Ottawa, 1979.

LeVine, Robert A., and Campbell, Donald T. *Ethnocentrism: Theories of Conflict, Ethnic Attitudes, and Group Behavior*. New York: Wiley, 1972.

Lijphart, Arend. *Democracy in Plural Societies: A Comparative Exploration*. New Haven, Conn.: Yale University Press, 1977.

Link, Werner, and Feld, Werner J., eds. *The New Nationalism: Implications for Transatlantic Relations*. New York: Pergamon, 1979.

Litt, Edgar. *Beyond Pluralism: Ethnic Politics in America*. Glenview, Ill.: Scott, Foresman, 1970.

Lubell, Samuel. *The Future of American Politics*. 2nd rev. ed. New York: Doubleday Anchor, 1955.

Macartney, C. A. *National States and National Minorities*. New York: Russell and Russell, 1968.

Mackie, J. A. C., ed. *The Chinese in Indonesia*. Honolulu: University Press of Hawaii, 1976.

Mazrui, Ali A. *Post-Imperial Fragmentation: The Legacy of Ethnic and Racial Conflict*. Denver: University of Denver; Center on International Race Relations, 1969.

Mill, John Stuart. *Considerations on Representative Government*. London: Routledge, 1904.

Mittelman, James H., and Marwah, Onkar S. *Asian Alien Pariahs: A Cross-Regional Perspective*. Denver: University of Denver; Center on International Race Relations, 1975.

Nairn, Tom. *The Break-Up of Britain: Crisis and Neo-Nationalism*. London: New Left Books, 1977.

Nakanishi, Don T. *In Search of a New Paradigm: Minorities in the Context of International Politics*. Denver: University of Denver; Center on International Race Relations, 1975.

Nordlinger, Eric A. *Conflict Regulation in Divided Societies*. Cambridge, Mass.: Harvard University Center for International Affairs; Occasional Papers, No. 29, 1972.

Obler, Jeffrey; Steiner, Jürg; Dierickx, Guido. *Decision-Making in Smaller Democracies: The Consociational "Burden"*. Beverly Hills, Calif.: Sage, 1977.

Patterson, Orlando. *Ethnic Chauvinism: The Reactionary Impulse*. New York: Stein and Day, 1977.

Psomiades, Harry J. *The Eastern Question: The Last Phase*. Thessaloniki: Institute for Balkan Studies, 1968.

Rabushka, Alvin, and Shepsle, Kenneth A. *Politics in Plural Societies*. Columbus, Ohio: Merrill, 1972.

Rhoodie, Nic, ed. *Intergroup Accommodation in Plural Societies*. London: Macmillan, 1978.

Richmond, Anthony H., ed. *Readings in Race and Ethnic Relations*. Oxford: Pergamon, 1972.

Ronen, Dov. *The Quest for Self-Determination*. New Haven, Conn.: Yale University Press, 1979.

Rose, Richard, and Urwin, Derek W. *Regional Differentiation and Political Unity in Western Nations*. Beverly Hills, Calif.: Sage, 1975.

Rothschild, Joseph. *Pilsudski's Coup d'Etat*. New York: Columbia University Press, 1966.

——. *East Central Europe Between the Two World Wars*. Seattle: University of Washington Press, 1974.

Said, Abdul A., ed. *Ethnicity and U.S. Foreign Policy*. New York: Praeger, 1977.

Said, Abdul A., and Simmons, Luiz R., eds. *Ethnicity In An International Context*. New Brunswick, N.J.: Transaction, 1976.

Schermerhorn, R. A. *Comparative Ethnic Relations*. New York: Random House, 1970.

Schoenberg, Harris O. *The Concept of "People" in the Principle of Self-Determination*. New York: Columbia University; Faculty of Political Science, Department of Political Science, doctoral dissertation, 1975.

Schweigler, Gebhard L. *National Consciousness in Divided Germany*. Beverly Hills, Calif.: Sage, 1975.

Shibutani, Tamotsu, and Kwan, Kian M. *Ethnic Stratification: A Comparative Approach*. New York: Macmillan, 1965.

Smith, Anthony D. *Theories of Nationalism*. New York: Harper and Row, 1972.

——. *Nationalism in the Twentieth Century*. Oxford: Robertson, 1979.

Smith, Anthony D., ed. *Nationalist Movements*. London: Macmillan, 1976.

Smith, Carol A., ed. *Regional Analysis*. 2 vols. New York: Academic Press, 1976.

Stone, John, ed. *Race, Ethnicity, and Social Change*. North Scituate, Mass.: Duxbury Press, 1977.

Suhrke, Astri, and Noble, Lela Garner, eds. *Ethnic Conflict in International Relations*. New York: Praeger, 1977.

Van Den Berghe, Pierre L. *Race and Ethnicity: Essays in Comparative Sociology*. New York: Basic Books, 1970.

Volkan, Vanik D. *Cyprus—War and Adaptation: A Psychoanalytic History of Two Ethnic Groups in Conflict*. Charlottesville: University Press of Virginia, 1979.

Wallman, Sandra, ed. *Ethnicity At Work*. London: Macmillan, 1979.

Weed, Perry L. *The White Ethnic Movement and Ethnic Politics*. New York: Praeger, 1973.

Weiner, Myron. *Sons of the Soil: Migration and Ethnic Conflict in India*. Princeton, N.J.: Princeton University Press, 1978.

Yinger, J. Milton, and Cutler, Stephen J., eds. *Major Social Issues: A Multidisciplinary View*. New York: Free Press, 1978.

Young, Crawford. *The Politics of Cultural Pluralism*. Madison: University of Wisconsin Press, 1976.

B. *Articles*

Abbott, George C. "Size, Viability, Nationalism, and Politico-Economic Development." *International Journal* 25, no. 1 (Winter 1969–70): 56–68.

Adekson, J. 'Bayo. "Ethnicity and Army Recruitment in Colonial Plural Societies." *Ethnic and Racial Studies* 2, no. 2 (April 1979): 151–65.

——. "Military Organization in Multi-Ethnically Segmented Societies." *Research in Race and Ethnic Relations* 1 (1979): 109–25.

Amersfoort, Hans van. "'Minority' As a Sociological Concept." *Ethnic and Racial Studies* 1, no. 2 (April 1978): 218–34.

Anderson, Malcolm. "The Rennaissance of Territorial Minorities in Western Europe." *West European Politics* 1, no. 2 (May 1978): 128–43.

Argyle, W. J. "Size and Scale as Factors in the Development of Nationalist Movements." In *Nationalist Movements*, edited by Anthony D. Smith, pp. 31–53. London: Macmillan, 1976.

Ashford, Douglas E. "Are Britain and France 'Unitary'?" *Comparative Politics* 9, no. 4 (July 1977): 483–99.

Ballard, Roger. "Ethnicity: Theory and Experience (A Review Article)." *New Community* 5, no. 3 (Autumn 1976): 196–202.

Beals, Ralph C. "The Rise and Decline of National Identity." *Canadian Review of Studies in Nationalism* 4, no. 2 (Spring 1977): 147–66.

Beckett, J. C. "Northern Ireland." *Journal of Contemporary History* 6, no. 1 (1971): 121–34.

Beer, William R. "The Social Class of Ethnic Activists in Contemporary France." In *Ethnic Conflict in the Western World*, edited by Milton J. Esman, pp. 143–58. Ithaca, N.Y.: Cornell University Press, 1977.

Begg, H. M., and Stewart, J. A. "The Nationalist Movement in Scotland." *Journal of Contemporary History* 6, no. 1 (1971): 135–52.

Bell, Daniel. "Ethnicity and Social Change." In *Ethnicity*, edited by Nathan Glazer and Daniel P. Moynihan, pp. 141–74. Cambridge, Mass.: Harvard University Press, 1975.

Berger, Suzanne. "Bretons, Basques, Scots, and Other European Nations." *Journal of Interdisciplinary History* 3, no. 1 (Summer 1972): 167–75.

——. "Bretons and Jacobins: Reflections on French Regional Ethnicity." In *Ethnic Conflict in the Western World*, edited by Milton J. Esman, pp. 159–78. Ithaca, N.Y.: Cornell University Press, 1977.

——. "Politics and Antipolitics in Western Europe in the Seventies." *Daedalus* 108, no. 1 (Winter 1979): 27–50.

Bialer, Seweryn. "The Soviet Political Elite and Internal Developments in the USSR." In *The Soviet Empire: Expansion and Détente*, edited by William E. Griffith, pp. 25–56. Lexington, Mass.: Lexington Books, 1976.

Birch, Anthony. "Minority Nationalist Movements and Theories of Political Integration." *World Politics* 30, no. 3 (April 1978): 325–44.

Blumer, Herbert. "Industrialisation and Race Relations." In *Industrialisation and Race Relations*, edited by Guy Hunter, pp. 220–53. London: Oxford University Press, 1965.

Bonacich, Edna. "A Theory of Ethnic Antagonism: The Split Labor Market." *American Sociological Review* 37, no. 5 (October 1972): 547–59.

——. "The Past, Present, and Future of Split Market Theory." *Research in Race and Ethnic Relations* 1 (1979): 17–64.

Borowiec, Walter A. "Perceptions of Ethnic Voters by Ethnic Politicians." *Ethnicity* 1, no. 3 (October 1974): 267–78.

Boulding, Elise. "Ethnic Separatism and World Development." In *Research in Social Movements, Conflicts and Change*, edited by Louis Kriesberg, vol. 2, pp. 259–81. Greenwich, Conn.: JAI Press, 1979.

Bram, Joseph. "Change and Choice in Ethnic Identification." *Transactions of the New York Academy of Sciences*, series 2, 28, no. 2 (December 1965): 242–48.

Brass, Paul R. "Ethnicity and Nationality Formation." *Ethnicity* 3, no. 3 (September 1976): 225–41.

Breton, Raymond. "The Structure of Relationships Between Ethnic Collectivities." In *The Canadian Ethnic Mosaic*, edited by Leo Driedger, pp. 55–73. Toronto: McClelland and Stewart, 1978.

Bryce-Laporte, Roy S. "On Models of Multiethnic Societies." In *Major Social Issues*, edited by J. Milton Yinger and Stephen J. Cutler, pp. 66–77. New York: Free Press, 1978.

Burgess, M. Elaine. "The Resurgence of Ethnicity: Myth or Reality?" *Ethnic and Racial Studies* 1, no. 3 (July 1978): 265–85.

Cho, Soon Sung. "The Changing Pattern of Asian International Relations: Prospects for the Unification of Korea." *Journal of International Affairs* 27, no. 2 (1973): 213–31.

Cloutier, Edouard. "Les Fondements Micro-Economiques du Nationalisme Canadien-Français: Une Hypothese." *Canadian Review of Studies in Nationalism* 2, no. 1 (Fall 1974): 145–47.

Connor, Walker. "Ethnonationalism in the First World: The Present in Historical Perspective." In *Ethnic Conflict in the Western World*, edited by Milton J. Esman, pp. 19–45. Ithaca, N.Y.: Cornell University Press, 1977.

——. "Nation-Building or Nation-Destroying?" *World Politics* 24, no. 3 (April 1972): 319–55.

——. "A Nation is a Nation is a State, is an Ethnic Group, is a. . . ." *Ethnic and Racial Studies* 1, no. 4 (October 1978): 377–400.

——. "The Politics of Ethnonationalism." *Journal of International Affairs* 27, no. 1 (1973): 1–21.

——. "Self-Determination: The New Phase." *World Politics* 20, no. 1 (October 1967): 30–53.

Connor, Walter D. "Social Change and Stability in Eastern Europe." *Problems of Communism* 26, no. 6 (November–December 1977): 16–32.

Corrado, Raymond R. "Nationalism and Communalism in Wales." *Ethnicity* 2, no. 4 (December 1975): 360–81.

Coulon, Christian. "French Political Science and Regional Diversity: A Strategy of Silence." *Ethnic and Racial Studies* 1, no. 1 (January 1978): 80–99.

Coulon, Christian. and Morin, Françoise. "Occitan Ethnicity and Politics." *Critique of Anthropology* 4, nos. 13 and 14 (Summer 1979): 105–22.

Cross, Malcolm. "Colonialism and Ethnicity." *Ethnic and Racial Studies* 1, no. 1 (January 1978): 37–59.

Daalder, Hans. "Building Consociational Nations." In *Building States and Nations*, edited by S. N. Eisenstadt and Stein Rokkan, vol. 2, pp. 14–31. Beverly Hills, Calif.: Sage, 1973.

——. "The Netherlands: Opposition in a Segmented Society." In *Political Oppositions in Western Democracies*, edited by Robert A. Dahl, pp. 188–236. New Haven, Conn.: Yale University Press, 1966.

Dahl, Robert. "Pluralism Revisited." *Comparative Politics* 10, no. 2 (January 1978): 191–203.

Da Silva, Milton M. "Modernization and Ethnic Conflict." *Comparative Politics* 7, no. 2 (January 1975): 227–51.

Das Gupta, J. "Ethnicity, Language Demands, and National Development in India." In *Ethnicity*, edited by Nathan Glazer and Daniel P. Moynihan, pp. 466–88. Cambridge, Mass.: Harvard University Press, 1975.

Dekmejian, Richard H. "Consociational Democracy in Crisis: The Case of Lebanon." *Comparative Politics* 10, no. 2 (January 1978): 251–65.

Devereux, George. "Ethnic Identity: Its Logical Foundations and Its Dysfunctions." In *Ethnic Identity*, edited by George De Vos and Lola Romanucci-Ross, pp. 42–70. Palo Alto, Calif.: Mayfield, 1975.

De Vos, George. "Ethnic Pluralism: Conflict and Accommodation." In *Ethnic Identity*, edited by George De Vos and Lola Romanucci-Ross, pp. 5–41. Palo Alto, Calif.: Mayfield, 1975.

——. "Selective Permeability and Reference Group Sanctioning: Psychocultural Continuities in Role Degradation." In *Major Social Issues*, edited by J. Milton Yinger and Stephen J. Cutler, pp. 7–24. New York: Free Press, 1978.

De Vos, George. and Romanucci-Ross, Lola. "Ethnicity: Vessel of Meaning and Emblem of Contrast." In *Ethnic Identity*, edited by George De Vos and Lola Romanucci-Ross, pp. 363–90. Palo Alto, Calif.: Mayfield, 1975.

Donoghue, John. "The Social Persistence of an Outcaste Group." In *Japan's Invisible Race*, edited by George De Vos and Hiroshi Wagatsuma, pp. 137–52. Berkeley: University of California Press, 1967.

Duchacek, Ivo. "Antagonistic Cooperation: Territorial and Ethnic Communities." *Publius* 7, no. 4 (Fall 1977): 3–29.

Edelstein, Joel C. "Pluralist and Marxist Perspectives on Ethnicity and Nation-Building." In *Ethnicity and Nation-Building*, edited by Wendell Bell and Walter E. Freeman, pp. 45–57. Beverly Hills, Calif.: Sage, 1974.

Enloe, Cynthia. "Ethnicity, Bureaucracy, and State-Building in Africa and Latin America." *Ethnic and Racial Studies* 1, no. 3 (July 1978): 336–51.

——. "Internal Colonialism, Federalism, and Alternative State-Development Strategies." *Publius* 7, no. 4 (Fall 1977): 145–60.

——. "The Issue Saliency of the Military-Ethnic Connection." *Comparative Politics* 10, no. 2 (January 1978): 267–85.

——. "The Military Uses of Ethnicity." *Millennium* 4, no. 3 (Winter 1975–76): 220–34.

——. "Multinational Corporations in the Making and Unmaking of Ethnic Groups." In *Ethno-Nationalism, Multinational Corporations, and the Modern State*, edited by Ronald M. Grant and E. Spencer Wellhofer, pp. 9–32. Denver: University of Denver; Monograph Series in World Affairs, 1979.

——. "Police and Military in the Resolution of Ethnic Conflict." *The Annals* 433 (September 1977): 137–49.

Esman, Milton J. "The Management of Communal Conflict." *Public Policy* 21, no. 1 (Winter 1973): 49–78.

——. "Perspectives on Ethnic Conflict in Industrialized Societies." In *Ethnic Conflict in the Western World*, edited by Milton J. Esman, pp. 371–90. Ithaca, N.Y.: Cornell University Press, 1977.

——. "Scottish Nationalism, North Sea Oil, and the British Response." In *Ethnic Conflict in the Western World*, edited by Milton J. Esman, pp. 251–86. Ithaca, N.Y.: Cornell University Press, 1977.

Feld, Werner J. "Subnational Regionalism and the European Community." *Orbis* 18, no. 4 (Winter 1975): 1176–92.

Fisher, Maxine P. "Creating Ethnic Identity: Asian Indians in the New York City Area." *Urban Anthropology* 7, no. 3 (1978): 271–85.

Foltz, William J. "Ethnicity, Status, and Conflict." In *Ethnicity and Nation-Building*, edited by Wendell Bell and Walter E. Freeman, pp. 103–16. Beverly Hills, Calif.: Sage, 1974.

Forbes, H.D. "Two Approaches to the Psychology of Nationalism." *Canadian Review of Studies in Nationalism* 2, no. 1 (Fall 1974): 172–81.

Forsythe, Dennis. "Race Relations from Liberal, Black, and Marxist Perspectives." *Research in Race and Ethnic Relations* 1 (1979): 65–85.

Freedman, Maurice. "Ethnic Puzzles." *New Community* 5, no. 3 (Autumn 1976): 181–88.

Galtung, Johan. "A Structural Theory of Imperialism." *Journal of Peace Research* 8, no. 2 (1971): 81–117.

Gans, Herbert J. "Symbolic Ethnicity: The Future of Ethnic Groups and Cultures in America." In *On the Making of Americans: Essays in Honor of David Riesman*, edited by Herbert J. Gans et al., pp. 193–220. Philadelphia: University of Pennsylvania Press, 1979.

Glass, Harold E. "Consensus and Opposition in Switzerland: A Neglected Consideration." *Comparative Politics* 10, no. 3 (April 1978): 361–72.

——. "Ethnic Diversity, Elite Accommodation and Federalism in Switzerland." *Publius* 7, no. 4 (Fall 1977): 31–48.

Glazer, Nathan, and Moynihan, Daniel P. "Why Ethnicity?" *Commentary* 58, no. 4 (October 1974): 33–39.

Goering, John M. "The Emergence of Ethnic Interests: A Case of Serendipity." *Social Forces* 49, no. 3 (March 1971): 379–84.

Gordon, Milton M. "Toward a General Theory of Racial and Ethnic Group Relations." In *Ethnicity*, edited by Nathan Glazer and Daniel P. Moynihan, pp. 84–110. Cambridge, Mass.: Harvard University Press, 1975.

Grabb, Edward G. "Subordinate Group Status and Perceived Chances for Success: The French Canadian Case." *Ethnicity* 6, no. 3 (September 1979): 268–80.

Grove, D. John. "A Test of the Ethnic Equalization Hypothesis: A Cross-National Study." *Ethnic and Racial Studies* 1, no. 2 (April 1978): 175–95.

——. "Ethnic Socioeconomic Redistribution." *Comparative Politics* 12, no. 1 (October 1979): 87–98.

Haaland, Gunnar. "Economic Determinants in Ethnic Processes." In *Ethnic Groups and Boundaries*, edited by Fredrik Barth, pp. 58–73. Boston: Little, Brown, 1969.

Hagy, James W. "René Lévesque and the Quebec Separatists." *Western Political Quarterly* 24, no. 1 (March 1971): 55–58.

Hah, Chong-do, and Martin, Jeffrey. "Toward a Synthesis of Conflict and Integration Theories of Nationalism." *World Politics* 27, no. 3 (April 1975): 361–86.

Halsey, A. H. "Ethnicity: A Primordial Social Bond?" *Ethnic and Racial Studies* 1, no. 1 (January 1978): 124–28.

Hanhardt, Arthur M., Jr. "Socialization and Integration Strategies: The Case of the Federal Republic of Germany and the German Democratic Republic." In *The Politics of Division, Partition, and Unification*, edited by Ray E. Johnston, pp. 40–54. New York: Praeger, 1976.

Hannerz, Ulf. "Ethnicity and Opportunity in Urban America." In *Urban Ethnicity*, edited by Abner Cohen, pp. 37–76. London: Tavistock, 1974.

Hargrove, Erwin C. "Nationality, Values, and Change: Young Elites in French Canada." *Comparative Politics* 2, no. 3 (April 1970): 473–99.

Hechter, Michael. "Ethnicity and Industrialization: On the Proliferation of the Cultural Division of Labor." *Ethnicity* 3, no. 3 (September 1976): 214–24.

——. "Group Formation and the Cultural Division of Labor." *American Journal of Sociology* 84, no. 2 (September 1978): 293–318.

——. "Towards a Theory of Ethnic Change." *Politics and Society* 2, no. 1 (Fall 1971): 21–45.

Hechter, Michael. and Levi, Margaret. "The Comparative Analysis of Ethnoregional Movements." *Ethnic and Racial Studies* 2, no. 3 (July 1979): 260–74.

Heisler, Martin O. "Managing Ethnic Conflict in Belgium." *The Annals* 433 (September 1977): 32–46.

Henderson, Gregory. "Korea: The Preposterous Division." *Journal of International Affairs* 27, no. 2 (1973): 204–12.

Hill, Robert F., and Stein, Howard F. "Ethnic Stratification and Social Unrest in Contemporary Eastern Europe and America." *Nationalities Papers* 1, no. 1 (Fall 1972): 1–28.

——. "The New Ethnicity and the White Ethnic in the United

States." *Canadian Review of Studies in Nationalism* 1, no. 1 (Fall 1973): 81–105.

Hoetink, Harmannus. "Resource Competition, Monopoly and Socioracial Diversity." In *Ethnicity and Resource Competition in Plural Societies*, edited by Leo A. Despres, pp. 9–25. The Hague: Mouton, 1975.

Horowitz, Donald L. "Direct, Displaced, and Cumulative Ethnic Aggression." *Comparative Politics* 6, no. 1 (October 1973): 1–16.

——. "Ethnic Identity." In *Ethnicity*, edited by Nathan Glazer and Daniel P. Moynihan, pp. 111–40. Cambridge, Mass.: Harvard University Press, 1975.

——. "Three Dimensions of Ethnic Politics." *World Politics* 23, no. 2 (January 1971): 232–44.

Horowitz, Irving Louis. "Ethnic Politics and U.S. Foreign Policy." In *Ethnicity and U.S. Foreign Policy*, edited by Abdul A. Said, pp. 178–80. New York: Praeger, 1977.

Hudson, Michael C. "Democracy and Social Mobilization in Lebanese Politics." *Comparative Politics* 1, no. 2 (January 1969): 245–63.

Huntington, Samuel P. "The Change to Change: Modernization, Development, and Politics." *Comparative Politics* 3, no. 3 (April 1971): 283–322.

——. "Political Development and Political Decay." *World Politics* 17, no. 3 (April 1965): 386–430.

Isajiw, Wsevolod W. "Definitions of Ethnicity." *Ethnicity* 1, no. 2 (July 1974): 111–24.

——. "Olga in Wonderland: Ethnicity in a Technological Society." In *The Canadian Ethnic Mosaic*, edited by Leo Driedger, pp. 29–39. Toronto: McClelland and Stewart, 1978.

Kasfir, Nelson. "Explaining Ethnic Political Participation." *World Politics* 31, no. 3 (April 1979): 365–88.

Katzenstein, Peter J. "Ethnic Political Conflict in South Tyrol." In *Ethnic Conflict in the Western World*, edited by Milton J. Esman, pp. 287–323. Ithaca, N.Y.: Cornell University Press, 1977.

Katznelson, Ira. "Comparative Studies of Race and Ethnicity." *Comparative Politics* 5, no. 1 (October 1972): 135–54.

Keech, William R. "Linguistic Diversity and Political Conflict." *Comparative Politics* 4, no. 3 (April 1972): 387–404.

Keyes, Charles F. "Towards a New Formulation of the Concept of Ethnic Group." *Ethnicity* 3, no. 3 (September 1976): 202–13.

Khleif, Bud B. "Language as Identity: Toward an Ethnography of Welsh Nationalism." *Ethnicity* 6, no. 4 (December 1979): 346–57.

Kihl, Young Whan. "International Integration Theories and Problems of Unifying A Divided Nation: The Case of Korea." In *The Politics of Division, Partition, and Unification*, edited by Ray E. Johnston, pp. 55–66. New York: Praeger, 1976.

Klein, George. "The Role of Ethnic Politics in the Czechoslovak Crisis of 1968 and the Yugoslav Crisis of 1971." *Studies in Comparative Communism* 8, no. 4 (Winter 1975): 339–69.

Krejci, Jaroslav. "Ethnic Problems in Europe." In *Contemporary Europe*. 2d ed., edited by Salvador Giner and Margaret S. Archer, pp. 124–71. London: Routledge and Kegan Paul, 1978.

Kristof, Ladis K. "The State-Idea, the National Idea, and the Image of the Fatherland." *Orbis* 11, no. 1 (Spring 1967): 238–55.

Kuper, Leo. "On Theories of Race Relations." In *Ethnicity and Nation-Building*, edited by Wendell Bell and Walter E. Freeman, pp. 19–28. Beverly Hills, Calif.: Sage, 1974.

——. "Race, Class, and Power: Some Comments on Revolutionary Change." *Comparative Studies in Society and History* 14, no. 4 (September 1972): 400–21.

——. "Theories of Revolution and Race Relations." In *Ethnic Conflicts and Power: A Cross-National Perspective*, edited by Donald E. Gelfand and Russell D. Lee, pp. 48–66. New York: Wiley, 1973.

Leff, Nathaniel H. "Bengal, Biafra, and the Bigness Bias." *Foreign Policy*, no. 3 (Summer 1971): 129–39.

Leggon, Cheryl B. "Theoretical Perspectives on Race and Ethnic

Relations: A Socio-Historical Approach." *Research in Race and Ethnic Relations* 1 (1979): 1–16.

Levine, Marc V. "Institution Design and the Separatist Impulse: Quebec and the Antebellum American South." *The Annals* 433 (September 1977): 60–72.

Lieberson, Stanley. "Stratification and Ethnic Groups." In *Readings in Race and Ethnic Relations*, edited by Anthony H. Richmond, pp. 199–209. Oxford: Pergamon, 1972.

Lijphart, Arend. "Political Theories and the Explanation of Ethnic Conflict in the Western World: Falsified Predictions and Plausible Postdictions." In *Ethnic Conflict in the Western World*, edited by Milton J. Esman, pp. 46–64. Ithaca, N.Y.: Cornell University Press, 1977.

Linz, Juan. "Early State-Building and Late Peripheral Nationalisms Against the State: The Case of Spain." In *Building States and Nations*, edited by S. N. Eisenstadt and Stein Rokkan, vol. 2, pp. 32–116. Beverly Hills, Calif.: Sage, 1973.

Lipsky, Michael. "Protest as a Political Resource." *American Political Science Review* 62, no. 4 (December 1968): 1144–58.

Lorwin, Val R. "Belgium: Religion, Class, and Language in National Politics." In *Political Oppositions in Western Democracies*, edited by Robert A. Dahl, pp. 147–87. New Haven, Conn.: Yale University Press, 1966.

——. "Segmented Pluralism." *Comparative Politics* 3, no. 2 (January 1971): 141–75.

Ludz, Peter C. "The SED's Concept of Nation: Deviations and Political Meanings." *Canadian Review of Studies in Nationalism* 4, no. 2 (Spring 1977): 206–24.

Lustick, Ian. "Stability in Deeply Divided Societies: Consociationalism versus Control." *World Politics* 31, no. 3 (April 1979): 325–44.

McBeath, Gerald A. "Political Behavior of Ethnic Leaders." *Comparative Politics* 10, no. 3 (April 1978): 393–417.

McKay, James, and Lewins, Frank. "Ethnicity and the Ethnic Group: A Conceptual Analysis and a Reformulation." *Ethnic and Racial Studies* 1, no. 4 (October 1978): 412–27.

McNeill, William H. "On National Frontiers: Ethnic Homogeneity and Pluralism." In *Small Comforts for Hard Times: Humanists on Public Policy*, edited by Michael Mooney and Florian Stuber, pp. 207–19. New York: Columbia University Press, 1977.

McRoberts, Kenneth. "Internal Colonialism: The Case of Quebec." *Ethnic and Racial Studies* 2, no. 3 (July 1979): 293–318.

——. "Social Communication and Mass Nationalism." *Canadian Review of Studies in Nationalism* 2, no. 1 (Fall 1974): 148–51.

Mansbach, Richard W. "The Scottish National Party: A Revised Political Profile." *Comparative Politics* 5, no. 2 (January 1973): 185–210.

Melson, Robert, and Wolpe, Howard. "Modernization and the Politics of Communalism: A Theoretical Perspective." *American Political Science Review* 64, no. 4 (December 1970): 1112–30.

Miller, Abraham. "Ethnicity and Political Behavior: A Review of Theories and an Attempt at Reformulation." *Western Political Quarterly* 24, no. 3 (September 1971): 483–500.

Morgan, Kenneth O. "Welsh Nationalism: The Historical Background." *Journal of Contemporary History* 6, no. 1 (1971): 153–72.

Mughan, Anthony. "Modernisation, Deprivation, and the Distribution of Power Resources: Towards a Theory of Ethnic Conflict." *New Community* 5, no. 4 (Spring-Summer 1977): 360–70.

Nelson, Dale C. "Ethnicity and Socioeconomic Status as Sources of Participation: The Case for Ethnic Political Culture." *American Political Science Review* 73, no. 4 (December 1979): 1024–38.

Newman, William M. "Theoretical Perspectives for the Analysis of Social Pluralism." In *The Canadian Ethnic Mosaic*, edited by Leo Driedger, pp. 40–54. Toronto: McClelland and Stewart, 1978.

Noel, Donald L. "A Theory of the Origin of Ethnic Stratification." *Social Problems* 16, no. 2 (Fall 1968): 157–72.

Parel, Anthony J. "Humanism and Nationalism." *Canadian Review of Studies in Nationalism* 4, no. 1 (Fall 1976): 1–14.

Parenti, Michael. "Ethnic Politics and the Persistence of Ethnic Identification." *American Political Science Review* 61, no. 3 (September 1967): 717–26.

Parsons, Talcott. "Some Theoretical Considerations on the Nature and Trends of Change of Ethnicity." In *Ethnicity*, edited by Nathan Glazer and Daniel P. Moynihan, pp. 53–83. Cambridge, Mass.: Harvard University Press, 1975.

Patterson, Orlando. "Context and Choice in Ethnic Allegiance: A Theoretical Framework and a Caribbean Case Study." In *Ethnicity*, edited by Nathan Glazer and Daniel P. Moynihan, pp. 305–49. Cambridge, Mass.: Harvard University Press, 1975.

Payne, Stanley. "Catalan and Basque Nationalism." *Journal of Contemporary History* 6, no. 1 (1971): 15–51.

Petersen, William. "A Comparison of a Racial and of a Language Subnation: American Negroes and Flemish." *Ethnicity* 3, no. 2 (June 1976): 145–73.

——. "On the Subnations of Western Europe." In *Ethnicity*, edited by Nathan Glazer and Daniel P. Moynihan, pp. 177–208. Cambridge, Mass.: Harvard University Press, 1975.

Pettigrew, Thomas F. "Three Issues in Ethnicity: Boundaries, Deprivations, and Perceptions." In *Major Social Issues*, edited by J. Milton Yinger and Stephen J. Cutler, pp. 25–49. New York: Free Press, 1978.

Pinard, Maurice. "Communal Segmentation and Communal Conflict: A Summary Presentation." *Canadian Review of Studies in Nationalism* 2, no. 2 (Spring 1975): 361–63.

Pious, Richard. "Canada and the Crisis of Quebec." *Journal of International Affairs* 27, no. 1 (1973): 53–65.

Plax, Martin. "On Group Behavior and the Ethnic Factor in Politics." *Ethnicity* 1, no. 3 (October 1974): 295–316.

——. "Towards a Redefinition of Ethnic Politics." *Ethnicity* 3, no. 1 (March 1976): 19–33.

Pollis, Adamantia. "Intergroup Conflict and British Colonial Policy: The Case of Cyprus." *Comparative Politics* 5, no. 4 (July 1973): 575–99.

Porter, John. "Ethnic Pluralism in Canadian Perspective." In

Ethnicity, edited by Nathan Glazer and Daniel P. Moynihan, pp. 267–304. Cambridge, Mass.: Harvard University Press, 1975.

Pospielovsky, D. "Nationalism as a Factor in Dissent in the Contemporary Soviet Union." *Canadian Review of Studies in Nationalism* 2, no. 1 (Fall 1974): 91–116.

Ragin, Charles. "Class, Status, and 'Reactive Ethnic Cleavages': The Social Bases of Political Regionalism." *American Sociological Review* 42, no. 3 (June 1977): 438–50.

Rakowska-Harmstone, Teresa. "The Dialectics of Nationalism in the USSR." *Problems of Communism* 23, no. 3 (May–June 1974): 1–22.

Rawkins, Phillip M. "The Global Corporation, Ethno-Nationalism, and the Changing Face of the Western European State." In *Ethno-Nationalism, Multinational Corporations, and the Modern State*, edited by Ronald M. Grant and E. Spencer Wellhofer, pp. 73–84. Denver: University of Denver; Monograph Series in World Affairs; Vol. 15, book 4, 1979.

——. "Outsiders as Insiders: The Implications of Minority Nationalism in Scotland and Wales." *Comparative Politics* 10, no. 4 (July 1978): 519–34.

Reece, Jack E. "Internal Colonialism: The Case of Brittany." *Ethnic and Racial Studies* 2, no. 3 (July 1979): 275–92.

Rejai, Mostafa, and Enloe, Cynthia. "Nation-States and State-Nations." *International Studies Quarterly* 13, no. 2 (June 1969): 140–58.

Remak, Joachim. "Two Germanies—and Then?" *Journal of International Affairs* 27, no. 2 (1973): 175–86.

Rothchild, Donald. "Ethnicity and Conflict-Resolution." *World Politics* 22, no. 4 (July 1970): 597–616.

Rudolph, Joseph R., Jr. "Ethnic Sub-States and the Emergent Politics of Tri-Level Interaction in Western Europe." *Western Political Quarterly* 30, no. 4 (December 1977): 537–57.

——. "Ethnonational Parties and Political Change: The Belgian and British Experience." *Polity* 9, no. 4 (Summer 1977): 401–26.

Rutan, Gerard F. "Two Views of the Concept of Sovereignty:

Canadian-Canadien." *Western Political Quarterly* 24, no. 3 (September 1971): 456–66.

Rywkin, Michael. "Central Asia and Soviet Manpower." *Problems of Communism* 28, no. 1 (January-February 1979): 1–13.

St. Leger, F. Y. "The Mass Media and Minority Cultures." In *The Future of Cultural Minorities*, edited by Antony E. Alcock, Brian K. Taylor, and John M. Welton, pp. 63–81. London: Macmillan, 1979.

Salibi, Kamal S. "The Lebanese Identity." *Journal of Contemporary History* 6, no. 1 (1971): 76–86.

Scheinman, Lawrence. "The Interfaces of Regionalism in Western Europe: Brussels and the Peripheries." In *Ethnic Conflict in the Western World*, edited by Milton J. Esman, pp. 65–78. Ithaca, N.Y.: Cornell University Press, 1977.

Seton-Watson, Hugh. "Unsatisfied Nationalisms." *Journal of Contemporary History* 6, no. 1 (1971): 3–14.

Shafarevich, Igor. "Separation or Reconciliation? The Nationalities Question in the USSR." In *From Under the Rubble*, edited by Alexander Solzhenitsyn et al., pp. 88–104. Boston: Little, Brown, 1975.

Shils, Edward, "Primordial, Personal, Sacred, and Civil Ties." *British Journal of Sociology* 8, no. 2 (June 1957): 130–45.

Smith, Anthony D. "Towards a Theory of Ethnic Separatism." *Ethnic and Racial Studies* 2, no. 1 (January 1979): 21–37.

Snetsinger, John. "Ethnicity and Foreign Policy." In *Encyclopedia of American Foreign Policy*, edited by Alexander De Conde, vol. 1, pp. 322–29. New York: Scribner's, 1978.

Starrels, John. "Nationalism in the German Democratic Republic." *Canadian Review of Studies in Nationalism* 2, no. 1 (Fall 1974): 23–37.

Steiner, Jürg, and Obler, Jeffrey. "Does Consociational Theory Really Hold for Switzerland?" In *Ethnic Conflict in the Western World*, edited by Milton J. Esman, pp. 324–42. Ithaca, N.Y.: Cornell University Press, 1977.

Streib, Gordon F. "The Restoration of the Irish Language: Behavioral and Symbolic Aspects." *Ethnicity* 1, no. 1 (April 1974): 73–89.

Suhrke, Astri. "Irredentism Contained." *Comparative Politics* 7, no. 2 (January 1975): 187–203.

Tajfel, Henri. "The Social Psychology of Minorities." *Minority Rights Group Report*, no. 38 (n.d.): 3–20.

Thornberry, Patrick. "Minority Rights, Human Rights and International Law." *Ethnic and Racial Studies* 3, no. 3 (July 1980): 249–63.

Tillett, Lowell. "The National Minorities Factor in the Sino-Soviet Dispute." *Orbis* 21, no. 2 (Summer 1977): 241–60.

Trent, John. "The Politics of Nationalist Movements—A Reconsideration." *Canadian Review of Studies in Nationalism* 2, no. 1 (Fall 1974): 157–71.

Turner, Jonathan H., and Bonacich, Edna. "Toward a Composite Theory on Middleman Minorities." *Ethnicity* 7, no. 2 (June 1980): 144–58.

Van Dyke, Vernon. "The Individual, the State, and Ethnic Communities in Political Theory." *World Politics* 29, no. 3 (April 1977): 343–69.

Vincent, Joan. "The Structuring of Ethnicity." *Human Organization* 33, no. 4 (Winter 1974): 375–79.

Wallerstein, Immanuel. "The Two Modes of Ethnic Consciousness." In *The Nationality Question in Soviet Central Asia*, edited by Edward Allworth, pp. 168–75. New York: Praeger, 1973.

Wei, Yung. "Unification or Confrontation: An Assessment of Future Relations Between Mainland China and Taiwan." In *The Politics of Division, Partition, and Unification*, edited by Ray E. Johnston, pp. 67–79. New York: Praeger, 1976.

Weil, Martin. "Can the Blacks Do for Africa What the Jews Did for Israel?" *Foreign Policy*, no. 15 (Summer 1974): 109–30.

Weiner, Myron. "The Macedonian Syndrome: An Historical Model of International Relations and Political Development." *World Politics* 23, no. 4 (July 1971): 665–83.

Weinstein, Brian. "Language Strategists: Redefining Political Frontiers on the Basis of Linguistic Choices." *World Politics* 31, no. 3 (April 1979): 345–64.

Wiley, Norbert F. "The Ethnic Mobility Trap and Stratification Theory." *Social Problems* 15, no. 2 (Fall 1967): 147–59.

Williams, Colin H. "Cultural Nationalism in Wales." *Canadian Review of Studies in Nationalism* 4, no. 1 (Fall 1976): 15–37.

Williamson, Jeffrey G. "Regional Inequality and the Process of National Development: A Description of the Patterns." *Economic Development and Cultural Change* 13, no. 4, part 2 (July 1965): 3–84.

Wright, Frank. "Protestant Ideology and Politics in Ulster." *Archives Européennes de Sociologie* 14, no. 2 (1973): 213–80.

Yinger, J. Milton. "Ethnicity in Complex Societies: Structural, Cultural, and Characterological Factors." In *The Uses of Controversy in Sociology*, edited by Lewis A. Coser and Otto N. Larsen, pp. 197–216. New York: Free Press, 1976.

Zolberg, Aristide. "Splitting the Difference: Federalization Without Federalism in Belgium." In *Ethnic Conflict in the Western World*, edited by Milton J. Esman, pp. 103–42. Ithaca, N.Y.: Cornell University Press, 1977.

INDEX